BIOGRAPHICAL STUDIES

BIOGRAPHICAL
STUDIES

BY

JOHN VISCOUNT MORLEY

Essay Index Reprint Series

 BOOKS FOR LIBRARIES PRESS
FREEPORT, NEW YORK

First Published 1923
Reprinted 1969

STANDARD BOOK NUMBER:
8369-1186-5

LIBRARY OF CONGRESS CATALOG CARD NUMBER:
78-86773

PRINTED IN THE UNITED STATES OF AMERICA

CONTENTS.

TURGOT.

I

II

III

CONDORCET.

THE CHAMPION OF SOCIAL REACTION.

ROBESPIERRE.

I

II

VICTOR HUGO'S 'NINETY-THREE'

TURGOT.

I.

ANNE-ROBERT-JACQUES TURGOT was born in Paris on the 10th of May 1727. He died in 1781. His life covered rather more than half a century, extending, if we may put it a little roughly, over the middle fifty years of the eighteenth century. This middle period marks the exact date of the decisive and immediate preparation for the Revolution. At its beginning neither the intellectual nor the social elements of the great disruption had distinctly appeared, or begun their active fermentation.

In 1727 Voltaire was returning from his exile in England, to open the long campaign of which he was from that time forth to the close of his days the brilliant and indomitable captain. He died in 1778, bright, resolute, humane, energetic, to the last. Thus Turgot's life was almost exactly contemporary with the pregnant era of Voltaire's activity. In the same spring in which Turgot died, Maurepas too came to his end, and Necker was dismissed. The last event was the signal at which the floods of the

deluge fairly began to rise, and the revolutionary tide
to swell.

Turgot was born half a generation after the first
race of the speculative revolutionists. Rousseau,
Diderot, Helvétius, Condillac, D'Alembert, as well as
the foreign Hume, so much the greatest of the whole
band of innovators, because penetrating so much
nearer to the depths, all came into the world they
were to confuse so unspeakably, in the half-dozen
years between 1711 and 1717. Turgot was of later
stock and comes midway between these fathers of
the new church, between Hume, Rousseau, Diderot,
Leibnitz, Lessing, and the generation of its fiery
practical apostles, Condorcet, Mirabeau, Robespierre.[1]
The only other illustrious European of this decade
was Adam Smith, born in 1723, between whose
labours and some of the most remarkable of Turgot's
there was so much community. We cannot tell how
far the gulf between Turgot and the earlier band was
fixed by the accident that he did not belong to their
generation in point of time. The accident is in itself
only worth attention in connection with his distance
from them in other and more important points than
time.

The years of Turgot exactly bridge the interval
between the ministry of Dubois and that of Calonne ;
between the despair and confusion of the close of
the Regency, and that of the last ten years of
the monarchy. In 1727 we stand on the threshold

[1] Born in 1743, 1749, and 1759 respectively.

of that far-resounding workshop, where a hundred hands wrought the cunning implements and encyclopædic engines that were to serve in storming the hated citadels of superstition and injustice. In 1781 we emerge from these subterranean realms into the open air, to find ourselves surrounded by all the sounds and portents of imminent ruin. This, then, is the significance of the date of Turgot's birth.

His stock was Norman, and those who amuse themselves by finding a vital condition of the highest ability in antiquity of blood, may quote the descent of Turgot. His biographers speak of one Togut, a Danish prince, who walked the earth some thousand years before the Christian era; and of Saint Turgot in the eleventh century, the Prior of Durham, biographer of Bede, and first minister of Malcolm III. of Scotland. Let us pass over Togut and Saint Turgot; and the founder of a hospital in the thirteenth century; and the great-great-grandfather who sat as president of the Norman nobles in the States-General of 1614, and the grandfather who deserted arms for the toga. History is hardly concerned in this solemn marshalling of shades.

Even with Michel-Étienne, the father of Turgot, we have here no dealing. Let it suffice to say that he held high municipal office in Paris, and performed its duties with exceptional honour and spirit, giving sumptuous fêtes, constructing useful public works, and on one occasion jeoparding his life with a fine intrepidity that did not fail in his son, in appeasing a bloody struggle between two bodies of Swiss and French guards. There is in the library of the British Museum a folio of 1740, containing elaborate plates and letterpress, descriptive of the fêtes celebrated by the city of Paris with Michel-Étienne Turgot as its chief officer, on the occasion of the marriage of Louise-Elizabeth of. France to Don Philip of Spain (August 1739). As one contemplates these courtly sumptuosities, La Bruyère's famous picture recurs, of far other scenes in the same gay land. ' We see certain wild animals, male and female, scattered over the fields, black, livid, all burnt by the sun, bound to the earth they dig and work with unconquerable pertinacity ; they have a sort of articulate voice, and when they rise on their feet, they show a human face ; in fact they are men.' That these violent and humiliating contrasts are eternal and inevitable, is the last word of the dominant philosophy of society ; and one of the reasons why Turgot's life is worth studying, is that he felt in so pre-eminent a degree the urgency of lightening the destiny of that wild, hardly articulate, ever-toiling multitude.

The sum of the genealogical page is that Turgot inherited the position that, falling to worthy souls, is of its nature so invaluable, a family tradition of exalted courage and generous public spirit.

Turgot was the third son of his father. As the employments that persons of respectable family could enter were definite and stereotyped, there was little room for debate as to the calling for which a youth should prepare himself. Arms, civil administration, and the church furnished the only three openings for a gentleman. To identify the interests of the richest and most powerful class with the interests of the church, of the army, and of a given system of civil government, was indeed to give to that class the strongest motives for leaving the existing social order undisturbed. It unfortunately went too far in this direction, by fostering the strongest possible motives of hostility to such modifications in these gigantic departments as changing circumstances might make needful, in the breasts of the only men who could produce these modifications without a violent organic revolution. Such a system left too little course to spontaneity. Some of its evil effects were obvious and on the surface. The man who should have been a soldier found himself saying mass and hearing confessions. Vauvenargues, who was born for diplomacy or literature, passed the flower of his days in the organised dreariness of garrisons and marches. The eldest son usually preserved the rank and status of the family, whether civil or military. Turgot's eldest brother was to devote himself to civil administration, the next to be a soldier, and Turgot himself to be an ecclesiastic.

The second of the brothers, who began by following arms, had as little taste for them as the future minister had for the church. He persuaded the government after the loss of Canada that Guiana, to be called

Equinoctial France, would if well governed become
some sort of equivalent for the northern possession.
He was made Governor-General, but he had forgotten
the climate, and the scheme came to an abortive end,
involving him in a mass of confused quarrels which
lasted some years. He had a marked love for botany,
agriculture, and the like ; was one of the founders
of the Society of Agriculture in 1760 ; and was
the author of various pieces on points of natural
history.[1]

Turgot went as a boarder first to the college of
Louis-le-Grand, then to that of Plessis ; thence to the
seminary of Saint-Sulpice, where he took the degree
of bachelor in theology ; and from Saint-Sulpice to
the Sorbonne. His childhood and youth, like those
of other men who have afterwards won love and
admiration, have their stories. The affection of one
biographer records how the pocket-money with which
the young Turgot was furnished, used always instantly
to disappear, no one knew how or on what. It was
discovered that he gave it to poor schoolfellows to
enable them to buy books. Condorcet remarks on
this, that ' goodness and even generosity are not
rare sentiments in childhood ; but for these sentiments to be guided by such wisdom, this really seems
the presage of an extraordinary man, all whose
sentiments should be virtues, because they would

[1] Among others, of a little volume still to be met with in
libraries, *Sur la manière de préparer les diverses curiosités
d'histoire naturelle* (1758).

always be controlled by reason.'[1]   It is at any rate
certain that the union of head and heart, which this
story prefigures, was the distinction of Turgot's
character.   It is less pleasant to learn that Turgot
throughout his childhood was always repulsed by his
mother, who deemed him sullen, because he failed to
make his bow with good grace, and was shy and
taciturn.   He fled from her visitors, and would hide
himself behind sofa or screen, until dragged forth
for inspection.[2]   This is only worth recording, because
the same awkwardness and lack of grace remained
with Turgot to the end, and had to do with the unpopularity that caused his fall.   Perhaps he was
thinking of his own childhood, when he wrote that
fathers are often indifferent, or incessantly occupied
with the details of business, and that he had seen the
very parents who taught their children that there is
nothing so noble as to make people happy, yet repulse
the same children when urging some one's claim to
favour, and intimidate their young sensibility, instead
of encouraging and training it.[3]

Morellet, one of the best known of the little group
of friends and brother-students at the Sorbonne, has
recorded other authentic traits.   Turgot, he says,
united the simplicity of a child to a peculiar dignity
that forced the respect of his comrades.   His modesty
and reserve were those of a girl, and those equivocal

[1] *Vie de Turgot*, p. 8 (ed. 1847).
[2] *Mémoires de Morellet*, i. 12 (ed. 1822).
[3] *Lettre à Madame de Graffigny. Œuvres*, ii. 793.

references in which the undisciplined animalism of
youth often has a stealthy satisfaction, always called
the blood to his cheeks and covered him with embarrassment.   For all that, his spirit was full of a frank
gaiety, and he would indulge in long bursts of laughter
at a pleasantry or frolic that struck him.   We may
be glad to know this, because without express testimony to the contrary, there would have been some
reason for suspecting that Turgot was defective in
that most wholesome and human quality of a capacity
for laughter.

With the moral quality we have seen, Morellet adds
that for the intellectual side Turgot as a boy had
a prodigious memory.   He could retain as many as
a hundred and eighty lines of verse, after hearing
them twice, or sometimes even once.   He knew by
heart most of Voltaire's fugitive pieces, and long
passages in his poems and tragedies.   His predominant
characteristics are described as penetration, and that
other valuable faculty to which penetration is an
indispensable adjunct, but which it by no means
invariably implies—a spirit of broad and systematic
co-ordination.   The unusual precocity of his intelligence was perhaps imperfectly appreciated by
his fellow-students, since it led him so far beyond
any point within their sight.   It has been said of
him that he passed at once from infancy to manhood,
and was in the rank of sages before he had shaken off
the dust of the playground.

To a certain extent his temperament, which

from the earliest hours consumed him with eager
desire for knowledge, was the mark of all the best
minds of the epoch ; from Voltaire downwards, they
were inflamed by an inextinguishable and universal curiosity. Voltaire hardly left a single corner
of the field entirely unexplored in science, poetry,
history, philosophy. Rousseau wrote a comic opera
and was an ardent botanist. Diderot wrote well
and intelligently *de omni scibili*, and was the author
alike of the *Letter on the Blind* and of *Jacques le
fataliste*. No era was ever so little the era of the
specialist.

The society of the Sorbonne corresponded exactly
to a college at one of our universities, and will be
distinguished by the careful reader from the faculty
of theology in the university, which was usually, but
not always, composed of *docteurs de Sorbonne*. It
consisted of a large number of learned men in the
position of fellows, and a smaller number of younger
students, who lived together just as our under-
graduates do, in separate apartments, but with
common hall, library, and garden. One of Turgot's
masters, Sigorgne, was the first to teach in the university the Newtonian principles of astronomy, instead
of the Cartesian hypothesis of vortices. As is well
known, Cartesianism had for various reasons taken
a far deeper root in France than it ever did here,
and held its place a good generation after Newtonian
ideas were accepted and taught at Oxford and Cam-

bridge.[1] Voltaire's translation of the *Principia*, which he was prevented by the Cartesian chancellor, D'Aguesseau, from publishing until 1738, overthrew the reigning system, and gave a strong impulse to scientific inquiry.

Turgot mastered the new doctrine with avidity. In the acute letter of criticism that, while still at the Sorbonne, he addressed to Buffon, he pointedly urged it as the first objection to the writer's theory of the formation and movements of the planets, that any attempt at fundamental explanations of this kind was a departure from ' the simplicity and safe reserve of the philosophy of Newton.'[2] He only, however, made a certain advance in mathematics. He appears to have had no peculiar or natural aptitude for them, though he is said to have constantly blamed himself for not having gone deeply into the subject. It is hardly to be denied that mathematical and philosophic genius do not always go together. The precision, definiteness, and accurate limitations of the method of the one, are usually unfriendly to the brooding, tentative, uncircumscribed meditation that is the productive humour in the other. Turgot was essentially of the philosophising temper. Though the activity of his intelligence was incessant, his manner of work was the reverse of quick. ' When he applied himself to work,'

---

[1] Whewell's *Hist. Induct. Sciences*, ii. 147-159.

[2] *Œuvres de Turgot*, ii. 783. (Edition of Messrs. Eugène Daire and H. Dussard, published in the *Collection des principaux économistes*, published by Guillaumin, 1844.)

says Morellet, ' when it was a question of writing or doing, he was slow and loitering. Slow, because he insisted on finishing all he did perfectly, according to his own conception of perfection, which was most difficult of attainment, even down to the minutest detail; and because he would not receive assistance, being never contented with what he had not done himself. He also loitered a great deal, losing time in arranging his desk and cutting his pens, not that he was not thinking profoundly through all this trifling; but mere thinking did not advance his work.'[1]

We know the books that Turgot and his friends devoured with ardour. Locke, Bayle, Voltaire, Buffon, relieved Clarke, Leibnitz, Spinoza, Cudworth; and constant discussions among themselves both cleared up and enlarged what they read.[2] One of the disputants, certainly not the least amiable, has painted his own part in these discussions : ' I was violent in discussion,' says the good Morellet, as he was pleasantly called, ' but without my antagonist being able to reproach me with a single insult; and sometimes I used to spit blood after a debate in which I had not allowed a single personality to escape me.'[3]

Another member of the circle was Loménie de Brienne, who, in long years after, was chief minister of France for a narrow space through the momentous winter of 1787 and the spring of the next year, filling

[1] *Mémoires*, i. 16. [2] *Ibid.* i. 20. [3] *Ibid.* i. 19.

the gap between Calonne and Necker in a desperate and fatal style. Loménie's ambition dated from his youth ; it was always personal. While Turgot, his friend, was earnestly meditating on the destinies of the race and the conditions of their development, Loménie was dreaming only of the restoration of his ancestral château of Brienne. Though quite without means, he planned this in his visions on a scale of extreme costliness and magnificence. The dreams fell true. Money came to the family, and the château was built exactly as he had projected it, at a cost of two million francs.[1] His career was splendid. He was clever, industrious, persevering, astute, lively, pretentious, a person ever by well-planned hints leading you to suppose his unrevealed profundity to be bottomless.[2] He espoused that richly dowered bride the church, rose to be Archbishop of Toulouse, and would have risen to be Archbishop of Paris, but for the king's over-scrupulous conviction that ' an Archbishop of Paris must at least believe in God.' He became an immense favourite with Marie Antoinette and the court, was made minister ' like Richelieu and Mazarin,' and after having postured and played tricks in face of the bursting deluge, and given the government the final impulse into the abyss of bankruptcy, was dismissed with the rich archbishopric of Sens and a cardinal's hat for

---

[1] Morellet's *Mémoires*, i. 17-21, 262-270 ; and ii. 15.

[2] Marmontel's *Mémoires*, bk. xiii. ; Morellet, however, with persevering friendliness, denies the truth of Marmontel's picture (ii. 465)

himself, and good sinecures for his kinsfolk. His last
official act was to send for the 20,000 livres for his
month's salary, not fully due. His brother, the
Count of Brienne, remained in office as Minister of
War. He was a person of no talent, his friends
allowed, but ' assisted by a good chief clerk, he would
have made a good minister ; he meant well.'

All his honour and glory Loménie de Brienne
enjoyed for a season, until the Jacobins laid violent
hands upon him. He poisoned himself in his own
palace, just as a worse thing was about to befall
him. Alas, poetic justice is the exception in history,
and only once in many generations does the drama
of the state criminal rise to an artistic fifth act.
This was in 1794. In 1750 a farewell dinner had
been given in the rooms of the abbé de Brienne at
the Sorbonne, and the friends made an appointment
for a game of tennis behind the church of the Sorbonne in the year 1800.[1] The year came, but no
Loménie, no Turgot, and the Sorbonne itself had
vanished.

When the time arrived for his final acceptance of
an ecclesiastical destination, Turgot felt the honourable repugnance that might have been anticipated
alike from his morality and his intelligence, to enter
into an engagement which would irrevocably bind
him for the rest of his life, either always to hold
exactly the same opinions, or else to continue to
preach them publicly after he had ceased to hold

[1] Morellet, i. 21.

them privately. No certainty of worldly comfort
and advantage could in his eyes counterbalance the
possible danger and shame of a position, which might
place him between the two alternatives of stifling
his intelligence and outraging his conscience—the
one by blind, unscrutinising, and immovable acceptance of all the dogmas and sentiments of the church;
the other by the inculcation as truths of what he
believed to be false, and the proscription as false-
hoods of what he believed to be true. The horror
and disgrace of such a situation were too striking
for one who used his mind and acted on principle,
to run any risk of that situation becoming his own.

At the close of his course at the Sorbonne, he
wrote a letter to his father giving the reasons for
this resolution to abandon all idea of an ecclesiastical
career and the advancement which it offered him,
and seeking his consent for the change from church
to law. His father approved of the resolution, and
gave the required consent. As Turgot had studied
law as well as theology, no time was lost, and he
formally entered the profession of the law as Deputy-
Counsellor of the Procureur-Général at the beginning
of 1752.

His college friends had remonstrated warmly at
this surrender of a brilliant prospect. A little deputation of young abbés, fresh from their vows, waited
on him at his rooms ; in the humour of blithe and
sagacious good-will that comes so naturally to men
who believe they have just found out Fortune's trick

and yoked her fast for ever to the car, they declared
that he was about to do something opposed to his
own interest, and inconsistent with his usual good
sense. In one profession he would waste his genius
in arguing trifling private affairs, while in the other
he would be of the highest usefulness to his country,
and would acquire the greatest reputation. Turgot,
however, insisted on placing genius and reputation
below the necessity of being honest. The object of
an oath might be of the least important kind, but
he could neither allow himself to play with it, nor
believe that a man could abase his profession in public
opinion, without at the same time abasing himself.
' *You shall do as you will*,' he said ; ' *for my own
part, it is impossible for me to wear a mask all my
life.*' [1]

We have said that Turgot disdained to fight under
a mask. There was one exception, and only one.
In 1754 there appeared two letters, nominally from
an ecclesiastic to a magistrate, and entitled *Le
Conciliateur*. Here it is enough to say that they
were intended to enforce the propriety and duty of
religious toleration. In a letter to a friend we find
Turgot saying, ' Although the *Conciliator* is of my
principles, and those of our friend, I am astonished
at your conjectures ; *it is neither his style nor mine.*' [2]
Yet Turgot had written it. This is his one public

---

[1] Dupont de Nemours. Condorcet's *Vie de Turgot*, pp. 8-10.
[2] *Œuvres*, ii. 685. Morellet says that it was written by
Loménie de Brienne, 19.

literary equivocation. Let us, at all events, allow
that it was resorted to, not to break the law with
safety, nor to cloak a malicious attack on a person,
but to give additional weight by means of a harmless
prosopopœia, to an argument for the noblest of
principles.[1]

Before Turgot entered the great world, he had
already achieved an amount of success in philosophic
speculation that placed him in the front rank of
social thinkers. To that passion for study and the
acquisition of knowledge, not uncommon in youth,
and one of the most attractive of youth's qualities,
there was added in him what is unhappily not common
in men and women of any age—an active impulse
to use his own intelligence upon the information
he gained from books and professors. He was no
conceited or froward caviller at authority, nor born
rebel against established teachers and governors.
His understanding seriously craved a full and independent satisfaction, and could draw this only from
laborious meditation that should either disclose the
inadequacy of the grounds for an opinion, or else
establish it with what would be to him a new and
higher, because an independently acquired, con-
clusiveness.

His letter to Buffon, to which we have already
referred, is an illustration of this wise, and never
captious nor ungracious, caution in receiving ideas.

[1] See the note of Dupont de Nemours, *ad loc.*

Neither Buffon's reputation, nor the glow of his style, nor the dazzling ingenuity and grandeur of his conceptions—all of them so well calculated, at one-and-twenty, to throw even a vigilant intelligence off its guard—could divert Turgot from the prime scientific duty of confronting a theory with facts. Buffon was for explaining the formation of the earth and the other planets, and their lateral movement, by the hypothesis that a comet had fallen obliquely on to the sun, driven off certain portions of its constituent matter in a state of fusion, and that these masses, made spherical by the mutual attraction of their parts, were carried to different distances in proportion to their mass and the force originally impressed on them. Buffon may have been actuated, both here and in his other famous hypothesis of reproduction, by a desire, less to propound a true and durable explanation, than to arrest by a bold and comprehensive generalisation that attention which is only imperfectly touched by mere collections of particular facts.[1]

Turgot was less sensible of these possible advantages than he was alive to the certain dangers. He perceived that to hold a theory otherwise than as an inference from facts, is to have a strong motive for looking at the facts in a predetermined light, or for ignoring them; an involuntary predisposition fatal to the discovery of truth, which is nothing

[1] See Condorcet's Éloge on Buffon (*Œuvres*, iii. 335); and a passage from Bourdon, quoted in Whewell's *Hist. Induct. Sci.* iii. 348.

more than the conformity of our conception of facts to their adequately observed order. Why, he asks, do you replunge us into the night of hypotheses, justifying the Cartesians and their three elements and their vortices ?   And whence comes your comet ?[1]

Before passing on to more scientific speculations, it is worth while to notice Turgot's letter to Madame de Graffigny, both for intrinsic merit and scope of ideas, and for proof of the interest, at once early and profound, that he took in moral questions lying at the very bottom, as well of sound character, as of a healthy society. Turgot's early passion for literature had made him seize an occasion of being introduced to even so moderately renowned a professor of it as Madame de Graffigny. He happened to be intimate with her niece, who afterwards became the lively and witty wife of Helvétius, somewhat to the surprise of Turgot's friends. For although he persuaded Mademoiselle de Ligniville to present him to her aunt, and though he assiduously attended Madame de Graffigny's literary gatherings, Turgot would constantly quit the circle of men of letters for the sake of a game of battledore with the comely and attractive niece. Hence the astonishment of men that from such familiarity there grew no stronger passion, and that whatever the causes of such reserve, the only issue was a tender and lasting friendship.[2]

Madame de Graffigny had begged Turgot's opinion upon the manuscript of a work composed, as so many

[1] October 1748. *Œuvres*, ii. 782-784.   [2] Morellet, i. 140.

others were, after the pattern of Montesquieu's *Lettres persanes*,—now nearly thirty years old,—and bearing the accurately imitative title of *Lettres péruviennes*. A Peruvian comes to Europe, and sends to a friend or mistress in Peru a series of remarks on civilisation. Goldsmith's delightful *Citizen of the World* is the best-known type in our own literature of this primitive form of social criticism. The effect upon common opinion of criticism cast in such a mould, presenting familiar habits, institutions, and observances, in a striking and unusual light, was to give a kind of Socratic stimulus to people's ideas about education, civilisation, conduct, and the other topics springing from a comparison between the manners of one community and another. That one of the two, whether Peru, or China, or Persia, was a community drawn mainly from the imagination, did not render the contrast any the less effective in stirring men's minds.

By the middle of the century the air was full of ideas upon these subjects. The temptation was irresistible to turn from the confusion of squalor, oppression, licence, distorted organisation, penetrative disorder, to ideal states comprising a little range of simple circumstances, and a small number of types of virtuous and unsophisticated character. Much came of the relief thus sought and found. It was the beginning of the subversive process, for it taught men to look away from ideas of practical amelioration. The genius of Rousseau gave these dreams the shape that, in many respects, so unfortunately for France, finally attracted the bulk of the national sentiment and sympathy. But the vivid, humane, and inspiring pages of *Émile* were not published until ten years after Turgot's *Letter to Madame de Graffigny* :[1] a circumstance that may teach us that in moral as in physical discoveries, though one man may take the final step and reap the fame, the conditions have been prepared beforehand.

The reader who remembers Locke's *Thoughts concerning Education* (published in 1690), and the particularly homely prescriptions upon the subjects of the infant body with which that treatise opens, will recognise the source of Turgot's inspiration. The same may be said of the wise passages in this letter, upon the right attitude of a father towards his child. It was not merely the metaphysics of the sage and positive Locke that laid the revolutionary train in France. This influence extended over the whole field, and even Rousseau confesses the obligations of the imaginary governor of Émile to the real Locke.

We are again plainly in the Lockian atmosphere when Turgot speaks of men being the dupes of ' general ideas, which are true because drawn from nature, but which people embrace with a narrow stiffness that makes them false, because they no longer combine them with circumstances, taking for absolute what is only the expression of a relation.'

[1] Written in 1751. *Œuvres*, ii. 785-794.

The merit of this and the other educational parts
of the piece is not their originality, but the kind of
complete and finished assimilation that is all but
tantamount to independent thought, and in certain
conditions may be much more practically useful.

Not less important to the happiness of men than
the manner of their education, is their own cultivation of a wise spirit of tolerance in conduct. ' I
should like to see explained,' Turgot says, ' the causes
of alienation and disgust between people who love
one another. I believe that after living awhile with
men, we perceive that bickerings, ill-humours,
teasings on trifles, perhaps cause more troubles and
divisions among them than serious things. How
many bitternesses have their origin in a word, in
forgetfulness of some slight observances! If people
would only weigh in an exact balance so many little
wrongs, if they would only put themselves in the
place of those who have to complain of them, if they
would only reflect how many times they have themselves given way to humours, how many things they
have forgotten! A single word spoken in disparagement of our intelligence is enough to make us irreconcilable, and yet how often have we been deceived
in the very same matter. How many persons of
understanding have we taken for fools! Why
should not others have the same privilege as ourselves ? . . . Ah, what address is needed to live
together, to be compliant without cringing, to expose a fault without harshness, to correct without

imperious air, to remonstrate without ill-temper!'
All wise and good, but, as Turgot had occasion by
and by to say, little comes of giving rules instead of
breeding habits.

We may notice too in this Letter, what so many
of Turgot's allies and friends were disposed to complain of, but what will commend him to a less newly
emancipated and therefore a less fanatical generation.
There is a conspicuous absence of that peculiar bound-
lessness of hope, that zealous impatience for the
instant realisation and fruition of all the aspirations
of philosophic intelligence, which carried others
immediately around him so excessively far in the
creed of Perfectibility. ' Liberty! I answer with a
sigh, maybe that men are not worthy of thee!
Equality! They would yearn after thee, but cannot
attain!' Compared with the confident exultation
and illimitable sense of the worth of man which
distinguished that time, there is something like
depression here, as in many other places in Turgot's
writings. It is usually less articulate, and rather
conveyed by a running undertone that so often
reveals more of a writer's true mood and temper
than is seen in his words, giving to them, by some
unconscious and inscrutable process, living effects
upon the reader's sense like those of eye and voice
and accompanying gesture.

Dejection, however, is not the proper word for
the humour of reserved and grave suspense, natural
in those rare spirits who have recognised how narrow

is the way of truth and how few there be that enter
therein, and what prolonged concurrence of favour-
ing hazards with gigantic endeavour is needed for
each smallest step in the halting advancement of
the race. With Turgot this was not the result of
mere sentimental brooding. It had a deliberate
and reasoned foundation in historical study. He
was patient and not hastily sanguine as to the speedy
coming of the millennial future, exactly because
history had taught him to measure the laggard paces
of the past. The secret of the intense hopefulness
of that time lay in the mournfully erroneous conviction that the one condition of progress is plenteous
increase of light. Turgot saw very early that this
is not so. ' *It is not error*,' he wrote, in a saying
that every champion of a new idea should have ever
in letters of flame before his eyes, ' *that opposes the
progress of truth : it is indolence, obstinacy, the spirit
of routine, everything that favours inaction.*' [1]

The others left these potent elements of obstruction out of calculation and account. With Turgot
they were the main facts to be considered, and the
main forces to be counteracted. It is the mark of
the highest kind of union between sagacious, firm,
and clear-sighted intelligence, and a warm and steadfast glow of social feeling, when a man has learnt how
little the effort of the individual can do either to
hasten or to direct the current of human destiny,
and yet finds in effort his purest pleasure and his

[1] *Œuvres*, ii. 672.

most constant duty.   If we owe honour to the social
endeavour that is stimulated and sustained by an
enthusiastic confidence in speedy and full fruition,
we surely owe it still more to those who, knowing
how remote and precarious and long beyond their
own days is the hour of fruit, yet need no other spur
nor sustenance than bare hope, and in this strive
and endeavour, and still endeavour.   It was the
possession of this strength and the constant call and
strain upon it, that gave Turgot in mien and speech
a gravity that revolted the frivolous or indifferent,
and seemed cold and timorous to the enthusiastic
and urgent.

II.

In 1750 Turgot, then only in his twenty-fourth
year, was appointed to the honorary office of Prior
of the Sorbonne, an elective distinction conferred
annually, as it appears, on some meritorious or highly-
connected student.   It was held in the following year
by Loménie de Brienne.   In this capacity Turgot read
two Latin dissertations, one at the opening of the
session, and the other at its close.   The first of these
was upon ' The Advantages that the Establishment
of Christianity has conferred upon the Human Race.'

Its value, as might well have been expected from
the circumstances of its production, is not very high.
It is pitched in a tone of exaltation that is eminently

unfavourable to the permanently profitable treatment of so vast a subject. There are in it too many of those eloquent and familiar commonplaces of orthodox history, by which the doubter tries to warm himself into belief, and the believer dreams that he is corroborating faith by reason. The assembly for whom his discourse was prepared, could hardly have endured the apparition in the midst of them of what both rigorous justice and accurate history required to have taken into account on the other side. It was not to be expected that a young student within the precincts of the Sorbonne should have any eyes for the evil with which the forms of the Christian religion, like other growths of the human mind, from the lowest forms of savage animism upwards, have ever alloyed its good. The absence of all reference to one half of what the annals of the various Christian churches have to teach us, robs the first of Turgot's Discourses of the serious and durable quality which belongs to his other writings.

The same vicious exclusiveness was practised by the enemies of the church, and if history was to one of the two contending factions an exaggerated enumeration of the blessings of Christianity, it was to their passionate rivals only a monotonous catalogue of curses. Of this temper we have a curious illustration in the circumstance that Dupont, Turgot's intimate friend of later years, who collected and published his works, actually took the trouble to suppress the opening of this very Discourse, in which

Turgot had replied to the reproach often made against Christianity, of being useful only for a future life.[1]

In the first Discourse, Turgot considers the influence of Christianity first upon human nature, and secondly on political societies. One feature at least deserves remark, and this is that, in spite both of a settled partiality and of a certain amount of the common form of theology, yet at bottom and putting some phrases apart, religion is handled, and its workings traced, much as they would have been if treated as admittedly secular forces. And this was something. Let us proceed to analyse what Turgot says.

1. Before the preaching and acceptance of the new faith, all nations alike were plunged into the most extravagant superstitions. The most frightful dissoluteness of manners was encouraged by the example of the gods themselves. Every passion and nearly every vice was the object of a monstrous deification. A handful of philosophers existed, who had learnt no better lesson from their reason than to despise the multitude of their fellows. In the midst of the universal contagion the Jews alone remained pure. Even the Jews were affected with a narrow and sterile pride, that proved how little they appreciated the priceless treasure entrusted to their keeping. What were the effects of the appearance of Christ, and the revelation of the gospel ? It inspired men with a tender zeal for the truth, and by establishing the

---

[1] *Œuvres*, ii. 586 *n.*

necessity of a body of teachers for the instruction of
nations, made studiousness and intellectual application indispensable in a great number of persons.

Consider, again, the obscurity, incertitude, and
incongruousness, that marked the ideas of the wisest
of the ancients upon the nature of man and of God,
and the origin of creation; the Ideas of Plato, for
instance, the Numbers of Pythagoras, the theurgic
extravagances of Plotinus and Porphyry and Iambli-
chus; and then measure the contributions made by
the scholastic theologians whose dry method has
undergone so much severe condemnation, to the
instruments by which knowledge is enlarged and
made accurate. It was the church, moreover, that
civilised the northern barbarians, and so preserved
the West from the same barbarism and desolation
with which the triumphs of Mahometanism replaced
the knowledge and arts and prosperity of the East.
It is to the services of the church that we owe the
perpetuation of a knowledge of the ancient tongues,
and if this knowledge, and the possession of the
masterpieces of thought and feeling and form, the
flower of the ancient European mind, remained so
long unproductive, still religious organisation deserves
our gratitude equally for keeping these great treasures
for happier times. They survived, as trees stripped
by winter of their leaves survive through frost and
storm, to give new blossoms in a new spring.

This much on the intellectual side; but how can
we describe the moral transformation which the new

faith brought to pass ?   Men who had hitherto only
regarded gods as beings to be entreated to avert ill or
bestow blessing, now learnt the nobler emotion of
devout love for a divinity of supreme power and
beneficence.   The new faith, besides kindling love for
God, inflamed the kindred sentiment of love for men,
all of whom it declared to be the children of God, one
vast family with a common father.   Julian himself
bore witness to the fidelity with which the Christians,
whose faith he hated or despised, tended the sick and
fed the poor, not only of their own association, but
those also who were without the fold.   The horrible
practice of exposing new-born infants, which outraged
nature, and yet did not touch the heart nor the
understanding of a Numa, an Aristotle, a Confucius,
was first proscribed by the holy religion of Christ.
If shame and misery still sometimes, in the hearts
of poor outcast mothers, overpower the horror that
Christianity first inspired, the same religion has
opened sheltering places for the unhappy victims
of such a practice, and provided means for rearing
foundlings into useful citizens.

Christian teaching, by reviving the principles of
sensibility within the breast, may be said ' to have in
some sort unveiled human nature to herself.'   If the
cruelty of old manners has abated, do we not owe the
improvement to such courageous priests as Ambrose,
who refused admission into the church to Theodosius,
because in punishing a guilty city he had hearkened
to the voice rather of wrath than of justice ; or as

that Pope who insisted that Louis the Seventh should expiate by a rigorous penance the sack and burning of Vitry ?[1]   It is not to a Titus, a Trajanus, an Antoninus, that we owe the abolition of the bloody gladiatorial games ; it is to Jesus Christ. Virtuous unbelievers have not seldom been the apostles of benevolence and humanity, but we rarely see them in the asylums of misery. Reason speaks, but it is religion that makes men act. How much dearer to us than the splendid monuments of antique taste, power, and greatness, are those Gothic edifices reared for the poor and the orphan, those far nobler monuments of the piety of Christian princes and the power of Christian faith. The rudeness of their architecture may wound the delicacy of our taste, but they will be ever beloved by feeling hearts. ' Let others admire in the retreat prepared for those who have sacrificed in battle their lives or their health for the state, all the gathered riches of the arts, displaying in the eyes of all the nations the magnificence of Louis the Fourteenth, and carrying our renown to the level of that of Greece and Rome. What I will admire is such a use of those arts ; the sublime glory of serving the weal of men raises them higher than they had ever been at Rome or at Athens.'

2. Let us turn from the action of the Christian faith in modifying the passions of the individual, to its influence upon societies of men. How has

[1] See Martin's *Hist. de la France*, iii. 422. Or Morison's *Life of Saint Bernard*, bk. iii. ch. vi.

Christianity ameliorated the art of government, with
reference to the two characteristic aims of that art,
the happiness of communities, and their stability?
'Nature has given all men the right of being happy,'
but the old lawgivers abandoned nature's wise
economy, by which she uses the desires and interests
of individuals to fulfil her general plans and ensure
the common weal. Men like Lycurgus destroyed all
idea of property, violated the laws of modesty, and
annihilated the tenderest ties of blood. A false and
mischievous spirit of system seduced them away from
the true method, the feeling after experience.[1] A
general injustice reigned in the laws of all nations;
among all of them what was called the public good
was confined to a small number of men. Love of
country was less the love of fellow-citizens than a
common hatred towards strangers. Hence the bar-
barities practised by the ancients upon their slaves,
hence that custom of slavery once spread over the
whole earth, those horrible cruelties in the wars of
the Greeks and the Romans, that barbarous inequality
between the two sexes which still reigns in the East;
hence the tyranny of the great towards the common
people in hereditary aristocracies, the profound degradation of subject peoples. In short, everywhere
the stronger have made the laws and have crushed
the weak; and if they have sometimes consulted the
interests of a given society, they have always forgotten

---

[1] *Les hommes en tout ne s'éclairent que par le tâtonnement
de l'expérience. Œuvres,* ii. 593.

those of the human race. To recall right and justice, a principle was necessary that could raise men above themselves and all around them, that could lead them to survey all nations and all conditions with an equitable gaze, and in some sort with the eyes of God himself. This is what religion has done. What other principle could have fought and vanquished both interests and prejudice united ?

If the history of the ancient republics shows that they hardly knew the difference between liberty and anarchy, and if even Aristotle seemed unable to reconcile monarchy with a mild government, is not the reason to be found in the fact that, before the Christian era, the various governments of the world only presented either an ambition without bound or limit, or else a blind passion for independence ? a perpetual balance between oppression on the one side, and revolt on the other ? In vain did law-givers attempt to arrest this incessant struggle of conflicting passions by laws too weak for the purpose, because in too imperfect an accord with opinions and manners. Religion, by placing man under the eyes of an all-seeing God, imposed on human passions the only rein capable of effectually bridling them. It gave men internal laws, that were stronger than all the external bonds of the civil laws. By means of this internal change, it has everywhere had the effect of weakening despotism, so that the limits of Christianity seem to mark also the limits of mild government and public felicity. Kings saw the supreme tribunal of a God who should judge them and the cause of their people. Thus the distance between them and their subjects became as nothing in the infinite distance between kings and subjects alike, and the divinity that was equally elevated above either. They were both in some sort equalised by a common abasement. ' Ye nations, be subject to authority,' cried the voice of religion to the one; and to the other it cried, ' Ye kings, who judge the earth, learn that God has only entrusted you with the image of power for the happiness of your peoples.'

An eloquent description of the efficacy of Christianity in raising human nature, and impressing on kings the obligation of pursuing above all things the well-being of their subjects, closes with a courtly official salutation of the virtues of that Very Christian King, Louis the Fifteenth.

' It is ill reasoning against religion,' an illustrious contemporary of Turgot's had said, in a deprecatory sentence that serves to mark the spirit of the time, ' to compile a long list of the evils it has inflicted, without doing the same for the blessings it has bestowed.' [1] Conversely we may well think it unphilosophical and unconvincing to enumerate all the blessings without any of the evils ; to tell us how the Christian doctrine enlarged the human spirit, without observing what narrowing limitations

---

[1] *Esprit des lois*, bk. xxiv. ch. ii.

it imposed; to dwell on all the mitigating influences
with which the Christian churches have been associated, while forgetting all the ferocities they have
inspired. The history of European belief offers a
double record since the decay of polytheism, and if
for a certain number of centuries this record shows
the civilisation of men's instincts by Christianity,
it reveals to us in the centuries subsequent, the
reverse process of the civilisation of Christianity by
men's instincts. Turgot's piece treats half the subject
as if it were the whole. He extends down to the
middle of the eighteenth century a number of propositions and implied inferences that are only true
up to the beginning of the fourteenth.

We now know how this long battle between the
champions of authority and the leaders of revolt,
which Turgot watched, but of which he did not see
the end, has gone. The churchmen lost their lead,
and were thrown back out of the civil and political
sphere. We know, too, what effect these blows to
the Catholic organisation have had upon the activity
of the Catholic idea. With the decline and extermination of the predominance of churchmen in civil
affairs, there began a tendency that has since become
deeper and stronger, in the church to withdraw herself and her sons from a sphere where she could no
longer be sovereign. This return of the leaders of
the Christian society upon the original conceptions
of the Christian faith, did not come to pass in Turgot's
time.

D

We may say, in fine, that if this first public
composition of Turgot's is imperfect, it was better
to exaggerate the services of Christianity, alike as
an internal faith and as a peculiar form of social
organisation, than to describe Gregory the Great and
Innocent, Hildebrand and Bernard, as artful and
vulgar tyrants, and Aquinas and Roger Bacon as
the products of a purely barbarous, stationary, and
dark age. There is at first sight something surprising
in the respect that Turgot's ablest contemporaries
paid to the contributions made to progress by Greece
and Rome, compared with their angry disparagement
of the Dark Ages. The reason of this contrast we
soon discover to be that the passions of present contests gave their own colour to men's interpretation
of the circumstances of the remote middle time
between the Roman Empire and the commencement
of the revolutionary period. Turgot escaped these
passions more completely than any man of his time
who was elevated enough to be endowed with the
capacity for passion. He never forgot that it is
as wise and just to confess the obligations of mankind to the Catholic monotheism of the West, as it
is shallow and unjust in professors of Christianity
to despise or hate the lower theological systems that
guide the humbler families of mankind.

Let us observe that only three years after this
academic discourse in praise of the religion of the
time, Turgot was declaring that ' the greatest of
the services of Christianity to the world was that

it had both enlightened and propagated *natural religion.*' [1]

III.

The second and more famous of the two Discourses at the Sorbonne was read in December 1750, and professes to treat the 'Successive Advances of the Human Mind.' [2] The opening lines are among the most pregnant, as they were among the most original, in the history of literature, and reveal in an outline, standing clear against the light, a thought which revolutionised old methods of viewing and describing the course of human affairs, and contained the germs of a new and most fruitful philosophy of society.

'The phenomena of nature, subjected as they are to constant laws, are enclosed in a circle of revolutions that remain the same for ever. All comes to life again, all perishes again ; and in these successive generations, by which vegetables and animals reproduce themselves, time does no more than bring back at each moment the image of what it has just dismissed.

'The succession of men, on the contrary, offers from age to age a spectacle of continual variations. Reason, freedom, the passions, are incessantly producing new events. *All epochs are fastened together by a sequence of causes and effects, linking the condition*

---

[1] *Lettres sur la tolérance,* II. vol. ii. 687.

[2] *Sur les progrès successifs de l'esprit humain. Œuvres,* ii. 597-611.

of the world to all the conditions that have gone before it.
The gradually multiplied signs of speech and writing,
giving men an instrument for making sure of the
continued possession of their ideas, as well as of
imparting them to others, have formed out of the
knowledge of each individual a common treasure,
which generation transmits to generation, as an inheritance constantly augmented by the discoveries of
each age ; and the human race, observed from its
first beginning, seems in the eyes of the philosopher
to be one vast whole, which, like each individual in
it, has its infancy and its growth.'

This was not a mere casual reflection in Turgot's
mind, taking a solitary and separate position among
those various and unordered ideas that spring up
and go on existing without visible fruit in every
active intelligence. It was one of the systematic
conceptions that shape and rule many groups of
facts, fixing a new and high place of their own for
them among the great divisions of knowledge. In a
word, it belonged to the rare order of truly creative
ideas, and was the root or germ of a whole body of
vigorous and connected thought. This quality marks
the distinction, in respect of the treatment of history,
between Turgot and both Bossuet and the great
writers of history in France and England in the
eighteenth century. Many of the sayings to which
we are referred for the origin of the modern idea of
history, such as Pascal's, for instance, are the fortuitous
glimpses of men of genius into a vast sea, whose

extent they have not been led to suspect, and only make a passing and momentary mark. Bossuet's talk of universal history, that has been so constantly applauded, was fundamentally, and in substance, no more than a theological commonplace splendidly decorated. He did indeed speak of ' the concatenation of human affairs,' but only in the same sentence with ' the sequence of the counsels of God.' The gorgeous rhetorician of the church was not likely to rise philosophically into the larger air of universal history, properly so called. His merit is that he did in a small and rhetorical way, what Montesquieu and Voltaire afterwards did in a truly comprehensive and philosophical way ; he pressed forward general ideas in connection with the recorded movements of the chief races of mankind. For a teacher of history to leave the bare chronicler's road so far as to declare, for example, the general principle, inadequate and over-stated as it may be, that ' religion and civil government are the two points on which human things revolve,'—even this was a clear step in advance. The dismissal of the long series of emperors from Augustus to Alexander Severus in two or three pages was to show historic proportion. Again, Bossuet's expressions of ' the concatenation of the universe,' of the interdependence of the parts of so vast a whole, of there coming no great change without having its causes in foregoing centuries, and of the true object of history being to observe, in connection with each epoch, those secret dispositions of events that prepared the way for great changes, as well as the momentous conjunctures which more immediately brought them to pass [1] — all these phrases point to a true and philosophic survey. But they end in themselves. The chain is an arbitrary and one-sided collection of facts. The writer does not follow and feel after the successive links, but forges and chooses and arrays them after a pattern of his own, that was fixed independently of them. A scientific term or two is not enough to disguise the purely theological essence of the treatise.

Montesquieu and Voltaire were both far enough removed from Bossuet's point of view, and the *Spirit of Laws* of the one, and the *Essay on the Manners and Character of Nations* of the other, mark a very different way of considering history from the lofty and confident method of the great divine. The *Spirit of Laws* was published in 1748, that is to say a couple of years before Turgot's Discourse at the Sorbonne. Voltaire's *Essay on Manners* did not come out until 1757, or seven years later than the Discourse; but Voltaire himself has told us that its composition dates from 1740, when he prepared this new presentation of European history for the service of Madame du Châtelet.[2] We may hence fairly consider the cardinal work of Montesquieu, and the cardinal historical work of Voltaire, as virtually belonging to the same time. And they possess a leading character in common that

---

[1] *Discours sur l'histoire universelle*, part iii. ch. ii.

[2] Preface to *Essai sur les mœurs*. *Œuvres*, xx.

separates them both from Turgot. In a word, Montesquieu and Voltaire, if we have to search their most distinctive quality, introduced into history systematically, and with full and decisive effect, a broad generality of treatment. They grouped the facts of history ; and they did not group them locally or in accordance with mere geographical or chronological division, but collected the facts in social classes and orders from many countries and times. Their work was a classification. It showed the possibility of arranging the manifold and complex facts of society, and of the movements of communities, under heads and with reference to definite general conditions.

There is no need here to enter into any criticism of Montesquieu, how far the merits of his execution equalled the merit of his design, how far his vicious confusion of the senses of the word ' law ' impaired the worth of his book, as a contribution to inductive or comparative history. We have only to seek the difference between the philosophic conception of Montesquieu and the philosophic conception of Turgot. The latter may be considered a more liberal completion of the former. Turgot not only sees the operation of law in the movements and institutions of society, but he interprets this law in a positive and scientific sense, as an ascertainable succession of social states, each of them being the cause and effect of other social states. He gives its deserved prominence to the fertile idea of there being an ordered movement

of growth or advance among societies ; in other words,
of the civilisation of any given portion of mankind
having fixed conditions analogous to those of a
physical organism. Finally, he does not limit his
thought by fixing it upon the laws and constitutions
only of countries, but refers historical philosophy to
its veritable and widest object and concern, the steps
and conditions of the progression of the human mind.

How, he inquires, can we seize the thread of the
progress of the human mind ?   How trace the road,
now overgrown and half-hidden, along which the race
has travelled ?   Two ideas suggest themselves, that
lay foundations for this inquiry.   For one thing, the
resources of nature and the fruitful germ of all sorts
of knowledge are to be found wherever men are to be
found. ' The sublimest attainments are not, and
cannot be, other than the first ideas of sense developed
or combined, just as the edifice whose height most
amazes the eye, of necessity reposes on the very earth
that we tread ; and the same senses, the same organs,
the spectacle of the same universe, have everywhere
given men the same ideas, as the same needs and the
same dispositions have everywhere taught them the
same arts.' Or it might be put in other words.
There is identity in human nature, and repetition in
surrounding circumstance means the reproduction of
social consequences. For another thing, ' the actual
state of the universe, by presenting at the same
moment on the earth all the shades of barbarism and
civilisation, discloses to us as in a single glance the

monuments, the footprints of all the steps of the human mind, the measure of the whole track along which it has passed, the history of all the ages.'

The progress of the human mind means to Turgot the progress of knowledge. Its history is the history of the growth and spread of science and the arts. Its advance is increased enlightenment of the understanding. From Adam and Eve down to Louis the Fourteenth, the record of progress is the chronicle of the ever-increasing additions to the sum of what men know, and the accuracy and fullness with which they know. The chief instrument in this enlightenment is the rising up from time to time of some lofty and superior intelligence; for though human character contains everywhere the same principle, yet certain minds are endowed with a peculiar abundance of talent that is refused to others. 'Circumstances develop these superior talents, or leave them buried in obscurity; and from the infinite variety of these circumstances springs the inequality among nations.' The agricultural stage goes immediately before a decisively polished state, because it is then first that there is that surplus of means of subsistence, which allows men of higher capacity the leisure for using it in the acquisition of knowledge, properly so called.

One of the greatest steps was the precious invention of writing, and one of the most rapid was the constitution of mathematical knowledge. The sciences that came next matured more slowly, because in mathematics the explorer has only to compare ideas among one another, while in the others he has to test the conformity of ideas to objective facts. Mathematical truths, becoming more numerous every day, and increasingly fruitful in proportion, lead to the development of hypotheses at once more extensive and more exact, and point to new experiments, that in their turn furnish new problems to solve. 'So necessity perfects the instrument; so mathematics finds support in physics, to which it lends its lamp; so all knowledge is bound together; so, notwithstanding the diversity of their advance, all the sciences lend one another mutual aid; and so, by force of feeling a way, of multiplying systems, of exhausting errors, so to speak, the world at length arrives at the knowledge of a vast number of truths.' It might seem as if a prodigious confusion, as of tongues, would arise from so enormous an advance along so many lines. 'The different sciences, originally confined within a few simple notions common to all, can now, after their advance into more extensive and difficult ideas, only be surveyed apart. But an advance, greater still, brings them together again, because that mutual dependence of all truths is discovered, which, while it links them one to another, throws light on one by another.'

Alas, the history of opinion is, in one of its most extensive branches, the history of error. The senses are the single source of our ideas, and furnish its models to the imagination. Hence the nearly in-

corrigible disposition to judge what we are ignorant
of by what we know ; hence the deceptive analogies
to which the primitive rudeness of men surrenders
itself. '*As they watched nature, as their eyes wandered
to the surface of a profound ocean, instead of the far-off
bed hidden under the waters, they saw nothing but their
own likeness.* Every object in nature had its god, and
this god formed after the pattern of men had men's
attributes and men's vices.' [1]   Here, in anthropo-
morphism, or the transfer of human quality to
things not human, and the invention of spiritual
existences to be the recipients of this quality, Turgot
justly touched the root of most of the wrong thinking
that has been as a manacle to science.

His admiration for those epochs in which new
truths were most successfully discovered, and old
fallacies most signally routed, did not prevent Turgot
from appreciating the ages of criticism and their
services to knowledge. He does full justice to
Alexandria, not only for its astronomy and geometry,
but for that peculiar studiousness ' that exercises
itself less on things than on books ; whose strength
lies less in producing and discovering, than in collecting and comparing and estimating what has been
produced and discovered ; that does not press forward, but gazes backward along the road that has
already been traversed. The studies that require
most genius, are not always those implying most
progress in the mass of men. There are minds to

[1] *Œuvres*, i. 601.

which nature has given a memory capable of comparing truths, of suggesting an arrangement that
places these truths in the fullest light ; but to which,
at the same time, she has refused the ardour of
genius that insists on inventing and opening out
for itself new lines of discovery. Made to unite
former discoveries under a single point of view, to
surround them with light, and to exhibit them in
entire perfection, if they are not luminaries that
burn and sparkle of themselves, at least they are
like diamonds that reflect with dazzling brilliance
a borrowed light.'

Thus Turgot's conception of progress regards it
mainly, if not entirely, as a gradual dawn and
diffusion of light, the spreading abroad of the rays
of knowledge. He does not assert, as some moderns
have asserted, that morality is of the nature of a
fixed quantity ; still he hints something of the kind.
' Morality,' he says, speaking of Greece in the time
of its early physical speculation, ' though still imperfect, still kept fewer relics of the infancy of reason.
Those ever-springing necessities that so incessantly
recall man to society, and force him to bend to its
laws ; the instinct, the sentiment of what is good and
right, which Providence has engraved in all hearts,
and which precedes reason, all lead the thinkers of
every time back to the same fundamental principles
of the science of morals.'

We meet with this limitation of the idea of progress
in every member of the school to which, more than

to any other, Turgot belonged. Even in the vindication of the claims of Christianity to the gratitude of mankind, he had forborne from laying stress on any original contribution supposed to be made by that religion to the precious stock of ethical ideas. He dwells upon the ' tender zeal for the progress of truth that the Christian religion inspired,' and recounts the various circumstances in which it spread and promoted the social and political conditions most favourable to intellectual or scientific activity. Whatever may be the truth or the value of Christianity as a dogmatic system, there can be little doubt that its weight as a historic force is to be looked for, not so much in the encouragement it gave to science and learning, in respect of which western Europe probably owes more to Mahometanism, as in the high and generous types of character it inspired. A man of rare moral depth, warmth, or delicacy, may be a more important element in the advance of civilisation, than the newest and truest deduction from what Turgot calls ' the fundamental principles of the science of morals.' The leading of souls to do what is right and humane, is always more urgent than mere instruction of the intelligence as to what exactly is the right and the humane. The saint after all has a place in positive history ; the men of the eighteenth century passionately threw him out from their calendar, as the wooden idol of superstition.

IV.

In 1761, Turgot, then in his thirty-fourth year, was appointed to the office of Intendant in the Generality of Limoges. There were three different divisions of France in the eighteenth century : first and oldest, the diocese or ecclesiastical circumscription ; second, the province or military government ; and third, the Generality, a district defined for fiscal and administrative purposes. The Intendant in the government was very much what the Prefect is in the government of our own time. Perhaps, however, we understand Turgot's position in Limousin best by comparing it to that of the Chief Commissioner of a great district in our Indian Empire. For example, the first task that Turgot had to perform was to execute a new land-assessment for purposes of imperial revenue. He had to construct roads, to build barracks, to administer justice, to deal with a famine, just as the English civilian has to do in Orissa or Behar. Much of his time was taken up in elaborate memorials to the central government, and the desk of the Controller-General at Versailles was loaded with minutes and reports exactly like the voluminous papers that fill the mahogany boxes of Members of Council at Calcutta. The fundamental conditions of the two systems of government were much alike ; absolute political authority, and an elaborately centralised civil administration for keeping order and raising a revenue. The direct authority of an

Intendant was not considerable. His chief functions were the settlement of detail in executing the general orders that he received from the minister; a provisional decision on certain kinds of minor affairs; and a power of judging some civil suits, subject to appeal to the Council.

Of all the thirty-two great districts in which the Intendant stood between the common people and the minister at Versailles, the Generality of Limoges was the poorest, the rudest, the most backward, and the most miserable. To the eye of the traveller with a mind for the picturesque, there were parts of this central region of France whose smiling undulations, delicious water-scenes, deep glens extending into amphitheatres, and slopes hung with woods of chestnut, all seemed to make a lovelier picture than the cheerful beauty of prosperous Normandy, or the olive-groves and orange-gardens of Provence. Arthur Young thought the Limousin the most beautiful part of France. Unhappily for the cultivator, these gracious conformations belonged to a harsh and churlish soil. For him the roll of the chalk and the massing of the granite would have been well exchanged for the fat loams of Picardy. The soil of the Limousin was declared by its inhabitants to be the most ungrateful in the whole kingdom, returning no more than four net for one of seed sown, while there was land in the vale of the Garonne that returned thirty-fold. The two conditions for raising tolerable crops were abundance of labour and abundance of manure. But misery drove the men away, and the stock were sold to pay the taxes. So the land lacked both the arms of the tiller, and the dressing whose generous chemistry would have transmuted the dull earth into fruitfulness and plenty. The extent of the district was estimated at a million and a half hectares, equivalent to nearly four millions of English acres : yet the population of this vast tract was only five hundred thousand souls.

The common food of the people was the chestnut, and to the great majority of them even the coarsest rye-bread was a luxury that they had never tasted. Maize and buckwheat were their chief cereals, and these, together with a coarse radish, took up hundreds of acres that might under a happier system have produced fine wheat and nourished fruit-trees. There had once been a certain export of cattle, but that had now come to an end, partly because the general decline of the district had impaired the quality of the beasts, and partly because the Parisian butchers, who were by much the greatest customers, had found the markets of Normandy more convenient. The more the trade went down, the heavier was the burden of the cattle-tax on the stock that remained. The stock-dealer was thus ruined from both sides. In the same way, the Limousin horses, whose breed had been famous all over France, had ceased to be an object of commerce, and the progressive increase of taxation had gradually extinguished the trade. Angoumois, which formed part of the Generality of Limoges, had

previously boasted of producing the best and finest
paper in the world, and it had found a market not
only throughout France, but all over Europe.   There
had been a time when this manufacture supported
sixty mills ; at the death of Louis XIV. their number
had fallen from sixty to sixteen.   An excise duty at
the mill, a duty on exportation at the provincial
frontier, a duty on the importation of rags over
the provincial frontier,—all these vexations had
reduced the trade with Holland, one of France's
best customers, to one-fourth of its previous dimensions.   Nor were paper and cattle the only branches
of trade blighted by fiscal perversity.   The same
burden arrested the transport of saffron across the
borders of the province, on its way to Hungary and
Prussia and the other cold lands where saffron was
a favourite condiment.   Salt, which came up the
Charente from the marshes by the coast, was stripped
of all its profit, first by the duty paid on crossing
from the Limousin to Périgord and Auvergne, and
next by the right possessed by certain of the great
lords on the banks of the Charente, to help themselves
at one point and another to portions of the cargo.
Iron was subject to a harassing excise in all those
parts of the country beyond the jurisdiction of the
parlement of Bordeaux.   The effect of such positive
hindrances as these to the transit of goods was
further aided, to the destruction of trade, by the
absence of roads.   There were four roads in the
province, but all of them so bad that the traveller

E

knew not whether to curse more lustily the rocks
or the swamps that interrupted his journey alter-
nately.   There were two rivers, the Vienne and the
Vézère, and these might seem to an enthusiast for the
argument from Design, as if Nature had intended
them for the transport of timber from the immense
forests that crowned the Limousin hills.   Unluckily,
their beds were so thickly bestrewn with rocks that
neither of them was navigable for any considerable
part of its long course through the ill-starred province.
   The inhabitants were as cheerless as the land on
which they lived.   They had none of the fiery energy,
the eloquence, the mobility of the people of the south.
Still less were they endowed with the apt intelligence,
the ease, the social amiability, the openness, of their
neighbours on the north.   ' The dwellers in Upper
Limousin,' said one who knew them, ' are coarse and
heavy, jealous, distrustful, avaricious.'   The dwellers
in Lower Limousin had a less repulsive address, but
they were at least as narrowly self-interested at heart,
and they added a capacity for tenacious and vindictive hatred.   The Limousins had the superstitious
doctrines of other semi-barbarous populations, and
they had their vices.   They passed abruptly and
without remorse from a penitential procession to the
tavern and the brothel.   Their Christianity was as
superficial as that of the peasant of the Eifel in our
own day, or of the Finnish converts of whom we are
told that they are even now not beyond sacrificing
a foal in honour of the Virgin Mary.   Saint Martial

and Saint Leonard were the patron saints of the country, and were the objects of an adoration in comparison with which the other saints fell into a secondary place.

They were deeply superstitious, violent in their prejudices, obstinate withstanders of all novelty, rude, hardly redeeming a narrow and blinding covetousness by stubborn industry. Their country has been fixed upon as the cradle of Celtic nationality in France, and there are some who believe that here the old Gaulish blood kept itself purer from external admixture than anywhere else in the land. In our own day, when an orator has occasion to pay a compliment to the townsmen of Limoges, he says that the genius of the people of the district has ever been faithful to its source ; it has ever held the balance true between the Frank tradition of the north, and the Roman tradition of the south. This makes an excellent period for a rhetorician, but the fact it conveys made Limousin the severer task for an administrator. Almost immediately after his appointment, Turgot had the chance of being removed to Rouen, and after that to Lyons. Either of these promotions would have had the advantages of a considerable increase of income, less laborious duties, and a much more agreeable residence. Turgot, with a sense of duty that probably seemed quixotic enough to the Controller-General, declined the preferment, on the very ground of the difficulty and importance of the task that he had already undertaken. *Poor peasants,*

poor kingdom!' had been Quesnay's constant exclamation, and it had sunk deep into the spirit of his
disciple. He could have little thought of high salary
or personal ease when he discerned an opportunity of
improving the hard lot of the peasant, and softening
the misfortunes of the realm.

Turgot was one of the men to whom good government is a religion. It might be said to be the religion
of all the best men of that century, and this was
natural. The decay of a theology that places our
deepest solicitudes in a sphere beyond this, is naturally
accompanied by a transfer of these high solicitudes
to a nearer scene. But though the desire for good
government, and a right sense of its cardinal importance, were common ideas of the time in all the best
heads from Voltaire downwards, yet Turgot had
a patience that in them was wanting. Though he
respected the writings of Rousseau and confessed his
obligations to them, Turgot abhorred declamation.
He had no hope of clearing society of the intellectual
and moral débris of ages at a stroke. Nor had he
abstract standards of human bliss. The keyword
to his political theory was not Pity nor Benevolence,
but Justice. 'We are sure to go wrong,' he said
once, when pressed to confer some advantage on
the poor at the cost of the rich, 'the moment we
forget that *justice alone can keep the balance true
among all rights and all interests.*'

As everybody knows, the great fiscal grievance of
old France was the *taille*, a tax raised on property and

income, but only on the property and income of the
unprivileged classes. In the Limousin Turgot's predecessor tried to substitute, for the arbitrary *taille*,
a tax systematically assessed in proportion to the
amount of the person's property. Such a design
involved a complete remeasurement and revaluation
of all the land of the Generality, and that was a task
of immense magnitude and difficulty. It was very
imperfectly performed, and Turgot found a province
groaning under a mass of fiscal anomalies and disorders. Assessment, collection, exemption, were all
alike conducted without definite principles or uniform
system. Besides these abuses, the total sum demanded
from the Generality by the royal government was
greatly in excess of the local resources. The district
was heavily overcharged, relatively to other districts
around it. No deduction had been made from the
sum exacted by the treasury, though the falling off
in prosperity was great and notorious. Turgot computed that ' the king's share ' was as large as that
of the proprietors ; in other words, taxation absorbed
one half of the net products of the land. The government listened to these representations, and conceded
to the Generality about half of the remissions that
Turgot had solicited. A greater operation was the
readjustment of the burden, thus lightened, within
the province. The people were so irritated by the
disorders introduced by the imperfect operation of
the proportional *taille* that, with the characteristic
impatience of a rude and unintelligent population,

they were heedlessly crying out for a return to the more familiar, and therefore more comfortable, disorders of the arbitrary *taille*. Turgot resisted this slovenly reaction, and applied himself with zealous industry to the immense and complex work of effecting a complete revision and settlement of the regulations for assessment, and, what was a more gigantic enterprise, of carrying out a new survey and new valuation of lands and property, to serve as a true base for the application of an equitable assessment. At the end of thirteen years of indomitable toil the work was still unfinished, chiefly owing to want of money. The court wasted more in a fortnight in the easy follies of Versailles than would have given to the Limousin the instrument of a finished scheme of fiscal order. Turgot's labour was not wholly thrown away. The worst abuses were corrected, and the most crying iniquities swept away, save that iniquity of the exemption of the privileged orders, which Turgot could not yet venture to touch.

Another of the master abuses of the old system was the introduction of the *corvée*, that, in the sense in which we have to speak of it, dates no further back than the beginning of the eighteenth century. It was an encroachment and an innovation on the part of the bureaucracy, and the odd circumstance has been remarked that the first mention of the road *corvées* in any royal Act is the famous edict of 1776, which suppressed them. Until the Regency this famous word had described only the services

owed by dependents to their lords. It meant so
many days' labour on the lord's lands, and so many
offices of domestic duty. When, in the early part
of the century, the advantages of a good system of
high-roads began to be perceived by the government, the convenient idea came into the heads of
the more ingenious among the Intendants of imposing, for the construction of the roads, a royal or
public *corvée* analogous to that of private feudalism.
Few more mischievous imposts could have been
devised.

That undying class who are contented with the
shallow presumptions of *a priori* reasoning in economic
matters, did, it is true, find specious pleas even for
the road *corvée*. There has never been an abuse in
the history of the world for which something good
could not be said. If men earned money by labour
and the use of their time, why not require from them
time and labour instead of money? By the latter
device, are we not assured against malversation of
the funds? Those who substitute words for things,
and verbal plausibilities for the observation of experience, could prolong these arguments indefinitely.
The evils of the road *corvée* meanwhile remained patent
and indisputable. In England at the same period,
it is true, the country people were obliged to give six
days in the year to the repair of the highways, under
the management of the justices of the peace. And
in England the business was performed without
oppression. But then this only illustrates the un-

wisdom of arguing about economic arrangements in
the abstract. All depends on the conditions by
which the given arrangement is surrounded, and a
practice that in England was merely clumsy, was in
France not only clumsy but a gross cruelty. The
French peasant had to give, not six, but twelve or
fifteen days of labour every year for the construction
and repair of the roads of his neighbourhood. If he
had a horse and cart, they too were pressed into the
service. He could not choose the time; he was
constantly carried away at the moment when his
own poor harvest needed his right arm and his
supervision. He received no pay, and his days on
the roads were days of hunger to himself and his
family. He had the bitterness of knowing that the
advantage of the high-road to himself was slight
and sometimes null, while it was direct and great
to the town merchants and the country gentlemen
who contributed not an hour nor a sou to the
work. It was exactly the most indigent upon whose
backs this slavish load was placed. There were a
hundred abuses of spite or partiality, of favouritism
or vengeance, in the allotment of the work. The
wretch was sent to the part of the road most distant
from his own house; or he was forced to work for a
longer time than fell fairly to his share; or he saw
a neighbour allowed to escape on payment of a sum
of money. And at the end of all, the roads were
vile. The labourers, having little heart in work for
which they had no wage, and weakened by want of

food, did badly what they had to do. There was no
scientific superintendence, no skilled direction, little
system in the construction, little watchfulness as to
the maintenance. The rains of winter and the storms
of summer did damage that one man could have
repaired by careful industry from day to day, and
that for lack of this one man went on increasing,
until the road fell into holes, the ditches got filled up,
and deep pools of water stood permanently in the
middle of the highway. The rich disdained to put
a hand to the work ; the poor, aware that they would
be forced to the hated task in the following autumn
or spring, naturally attended to their own fields, and
left the roads to fall to ruin.

It need not be said that barbarous slovenliness
and disorder meant incredible waste. It was calculated that a contractor would have provided and
maintained fine roads for little more than one-third
of the cost at which the *corvée* furnished roads
that were execrable. Condorcet was right in comparing the government in this matter to a simple-
ton who indulges in all the more lavish riot because
by paying for nothing, and getting everything at
a higher price on credit, he is never frightened
into sense by being confronted with a budget of his
prodigalities.

It takes fewer words to describe Turgot's way of
dealing with this oriental mixture of extravagance,
injustice, and squalor. The Intendant of Caen had
already proposed to the inhabitants of that district

the alternative plan of commuting the *corvee* into
money payment. Turgot adopted and perfected this
transformation. He substituted for personal service
on the roads a yearly rate, proportional in amount
to the *taille*. He instituted a systematic survey and
direction of the roads, existing or required in the
Generality, and he committed the execution of the
approved plans to contractors on exact and business-
like principles. The result of this change was not
merely an immense relief to the unfortunate men
who had been every year harassed to death and half-
ruined by the old method of forced labour, but so
remarkable an improvement in both the goodness and
the extension of the roads, that when Arthur Young
went over them five-and-twenty years afterwards, he
pronounced them by far the noblest public ways to be
found anywhere in France.

Two very instructive facts may be mentioned in
connection with the suppression of the *corvées* in the
Limousin. The first is that the central government
assented to the changes proposed by the young
Intendant as promptly as if it had been a committee
of the Convention, instead of being the nominee of
an absolute king. The other is that the people in
the country, when Turgot had his plans laid before
them in their parish meetings, held after mass on
Sundays, listened with the keenest distrust and
suspicion to what they insisted on regarding as a
sinister design for exacting more money. Well might
Condorcet say that very often it needs little courage

to do men harm, for they constantly suffer harm
tranquilly enough ; but when you take it into your
head to do them some service, then they accuse you
of being an innovator. It is fair, however, to remember how many good grounds the French country-
man had for distrusting the professions of any agent
of the government. This is only an illustration of
what is now a well-known fact, that revolution was
made necessary less by despotism than by privilege
on the one side, and by intense political distrust on
the other.

Turgot was thoroughly awake to the necessity of
penetrating public opinion. The first principle of
the school of Economists was an ' enlightened people.'
Nothing was to be done by them ; everything was to
be done for them. But they were to be trained to
understand the grounds of the measures that a
central authority conceived, shaped, and carried into
practice. Rousseau was the only writer of the
revolutionary school who had the modern democratic
faith in the virtue and wisdom of the common people.
Voltaire habitually spoke of their bigotry and prejudice with the natural bitterness of a cultivated
man towards incurable ignorance. The Economists
admitted Voltaire's view as true of an existing state
of things, but they looked to education, meaning
by that something more than primary instruction,
to lead gradually to the development of sound
political intelligence. Hence when Turgot came
into full power as the minister of Louis XVI., twelve

years after he first went to his obscure duties in the
Limousin, he introduced the method of prefacing his
edicts by an elaborate statement of the reasons on
which their policy rested. And on the same principle
he now adopted the only means at his disposal for
instructing and directing opinion. The book press
was at that moment doing tremendous work among
the classes with education and leisure. But the
newspaper press hardly existed, and even if it had
existed, however many official journals Turgot might
have had under his inspiration, the people whose
minds he wished to affect could not read. There
was only one way of reaching them, and that was
through the priests. Religious life among the
Limousins was, as we have seen, not very pure, but
it is a significant law of human nature that the less
pure a religion is, the more important in it is the
place of the priest and his office. Turgot pressed the
curés into friendly service. It is a remarkable fact,
not without a parallel in other parts of modern
history, that of the two great conservative corporations of society, the lawyers did all they could to
thwart his projects, and the priests did all they could
to advance them. In truth the priests are usually
more or less sympathetic towards any form of
centralised authority; it is only when the people
take their own government into their own hands that
the clergy are apt to turn cold or antipathetic towards
improvement. There is one other reservation, as
Turgot found out in 1775, when he had been trans-

ferred to a greater post, and the clergy had joined
his bitterest enemies. Then he touched the corporate
spirit, and perceived that for authority to lay a hand
on ecclesiastical privilege is to metamorphose good-
will into malignity. Meanwhile, the letters in which
Turgot explained his views and wishes to the curés,
by them to be imparted to their parishes, are masterpieces of the care, the patience, the interest, of a
good ruler. Those peremptory spirits who see in
Frederick or Napoleon the only born rulers of men,
might find in these letters, and in the acts to which
they refer, the memorials of a far more admirable
and beneficent type.

The *corvée*, vexatious as it was, yet excited less
violent heats and inflicted less misery than the abuses
of military service. There had been a militia in the
country as far back as the time of the Merovingians,
but the militia-service with which Turgot had to deal
only dated from 1726. Each parish was bound to
supply its quota of men to this service, and the
obligation was perhaps the most odious grievance,
though not the most really mischievous, of all that
then afflicted the realm. The hatred that it raised
was due to no failure of the military spirit in the
people. From Frederick the Great downwards,
everybody was well aware that the disasters to France,
that had begun with the shameful defeat of Rossbach,
and ended with the loss of Canada in the West and
the Indies in the East (1757–63), were due to no

want of valour in the common soldier. It was the
generals, as Napoleon said fifty years afterwards, who
were incapable and inept. And it was the ineptitude
of the administrative chiefs that made the militia at
once ineffective and abhorred. First, they allowed a
large number of classified exemptions from the ballot.
The noble, the tonsured clerk, the counsellor, the
domestic of noble, tonsured clerk, and counsellor, the
eldest son of the lawyer and the farmer, the tax-
collector, the schoolmaster, were all exempt. Hence
the curse of service was embittered by a sense of
injustice. This was one of the many springs in the
old régime that fed the swelling and vehement stream
of passion for social equality, until at length when the
day came, it made such short and furious work with
the structure of envious partition between citizen and
citizen.

Again, by a curious perversity of official pedantry,
the government insisted on each man who drew the
black ticket in the abhorred lottery, performing his
service in person. It forbade substitution. Under
a modern system of universal military service, this
is intelligible and just. But, as we have seen,
military service was only made obligatory on those
who were already ground down by hardships. As
a consequence of this prohibition, those who were
liable to be drawn lived in despair, and as no worse
thing than the black ticket could possibly befall
them, they had every inducement to run away from
their own homes and villages. At the approach of

the commissary of the government, they fled into the woods and marshes, as if they had been pursued by the plague. This was a signal for a civil war on a small scale. Those who were left behind, and whose chance of being drawn was thus increased, hastened to pursue the fugitives with such weapons as came to their hands. In the Limousin the country was constantly the scene of murderous disorders of this kind. What was worse, was not only that the land was infested by vagabonds and bad characters, but that villages became half depopulated, and the soil lost its cultivators. Finally, as is uniformly the case in the history of bad government, an unjust method produced a worthless machine. The *milice* supplied as bad troops as the *corvée* supplied bad roads. The force was recruited from the lowest class of the population, and as soon as its members had learned a little drill, they were discharged and their places taken by raw batches provided at random by lot.

Turgot proposed that a character both of permanence and of locality should be given to the provincial force; that each parish or union of parishes should be required to raise a number of men; that these men should be left at home and in their own districts, and only called out for exercise for a certain time each year; and that they should be retained as a reserve force by a small payment. In this way, he argued that the government would secure a competent force, and by stimulating local pride and point of honour would make service popular instead of hateful. As the government was too weak and distracted to take up so important a scheme as this, Turgot was obliged to content himself with evading the existing regulations ; and it is a curious illustration of the pliancy of Versailles, that he should have been allowed to do so openly and without official remonstrance. He permitted the victim of the ballot to provide a voluntary substitute, and he permitted the parish to tempt substitutes by payment of a sum of money on enrolment. This may seem a very obvious course to follow ; but no one who has tried to realise the strength and obstinacy of routine, will measure the service of a reformer by the originality of his ideas. In affairs of government, the priceless qualities are not merely originality of resource, but a sense for things that are going wrong, and a sufficiently vigorous will to set them right.

One general expression serves to describe this most important group of Turgot's undertakings. The reader has probably already observed that what Turgot was doing, was to take the step that is one of the most decisive in the advance of a society to a highly organised industrial stage. He displaced imposts in kind, that rudest and most wasteful form of contribution to the public service, and established in their stead a system of money payments, and of having the work of the government done on commercial principles. Thus, as if it were not enough to tear the peasant away from the soil to serve in

the militia ; as if it were not enough to drag away
the farmer and his cattle to the public highways, the
reigning system struck a third blow at agriculture by
requiring the people of the localities that happened
to be traversed by a regiment on the march, to supply
their waggons and horses and oxen for the purposes
of military transport. In this case, it is true, a
certain compensation in money was allowed, but
we may easily understand how inadequate was this
insignificant allowance. The payment was only for
one day, but the day's march was often of many
miles, and the oxen, which in the Limousin mostly
did the work of horses, were constantly seen to drop
down dead in the roads. There was not only the
one day's work. Often two, three, or five days were
needed to reach the place of appointment, and for
these days not even the paltry twenty sous were
granted. Nor could any payment of this kind recompense the peasant for the absence of his beasts
of burden on the great days when he wanted to
plough his fields, to carry the grain to the barns, or
to take his produce to market. The obvious remedy
here, as in the *corvées*, was to have the transport
effected by a contractor, and to pay him out of a
rate levied on the persons liable. This was what
Turgot ordered to be done.

Of one other burden of the same species he relieved
the cultivator. This unfortunate being was liable
to be called upon to collect, as well as to pay, the
taxes. Once nominated, he became responsible for

F

the amount at which his commune was assessed. If
he did not produce the sum, he lost his liberty. If
he advanced it from his own pocket, he lost at least
the interest on the money. In collecting the money
from his fellow taxpayers, he not only incurred bitter
and incessant animosities, but, what was harder to
bear, he lost the priceless time of which his own land
was only too sorely in need. In the Limousin the
luckless creature had a special disadvantage, for here
the collector of the *taille* had also to collect the
twentieths, and the twentieths were a tax for which
even the privileged classes were liable. They, as
might be supposed, cavilled, disputed, and appealed.
The appeal lay to a sort of county board, composed
of people of their own kind, before which they too
easily made out a plausible case against a clumsy
collector, who more often than not knew neither
how to read nor how to write. Turgot's reform
of a system that was always harassing and often
ruinous to an innocent individual, consisted in
the creation of the task of collection into a distinct
and permanent office, exercised over districts sufficiently large to make the poundage, out of which
the collectors were paid, an inducement to persons
of intelligence and spirit to undertake the office as
a profession.

Apart from these, the most difficult of all Turgot's
administrative reforms, we may notice his assi-
duity in watching for the smaller opportunities
of making life easier to the people. His private

benevolence was incessant and marked. One case of its exercise carries our minds at a word into the very midst of the storm of fire that purified France of the evil and sordid elements, that now and for his life lay like a mountain of lead on all Turgot's aims and efforts. A certain foreign contractor at Limoges was ruined by the famine of 1770. He had a clever son, whom Turgot charitably sent to school, and afterwards to college in Paris. The youth grew up to be the most eloquent and dazzling of the Girondins, the high-souled Vergniaud. It was not, however, in good works of merely private destination that Turgot exercised himself. In 1767 the district was infested by wolves. The Intendant imposed a small tax for the purpose of providing rewards for the destruction of these tormentors, and in reading the minutes on the subject we are reminded of the fact, that was not without its significance when the peasants rose in vengeance on their lords two-and-twenty years later, that the dispersion of the hamlets and the solitude of the farms had made it customary for the people to go about with fire-arms. Besides encouraging the destruction of noxious beasts, Turgot did something for the preservation of beasts not noxious. The first veterinary school in France had been founded at Lyons in 1762. To this he sent pupils from his province, and eventually he founded a similar school at Limoges. He suppressed a tax on cattle, which acted prejudicially on breeding and grazing ; and he introduced clover into the grass-

lands. The potato had been unknown in the Limousin.
It was not common in any part of France ; and perhaps this is not astonishing when we remember that
the first field crop even in Scotland is supposed only
to have been sown in the fourth decade of that
century. People would not touch it, though the
experiment of persuading them to cultivate this root
had been frequently tried. In the Limousin the
people were even more obstinate in their prejudice
than elsewhere. But Turgot persevered. The
ordinary view was that potatoes were hardly fit for
pigs, and that in human beings they would certainly
breed leprosy. Some of the English Puritans would
not eat potatoes because they are not mentioned in
the Bible, and that is perhaps no better reason than
the other. When, however, it was seen that the
Intendant had the hated vegetable served every day
at his own table, the opposition grew more faint.

This was the time when the passion for provincial
academies of all sorts was at its height. When we
consider that Turgot's society was not practical but
deliberative, and what themes he proposed for discussion by it, we may believe that it was one of the
less useful of his works. What the farmers needed
was something much more directly instructive in
the methods of their business, than could come of
discussions as to the effects of indirect taxation on
the revenues of landowners, or the right manner of
valuing the income of land in the different kinds of
cultivation. 'In that most unlucky path of French

exertion,' says Arthur Young, ' this distinguished patriot was able to do nothing. This society does like other societies ; they meet, converse, offer premiums, and publish nonsense. This is not of much consequence, for the people, instead of reading their memoirs, are not able to read at all. They can, however, *see*, and if a farm was established in that good cultivation which they ought to copy, something would be presented from which they *might* learn. I asked particularly if the members of this society had land in their own hands, and was assured that they had ; but the conversation presently explained it. They had *métayers* round their country seats, and this was considered as farming their own lands, so that they assume something of a merit from the identical circumstance, which is the curse and ruin of the whole country.'

To his superior enlightenment in another part of the commercial field we owe one of the most excellent of Turgot's pieces, his *Memorial on Loans of Money*. This plea for free trade in money has all the sense and liberality of the brightest side of the eighteenth-century illumination. It was suggested by circumstances. At Angoulême four or five rogues associated together, and drew bills on one another. On these bills they borrowed money, the average rate of interest being from eight to ten per cent. When the bills fell due, instead of paying them, they laid informations against the lenders for taking more than the legal rate of interest. The lenders were ruined, persons who had money were afraid to make advances, bills were protested, commercial credit was broken, and the trade of the district was paralysed. Turgot prevailed upon the Council of State to withdraw the cases from the local jurisdiction; the proceedings against the lenders were annulled, and the institution of similar proceedings forbidden. This was a characteristic course. The royal government was generally willing in the latter half of the eighteenth century to redress a given case of abuse, but it never felt itself strong enough, or had leisure enough, to deal with the general source from which the particular grievance sprang. Turgot's *Memorial* is as cogent an exposure of the mischief of Usury Laws to the public prosperity, as the more renowned pages of either Bentham or J. B. Say on the same subject.

After he had been eight years at his post, Turgot was called upon to deal with the harassing problems of a scarcity of food. In 1770 even the maize and black grain, and the chestnuts on which the people supported life, failed almost completely, and the failure extended over two years.

His first battle was on an issue that has been painfully familiar to our own Indian administrators. In 1764, an edict had been promulgated decreeing free trade in grain, not with foreign countries, but among the different provinces of the kingdom. This edict had not made much way in the minds either of the local officials or of the people at large, and the presence of famine made the free and unregulated

export of food seem no better than a cruel paradox. The parlement of Bordeaux at once suspended the edict of 1764. They ordered that all
dealers in grain, farmers of land, owners of land,
of whatever rank, quality, or condition, should
forthwith convey to the markets of their district
' *a sufficient quantity* ' of grain to provision the
said markets. The same persons were forbidden to
sell either by wholesale or retail any portion of the
said grain at their own granaries. Turgot at once
procured from the Council at Versailles the proper
instrument for checking this impolitic interference
with the free circulation of grain, and he contrived
this instrument in such conciliatory terms as to avoid
any breach with the parlement, whose motives, for
that matter, were respectable enough. In spite, however, of the action of the government, popular feeling
ran high against free markets. Tumultuous gatherings of famishing men and women menaced the
unfortunate grain-dealers. Waggoners engaged in
carrying grain away from a place where it was cheaper,
to another place where it was dearer, were violently
arrested in their business, and terrified from proceeding. Hunger prevented people from discerning the
unanswerable force of the argument that if the grain
commanded a higher price somewhere else, that was
a sure sign of the need there being sharper. The
local officials were as hostile as their humbler neighbours. At the town of Turenne, they forbade grain
to be taken away, and forced the owners of it to sell

it on the spot at the market rate. At the town of
Angoulême the lieutenant of police took upon himself
to order that all the grain destined for the Limousin
should be unloaded and stored at Angoulême. Turgot
brought a heavy hand to bear on these breakers of
administrative discipline, and readily procured such
sanction as his authority needed from the Council.

One of the measures to which Turgot resorted
in meeting the destitution of the country, was the
establishment of the Charitable Workshops. Some
of the advocates of the famous National Workshops of 1848 have appealed to this example of
the severe patriot, for a sanction to their own economic policy. It is not clear that the logic of the
Socialist is here more remorseless than usual. If
the State may set up workshops to aid people who
are short of food because the harvest has failed, why
should it not do the same when people are short of
food because trade is bad, work scarce, and wages
intolerably low? Of course Turgot's answer would
have been that remorseless logic is the most improper
instrument in the world for a business of rough
expedients. There is a vital difference in practice
between opening a public workshop in the exceptional
emergency of a famine, and keeping public workshops
open as a normal interference with the free course of
industrial activity. To invoke Turgot as a dabbler
in Socialism because he opened *ateliers de charité*, is
as unreasonable as it would be to make an English
minister, who should suspend the Bank Charter Act

in a crisis, into the champion of inconvertible
paper currency. Turgot always regarded the sums
paid in his works, not as wages, but as alms. All
that he urged was that ' the best and most useful
kind of alms consists in providing means for earning
them.' To prevent the workers from earning aid
with as little trouble to themselves as possible, he
recommended payment by the piece and not by the
day. To check workers from flocking in from their
regular employments, he insisted on the wages being
kept below the ordinary rate, and he urged the
propriety of driving as sharp bargains as possible in
fixing the price of the piece of work. To prevent the
dissipation of earnings at the tavern, he paid not in
money, but in leathern tokens, that were only current
in exchange for provisions. All these regulations
mark a wide enough gulf between the Economist of
1770 and the Socialist of 1848.

The story of the famine in the Limousin brings to
light some instructive facts as to the temper of the
lords and rich proprietors on the eve of the changes
that were to destroy them. Turgot had been specially
anxious that as much as possible of what was necessary for the relief of distress should be done by private
persons. He knew the straits of the government.
He knew how hard it would be to extract from it
the means of repairing a deficit in his own finances.
Accordingly he invited the landowners, not merely
to contribute sums of money in return for the public
works carried on in their neighbourhood, but also,

by way of providing employment to their indigent
neighbours, to undertake such works as they should
find convenient on their own estates. The response
was disappointing. ' The districts,' he wrote in 1772,
' where I have works on foot, do not give me reason
to hope for much help on the side of the generosity
of the nobles and the rich landowners. The Prince
de Soubise is so far the only person who has given
anything for the works that have been executed in
his duchy.' Nor was abstinence from generosity the
worst part of this failure in public spirit. The same
nobles and landowners who refused to give, did not
refuse to take away. Most of them proceeded at
once to dismiss their *métayers*, the people who farmed
their lands in consideration of a fixed proportion of
the produce. Turgot, in an ordinance of admirable
gravity, remonstrated against this harsh and impolitic proceeding. He pointed out that the unfortunate wretches, thus stripped of every resource,
would have to leave the district, abandoning their
wives and children to the charity of villages that
were already overburdened with the charge of their
own people.

Turgot's policy in this matter is more instructive
as to the social state of France, than it may at first
sight appear. At first sight we are astonished to
find the austere economist travelling so far from the
orthodox path of free contract as to order a land-
owner to furnish at his own cost subsistence for his
impoverished tenants. But the *métayer* was not a

free tenant in the sense which we attach to the word. ' *In the Limousin,*' says Arthur Young, ' *the métayers are considered as little better than menial servants.*' And it is not going beyond the evidence to say that they were even something lower than menial servants; they were really a kind of serf-caste. They lived in the lowest misery. More than half of them were computed to be deeply in debt to the proprietors. In many cases they were even reduced every year to borrow from their land-lord, before the harvest came round, such coarse bread of mixed rye and barley as he might choose to lend them. What Turgot therefore had in his mind was no relation of free contract, though it was that legally, but a relation which partly resembled that of a feudal lord to his retainer, and partly that of a planter to his negroes. It is less surprising, then, that Turgot should have enforced some of the responsibilities of the lord and the planter.

The nobles had resort to a still more indefensible measure than the expulsion of their *métayers*. Most of the lands in the Generality of Limoges were charged with dues in kind payable to the lords. As the cultivators had for the most part no grain even for their own bread, they naturally had no grain for the lords' dues. The lords then insisted on payment in cash, and they insisted on estimating this payment at the famine price of the grain. Most of them were really as needy as they were idle and proud, and nothing is so inordinately grasping as the indigence

of class-pride. The effect of their proceedings now
was to increase their revenue fourfold and fivefold
out of public calamity and universal misery. And
unfortunately the liability of the cultivators in a
given manor was *solidaire*; they were jointly and
severally responsible, and the effect of this was that
even those who were in circumstances to pay the
quadrupled dues, were ruined and destroyed without
mercy in consequence of having also to pay the
quadrupled dues of their beggared neighbours.
Turgot arrested this odious process by means of an
old and forgotten decree, that he prevailed upon
the parlement of Bordeaux to revive in good and due
form, to the effect that the arrears of dues in kind
for 1769 should be paid at the market price of grain
when the dues were payable; that is, before the
scarcity had declared itself.

When we consider the grinding and extortionate
spirit thus shown in face of a common calamity, we
may cease to wonder at the ferocity with which, when
the hour struck, the people tore away privilege, distinction, and property itself, from classes that had
used all three only to ruin the land and crush its
inhabitants into the dust. And the moment that
the lord had thus transformed himself into a mere
creditor, and a creditor for goods delivered centuries
ago, and long since consumed and forgotten, then it
was certain that, if political circumstances favoured
the growing economic sentiment, there would be
heard again the old cry of the Roman plebs for an

77

agrarian law and *novæ tabulæ*. Nay, something was heard that is amazingly like the cry of the modern Irish peasant. In 1776 two noteworthy incidents happened. A certain Marquis de Vibraye threw into prison a peasant who refused to pay the *droit de cens*. Immediately between thirty and forty peasants came to the rescue, armed themselves, besieged the château, took it and sacked it, and drove the Marquis de Vibraye away in terror. Still more significant is the second incident, shortly after. A relative of the Duke of Mortemart, shooting on his property, was attacked by peasants who insisted that he should cease his sport. They treated him with much brutality, and even threatened to fire on him and his attendants, '*claiming to be free masters of their lands.*' Here was the main root of the Revolution. A fair consideration of the details of such an undertaking as Turgot's administration of the Limousin helps us to understand two things : first, that all the ideas necessary for the pacific transformation of French society were there in the midst of it ; second, that the system of privilege had fostered such a spirit in one class, and the reaction against the inconsiderate manifestation of that spirit was so violent in the other class, that political ideas were vain and inapplicable.

It is curious to find that, in the midst of his beneficent administration, Turgot was rating practical work very low in comparison with the achievements of the student and the thinker. 'You are very fortunate,' Condorcet said to him, ' in having a

passion for the public good, and in being able to
satisfy it ; it is a great consolation, and of a very
superior order to the consolation of mere study.'
' Nay,' replied Turgot, in his next letter, ' whatever
you may say, I believe that the satisfaction derived
from study is superior to any other kind of satisfaction. I am perfectly convinced that one may be,
through study, a thousand times more useful to men
than in any of our subordinate posts. There we
torment ourselves, and often without any compensat-
ing success, to secure some small benefits, while we
are the involuntary instrument of evils that are by
no means small. All our small benefits are transitory,
while the light that a man of letters is able to diffuse
must, sooner or later, destroy all the artificial evils
of the human race, and place it in a position to enjoy
all the goods that nature offers.' It is clear that we
can only accept Turgot's preference, on condition
that the man of letters is engaged on work that
seriously advances social interests and adds something to human stature.[1]

Turgot himself, however, found time, in his industry at Limoges, to make a contribution to a kind
of literature that has seriously modified the practical
arrangements and social relations of the western
world. In 1766 he published his *Essay on the Formation and Distribution of Wealth*—a short but most
pithy treatise, in which he anticipated some of the
leading economic principles of the greater work by

[1] See *Critical Miscellanies*, p. 254.

Adam Smith, given to the world ten years later.
Turgot's essay has none of the breadth of historic
outlook, and none of the amplitude of concrete
illustrations from real affairs, that make the *Wealth
of Nations* so deeply fertile, so persuasive, so interesting, so thoroughly alive, so genuinely enriching to
the understanding of the judicious reader. But the
comparative dryness of Turgot's too concise form does
not blind the historian of political economy to the
merit of the substance of his propositions. It was
no small proof of originality and enlightenment to
precede Adam Smith by ten years in the doctrines
of free trade, of free industry, of loans on interest,
of the constitutive elements of price, of the effects of
the division of labour, of the processes of the formation
of capital.

V.

In May 1774 Louis XV. died. His successor was
only twenty years old; he was sluggish in mind,
vacillating in temper, and inexperienced in affairs.
Maurepas was recalled, to become the new king's
chief adviser; and Maurepas, at the suggestion of one
of Turgot's college friends, summoned the Intendant
from Limoges, and placed him at the head of the
department of marine. This post Turgot only held
for a couple of months; he was then preferred to the
high office of Controller-General. The condition of
the national finance made its administration the most
important of all the departments of the government.

Turgot's policy in this high sphere belongs to the general history of France, and there is no occasion for us to reproduce its details here. It was mainly an attempt to extend over the whole realm the kind of reforms that had been tried on a small scale in the Limousin. He suppressed the *corvées*, and he tacked the money payment which was substituted for that burden on to the twentieths, an impost from which the privileged class was not exempt. ' The weight of this charge,' he made the king say in the edict of suppression, ' now falls and must fall only on the poorest classes of our subjects.' This truth only added to the exasperation of the rich, and perhaps might well have been omitted. Along with the *corvées* were suppressed the *jurandes*, or exclusive industrial corporations or trade-guilds, whose monopolies and restrictions were so mischievous an impediment to the well-being of the country. In the preamble to this edict we seem to be breathing the air, not of Versailles in 1775, but of the Convention in 1793 :—' God, when he made man with wants, and rendered labour an indispensable resource, made the right of work the property of every individual in the world, and this property is the first, the most sacred, and the most imprescriptible of all kinds of property. We regard it as one of the first duties of our justice, and as one of the acts most of all worthy of our benevolence, to free our subjects from every infraction of that inalienable right of humanity.'

Again, Turgot removed a tax from certain forms

of lease, with a view to promote the substitution of a system of farming for the system of *métayers*. He abolished an obstructive privilege by which the Hôtel Dieu had the exclusive right of selling meat during Lent. The whole of the old incoherent and vexatious police of the corn-markets was swept away. Finally, he inspired the publication of a short but important writing, Boncerf's *Inconvénients des droits féodaux*, in which, without criticising the origin of the privileges of the nobles, the author showed how much it would be to the advantage of the lords to accept a commutation of their feudal dues. What was still more exasperating to both nobles and lawyers was the author's hardy assertion that if the lords refused the offer of their vassals, the king had the power to settle the question for them by his own legislative authority. This was the most important and decisive of the pre-revolutionary tracts.

Equally violent prejudices and more sensitive interests were touched by two other sets of proposals. The minister began to talk of a new territorial contribution, and a great survey and re-assessment of the land. Then followed an edict restoring in good earnest the free circulation of corn within the kingdom. Turgot was a partisan of free trade in its most entire application; but for the moment he contented himself with the free importation of grain and its free circulation at home, without sanctioning its exportation abroad.

The measures were all excellent in themselves.

G

They were steps towards the construction of a fabric of freedom and justice. But they provoked a host of bitter and irreconcilable enemies, while they raised up no corresponding host of energetic supporters. That the country clergy should denounce the Philosopher, as they called him, from the pulpit and the steps of the altar, was natural enough. Many even of his old colleagues of the Encyclopædia had joined Necker against the minister. The greatest of them all, it is true, stood by Turgot with unfailing staunchness ; a shower of odes, diatribes, dialogues, allegories, dissertations, came from the Patriarch of Ferney to confound and scatter the enemies of the new reforms. But the people were unmoved. If Turgot published an explanation of the high price of grain, they perversely took explanation for gratulation, and thought the Controller preferred to have bread dear. If he put down seditious risings with a strong hand, they insisted that he was in nefarious league with the corn-merchants and the bakers. How was it that the people did not recognise the hand of a benefactor ? The answer is that they suspected the source of the new reforms too virulently to judge them calmly. For half a century, as Condorcet says, they had been undergoing the evils of anarchy, while they supposed that they were feeling those of despotism. The error was grave, but it was natural, and one effect of it was to make every measure that proceeded from the court odious. Hence, when the parlements took up their judicial arms in defence of abuses and against reforms, the common people took sides with them, for no better reason than that this was to take sides against the king's government. Malesherbes in those days, and good writers since, held that the only safe plan was to convoke the States-General. They would at least have shared the responsibility with the crown. Turgot rejected this opinion. By doctrine, no less than by temperament, he disliked the control of a government by popular bodies. Everything for the people, nothing by the people : this was the maxim of the Economists, and Turgot held it in all its rigour. The royal authority was the only instrument that he could bring himself to use. Even if he could have counted on a Frederick or a Napoleon, the instrument would hardly have served his purposes ; as things were, it was a broken reed that he had to his hand, not a fine sword.

The National Assembly and the Convention went to work in exactly the same stiff and absolute spirit as Turgot. They were just as little disposed to gradual, moderate, and compromising ways as he. But with them the absolute authority on which they leaned was real and most potent ; with him it was a shadow. We owe it to Turgot that the experiment was complete : he proved that the monarchy of divine right was incapable of reform.[1] As it has been sententiously expressed, ' The part of the sages was played out ; there was now room for the men of destiny.'

[1] Foncin's *Ministère de Turgot*, p. 574.

If the repudiation of a popular assembly was a
cardinal error in Turgot's scheme of policy, there were
other errors added. The publication of Boncerf's
attack on the feudal dues, with the undisguised
sanction of the minister, has been justly condemned
as a grave imprudence, and as involving a forgetfulness of the true principles of government and administration, that would certainly not have been committed
either by Colbert, in whom Turgot professed to seek
his model, or by Gournai, who had been his master.
It was a broad promise of reforms which Turgot was
by no means sure of being able to persuade the king
and his council to adopt. By prematurely divulging
his projects, it augmented the number of his adversaries, without being definite enough to bring new
friends.[1] Again, Turgot did nothing to redeem it by
personal conciliatoriness in carrying out the designs
of a benevolent absolutism. The royal prince, long
afterwards Louis XVIII., wrote a satire on the
government during Turgot's ministry, and in it there
is a picture of the great reformer as he appeared to
his enemies : ' There was then in France an awkward,
heavy, clumsy creature ; born with more rudeness
than character, more obstinacy than firmness, more
impetuosity than tact ; a charlatan in administration
no less than in virtue, exactly formed to get the one
decried, and to disgust the world with the other ;
made harsh and distant by his self-love, and timid

[1] See Mauguin's *Études historiques sur l'administration de
l'agriculture*, i. 353.

by his pride ; as much a stranger to men, whom
he had never known, as to the public weal, which
he had never seen aright ; this man was called
Turgot.'

It is a cheap mistake to take the word of political
adversaries for a man's character, but adversaries
sometimes only say out aloud what is already suspected by friends. The coarse account given by
the Count of Provence shows us where Turgot's
weakness as a ruler may have lain. He was distant
and stiff in manner, and encouraged no approach.
Even his health went against him, for at a critical
time in his short ministry he was confined to bed
by gout for four months, and could see nobody
save clerks and secretaries. The very austerity,
loftiness, and purity, that make him so reverend
and inspiring a figure in the pages of the noble-
hearted Condorcet, may well have been impediments
in dealing with a society that, in the fatal words of
the Roman historian, could bear neither its disorders
nor their remedies.

The king had once said pathetically : ' It is only
M. Turgot and I who love the people.' But even with
the king, there were points at which the minister's
philosophic severity strained their concord. Turgot
was the friend of Voltaire and Condorcet ; he counted
Christianity a form of superstition ; and he, who as
a youth had refused to go through life wearing the
mask of the infidel abbé, had too much self-respect
in his manhood to practise the rites and uses of a

system he considered a degradation of the understanding. One day the king said to Maurepas : ' You
have given me a Controller-General who never goes
to mass.' ' Sire,' replied that ready worldling, ' the
abbé Terrai always went '—and Terrai had brought
the government to bankruptcy. But Turgot hurt
the king's conscience more directly than by staying
away from mass and confession. Faithful to the
long tradition of his ancestors, Louis XVI. wished
the ceremony of his coronation to take place at
Rheims. Turgot urged that it should be performed
at Paris, and as cheaply as possible. And he advanced
on to still more delicate ground. In the rite of con-
secration, the usage was that the king should take an
oath to pursue all heretics. Turgot demanded the
suppression of this declaration of intolerance. It
was pointed out to him that it was only a formality.
But Turgot was one of the scrupulous to whom a
wicked promise does not cease to be degrading by
becoming hypocritical. It was only by the gradual
extinction of the vestiges of her ancient barbarisms,
as occasion offered, that the church could have
escaped the crash of the Revolution. Meanwhile,
the king and the priests had their own way : the
king was crowned at Rheims, and the priests exacted
from him an oath to be unjust, oppressive, and cruel
towards a portion of his subjects. Turgot could only
remonstrate ; but the philosophic memorial in which
he protested in favour of religious freedom and
equality gave the king a serious shock.

He was dismissed in the beginning of May 1776, having been in power little more than twenty months. 'You are too hurried,' Malesherbes had said to him. 'You think you have the love of the public good; not at all; you have a rage for it, for a man must be nothing short of enraged to insist on forcing the hand of the whole world.' Turgot replied, more pathetically perhaps than reasonably, 'What, you accuse me of haste, and you know that in my family we die of gout at fifty!'

There is something tragic in the joy with which Turgot's dismissal was received on all sides. 'I seem,' said Marmontel, 'to be looking at a band of brigands in the forest of Bondy, who have just heard that the provost-marshal has been discharged.' Voltaire and Condorcet were not more dismayed by the fall of the minister than by the insensate delight that greeted the catastrophe. 'This event,' wrote Condorcet, 'has changed all nature in my eyes. I have no longer the same pleasure in looking at those fair landscapes over which he would have shed happiness and contentment. The sight of the gaiety of the people wrings my heart. They dance and sport, as if they had lost nothing. Ah, we have had a delicious dream, but it has been all too short.' Voltaire was equally inconsolable, and still more violent in the expression of his grief. When he had become calmer, he composed those admirable verses—*To a Man*:

Philosophe indulgent, ministre citoyen,
Qui ne cherchas le vrai que pour faire le bien,
Qui d'un peuple léger et trop ingrat peut-être
Préparais le bonheur et celui de son maître,
Ce qu'on nomme disgrâce a payé tes bienfaits.
Le vrai prix de travail n'est que de vivre en paix.

Turgot at first showed resentment at the levity
with which he had been banished from power, and
he put on no airs of theatrical philosophy. He would
have been untrue to the sincerity of his character if
he had affected indifference or satisfaction at seeing
his beneficent hopes for ever destroyed. But chagrin
did not numb his industry. Condorcet went to visit
him some months after his fall. He describes Turgot
as reading Ariosto, as making experiments in physics,
and as having forgotten all that had passed within
the last two years, save when the sight of evils that
he would have mitigated or removed happened to
remind him of it. He occupied himself busily with
chemistry and optics, with astronomy and mechanics,
and above all with meteorology, a new science in
those days, and the value of which to the study of
the conditions of human health, of the productions
of the earth, of navigation, excited his most ardent
anticipations. Turgot also was so moved by the
necessity for a new synthesis of life and knowledge
as to frame a plan for a great work ' on the human
soul, the order of the universe, the Supreme Being,
the principles of societies, the rights of men, political
constitutions, legislation, administration, physical
education, the means of perfecting the human race

relatively to the progressive advance and employment of their forces, to the happiness of which they
are susceptible, to the extent of the knowledge to
which they may attain.' While his mind was moving
through these immense spaces of thought, he did
not forget the things of the hour. He invented a
machine for serving ship's cables. He wrote a plea
for allowing Captain Cook's vessel to remain un-
molested during the American war. With Adam
Smith, with Dr. Price, with Franklin, with Hume,
he kept up a grave correspondence. Of his own
countrymen, Condorcet was his most faithful friend
and disciple.

We have already said that the keyword to Turgot's
political aims and social theory was not Pity nor
Benevolence, but Justice. It was Justice also, not
temporary Prejudice nor Passion, that guided his
judgment through the heated issues of the time.
This exact reasonableness it was impossible to surprise or throw off its guard. His intellectual probity
never suffered itself to be tempted. He protested
against the doctrines of Helvétius's book, *De l'esprit*,
and of D'Holbach's *Système de la Nature*, at a moment
when some of his best friends were enthusiastic in
admiration, for no better reason than that the
doctrines of the two books were hateful to the ecclesiastics and destructive of the teaching of the church.
Condorcet had maintained that scrupulous persons
are not fit for great things. A Christian, he said,
will waste, in subduing the darts of the flesh, time

he might have employed upon things that would have been useful to humanity ; he will never venture to rise against tyrants, for fear of having formed a hasty judgment, and so forth in other cases. ' No virtue,' replies Turgot, ' in whatever sense you take the word, can dispense with justice ; and I think no better of the people who do your *great things* at the cost of justice, than I do of poets who fancy that they can produce great wonders of imagination without order and regularity. I know that excessive precision tends to deaden the fire alike of action and of composition ; but there is a medium in everything. There has never been any question in our controversy of a capuchin wasting his time in quenching the darts of the flesh, though, by the way, in the whole sum of time wasted, the term expressing the time lost in satisfying the appetites of the flesh would probably be found to be decidedly the greater of the two.' This parenthesis is one of a hundred illustrations of Turgot's habitual refusal to be carried out of the path of exact rationality, or to take for granted a single word of the common form of the dialect even of his best friends and closest associates. And the readiness with which men fall into common form, the levity with which they settle the most complex and difficult issues, stirred in Turgot what Michelet calls *férocité*, and Matthew Arnold by the better name of *sæva indignatio*. ' Turgot was filled with an astonished, awful, oppressive sense of the *immoral thoughtlessness* of men ; of the heedless, hazardous way in which they deal with things of the greatest moment to them ; of the immense, incalculable misery which is due to this cause.'

He died on the 20th of March 1781, leaving to posterity the memory of a character more lofty, noble, and imposing than the chances of Time permitted to the summary of his performance. Condorcet saw in this harmonious union and fine balance of qualities the secret of his unpopularity. 'Envy,' he says, ' seems more closely to attend a character that approaches perfection, than one that, while astonishing men by its greatness, yet by exhibiting a mixture of defects and vices, offers a consolation that envy seeks.'

CONDORCET.

Of the illustrious thinkers and writers who for two generations had been actively scattering the seed of revolution in France, only Condorcet survived to behold the first bitter ingathering of the harvest. Those who had sown the wind were no more ; he only was left to see the reaping of the whirlwind, and to be swiftly and cruelly swept away by it. Voltaire and Diderot, Rousseau and Helvétius, had vanished, but Condorcet both assisted in the Encyclopædia and sat in the Convention ; the one eminent man, of those who had tended the tree, who also came in due season to partake of its fruit. In neither character has he attracted the good-will of any of those considerable sections and schools into which criticism of the Revolution has been mainly divided. As a thinker he is roughly classed as an Economist, and as a practical politician he figured first in the Legislative Assembly, and then in the Convention. As a rule, the political parties that have most admired the Convention have had least sympathy with the Economists, and the historians who are most favourable to Turgot and his followers are usually most

hostile to the actions and associations of the great
revolutionary chamber successively swayed by
Vergniaud, Danton, Robespierre. Between the two,
Condorcet's name has been allowed to lie hidden
for the most part in a certain obscurity, or else has
been covered with those taunts and innuendoes
that partisans are wont to lavish on men of whom
they do not know exactly whether they are with or
against them.

Generally the men of the Revolution are criticised
in blocks and sections, and Condorcet cannot be
accurately placed under any of these received schools.
He was an Economist, but he was something more ;
the most characteristic article in his creed was a
passionate belief in the infinite perfectibility of human
nature. He was more of a Girondin than a Jacobin,
yet he did not always act, any more than he always
thought, with the Girondins, and he did not fall when
they fell, but was proscribed by a decree specially
levelled at himself. Isolation of this kind is no
merit in political action, but it explains the coldness
with which Condorcet's memory has been treated ; it
flowed from some marked singularities both of character and opinion that are of the highest interest,
if we consider the position of the man and the lustre
of the time. ' Condorcet,' said D'Alembert, ' is a
volcano covered with snow.'   Said another, less
picturesquely : ' He is a sheep in a passion.' ' You
may say of the intelligence of Condorcet in relation
to his person,' wrote Madame Roland, ' that it is

a subtle essence soaked in cotton.' The curious
mixture disclosed by sayings like these, of warm
impulse and fine purpose with immovable reserve,
only shows that he of whom they were spoken
belonged to the natures that may be called
non-conducting. They are not effective, because
without this effluence of power and feeling from
within, the hearer or onlooker is stirred by no
sympathetic thrill. They cannot be the happiest,
because consciousness of the inequality between
the influence intended and the impression conveyed
must be as tormenting as to one who dreams
is the vain effort to strike a blow. If to be
of this non-conducting temperament is impossible
in the really greatest characters, like St. Paul,
St. Bernard, or Luther, at least it is no proper
object of blame, for it is constantly the companion
of lofty and generous aspiration. It was perhaps
unfortunate that Condorcet should have permitted
himself to be drawn into a position where his want
of that magical quality, by which even Marat
could gain the sympathies of men, should be so con-
spicuously made visible. The character of Condorcet
offers nothing to the theatrical instinct. None the
less on this account should we be willing to weigh
the contributions he made to the stock of science and
social speculation, and recognise the elevation of
his sentiments, his noble solicitude for human well-
being, his eager and resolute belief in its indefinite
expansion, and the devotion that sealed his faith

by a destiny as tragical as any in those sanguinary
days.

I.

Condorcet was born at a small town in Picardy,
in the year 1743. His father was a cavalry officer
who died when his son was only three years old.
Condillac was his uncle, but there is no record of any
intercourse between them. His mother was a devout
and trembling soul, who dedicated her child to the
Holy Virgin, and for eight years or more made him
wear the dress of a girl, by way of sheltering him
against the temptations and unbelief of a vile world.
Condorcet was weakened physically by much confinement and the constraint of cumbrous clothing;
and not even his dedication to the Holy Virgin prevented him from growing up the most ardent of the
admirers of Voltaire. His earliest instructors, as
happened to most of the sceptical philosophers, were
the Jesuits, then within a few years of their fall.
The Jesuits were the official instructors of France
for the first half of the eighteenth century. In 1764
the Order was thrust forth from the country, and they
left behind them an army of the bitterest enemies
that Christianity has ever had. To do them justice,
they were destroyed by weapons which they had
themselves supplied. The intelligence they had
developed and sharpened turned inevitably against
the incurable faults in their own system. They were
admirable teachers of mathematics. Condorcet,

instructed by the Jesuits at Rheims, was able when he was only fifteen years old to go through such performances in analysis as to win especial applause from illustrious judges like D'Alembert and Clairaut. It was impossible, however, for Jesuits, as it has ever been for all enemies of movement, to constrain within prescribed limits an activity once effectively stirred. Mathematics has always been in the eyes of the church a harmless branch of knowledge, but the mental energy that mathematics first touched is apt to turn itself by and by to more complex and dangerous subjects in the scientific hierarchy.

At any rate, Condorcet's curiosity was speedily drawn to problems beyond geometry and algebra. ' For thirty years,' he wrote in 1790, ' I have hardly ever passed a single day without meditating on the political sciences.' [1] Thus, at seventeen, when the ardour of even the choicest spirits is usually most purely intellectual, moral and social feeling was rising in Condorcet to that supremacy it afterwards attained in him. He wrote essays on integral calculus, but he was already beginning to reflect upon the laws of human societies and the conditions of moral obligation. At the root of Condorcet's nature was a profound sensibility of constitution. One of his biographers explains his early enthusiasm for virtue and human welfare as the conclusion of a kind of syllogism. It is possible that the syllogism was only the later shape into which an instinctive impulse

---

[1] *Œuvres de Condorcet* (12 vols., 1847-49), ix. 489.

threw itself by way of rational entrenchment. His sensibility caused him to abandon the pleasures of the chase that had at first powerfully attracted him.[1] To derive delight from what inflicts pain on any sentient creature revolted his conscience and offended his reason, because he perceived that the character which does not shrink from associating its own joy with the anguish of another, is either found or left mortally blunted to the finest impressions of humanity.

It is thus assured that from the beginning Condorcet was unable to satisfy himself with the mere knowledge of the specialist, but felt the necessity of placing social aims at the head and front of his life, and of subordinating to them all other pursuits. Such a temper of mind has penetrated no man more fully than Condorcet, though there are other thinkers to whom time and chance have been more favourable in making that temper permanently productive. There is a fine significance in his words, after the dismissal of Turgot from office : 'We have had a delightful dream, but it was too brief. Now I mean to apply myself to geometry. It is terribly cold to be for the future labouring only for the *gloriole*, after flattering oneself for a while that one was working for the public weal.' It is true that a geometer, too, works for the public weal ; but the process is tardy, and we may well pardon an impatience that sprang of reasoned zeal for the happiness of mankind. There is something much more attractive about Condorcet's

[1] *Œuvres de Condorcet*, i. 220.

undisguised disappointment at having to exchange active public labour for geometrical problems, than in the affected satisfaction conventionally professed by statesmen driven from place to their books. His correspondence shows that, even when his mind seemed to be most concentrated upon his special studies, he was incessantly on the alert for every new idea, book, transaction, likely to stimulate the love of virtue in individuals, or to increase the strength of justice in society. It would have been in one sense more fortunate for him to have cared less for high social interests, if we remember the contention of his latter days and the catastrophe that brought them to a frightful close. But Condorcet was not one of those natures who can think it happiness to look passively out from the tranquil literary watch-tower upon the mortal struggles of a society on the point of overthrow.

In 1769 Condorcet became connected with the Academy, to the mortification of his relations, who hardly pardoned him for not being a captain of horse like his father. About the same time, or a little later, he performed a pilgrimage of a kind that could hardly help making a mark upon a character so impressible. In company with D'Alembert he went to Ferney and saw Voltaire.[1] To the position of Voltaire in Europe in 1770 there has never been any other man's position in any age wholly comparable. It is true that there had been one or two of the great popes, and a great

[1] Sept. 1770. Voltaire's *Corr.* vol. lxxi. p. 147.

ecclesiastic like St. Bernard, who had exercised a
spiritual authority, pretty universally submitted to,
or even spontaneously invoked, throughout western
Europe. But these were the representatives of a
powerful organisation and an accepted system.
Voltaire filled a place before men's eyes in the eight-
teenth century as conspicuous and as authoritative
as that of St. Bernard in the twelfth. The difference
was that Voltaire's place was unofficial in its origin,
and indebted to no system nor organisation for its
maintenance. Again, there have been others, like
Bacon or Descartes, destined to make a far more
permanent contribution to the ideas that have
extended the powers and elevated the happiness of
men; but these great spirits for the most part
laboured for the generation that followed them, and
won comparatively slight recognition from their own
age. Voltaire during his life enjoyed to the full not
only the admiration belonging to the poet, but something of the veneration paid to the thinker, and
even something of the glory usually reserved for
captains and conquerors of renown. No other man
before or since ever hit so exactly the mark of his
time on every side, so precisely met the conditions
of fame for the moment, nor so thoroughly dazzled
and reigned over the foremost men and women who
were his contemporaries. Wherever else intellectual
fame has approached the fame of Voltaire, it has
been posthumous. With him it was immediate and
splendid. He was an unsurpassed master of the

art of literary expression in a country where that
art is more highly prized than anywhere else; he
was the most brilliant of wits among a people whose
relish for wit is a supreme passion; he won the admiration of the lighter souls by his plays, of the learned
by his interest in science, of the men of letters by his
never-ceasing flow of essays, criticisms, and articles,
not one of which lacks vigour and freshness and
sparkle; he was the most active, bitter, and telling
foe of what was then the most distracted and dis-
located of all institutions—the church. Add to these
remarkable titles to honour and popularity that he
was no mere declaimer against oppression and injustice in the abstract, but the strenuous, persevering,
and absolutely indefatigable champion of every
victim of oppression or injustice whose case was once
brought under his eye.

It is not difficult to perceive the fascination that
Voltaire, with this character, would have for a man
like Condorcet. He conceived the warmest attachment to Voltaire, and Voltaire in turn the highest
respect for him. Their correspondence (1770–78) is
perhaps as interesting as any letters of that period:
Voltaire is always bright, playful, and affectionate;
Condorcet more declamatory and less graceful, but
full of reverence and loyalty for his 'dear and illustrious' master, and of his own peculiar eagerness for
good causes and animosity against the defenders of
bad ones. Condorcet was younger than the patriarch
of Ferney by nearly half a century, but this did not

prevent him from loyal remonstrances on more than one occasion against conduct on Voltaire's part in this matter or that, which he held to be unworthy. He went so far as actually to decline to print in the *Mercure* a letter in which the writer in some fit of spleen placed Montesquieu below D'Aguesseau. ' My attachment,' he says, ' bids me say what will be best for you, and not what might please you most. If I loved you less, I should not have the courage to thwart you. I am aware of your grievances against Montesquieu ; it is worthy of you to forget them.' There was perhaps as much moral courage in doing this as in defying the Men of the Mountain in the days of the Terror. It dispels some false impressions of Voltaire's supposed intolerance of criticism, to find him thanking Condorcet for one of these friendly protests. ' One sees things ill,' he writes, ' when one sees them from too far off. After all, we ought never to blush to go to school if we are as old as Methuselah. I repeat my acknowledgments to you.' [1] Condorcet did not conceive that either to be blind to a man's errors or to compromise them is to prove yourself his friend. There is an integrity of friend-ship as in public concerns, and he adhered to it as manfully in one as in the other.

Perhaps we see him most characteristically in his correspondence with Turgot. What Turgot loved in him was his ' simplicity of character.' [2] Turgot was almost as much less vivacious than Condorcet, as

---

[1] *Œuvres*, i. 41. [2] *Œuvres de Turgot*, ii. 817.

Condorcet was less vivacious than Voltaire. They belonged to distinct types, but this may be a condition of the most perfect forms of sympathy. Turgot was one of those serene, capacious, and sure intelligences whose aspirations do not become low or narrow by being watchfully held under the control of reason; whose ideas are no less vigorous or exuberant because they move in a steady and ordered train ; and who, in their most fervent reactions against abuses or crimes, resist the vehement temptation to excess that is the besetting infirmity of generous natures. Condorcet was very different from this. Whatever he wished he wished unrestrainedly. As with most men of the epoch, the habit of making allowances was not his. We observe something theological in his hatred of theologians. Even in his letters the distant ground-swell of repressed passion sounds in the ear, and at every mention of false opinion or evil-doing a sombre and angry shadow seems to fall upon the page. Both he and Turgot clung to the doctrine of the infinite perfectibility of human nature, and the correspondingly infinite augmentation of human happiness; but Condorcet's ever-smouldering impetuosity would be content with nothing less than the arrival of at least a considerable instalment of this infinite quantity now and instantly. He went so far as to insist that by and by men would acquire the art of prolonging their lives for several generations, instead of being confined within the fatal span of threescore years and ten. He was impatient of any frittering away of life in scruple, tremors, and hesitations.

The main currents of opinion and circumstance in France, when Condorcet came to take his place among her workers, are now well understood. The third quarter of the century was just closing. Louis XV. died in 1774 ; and though his death was of little intrinsic consequence, except as the removal of every corrupt heart is of consequence, it is justly taken to mark the date of the beginning of the French Revolution. It was the accidental shifting of position that served to disclose the existing system to be smitten with a mortal paralysis. It is often said that what destroyed the French kingdom was despotism. A sounder explanation discovers the causes less in despotism than in anarchy—anarchy in every department where it could be most ruinous. No substantial reconstruction was possible, because all the evils came from the sinister interests of the nobles, the clergy, or the financiers ; and these classes, informally bound together against the common weal, were too strong for either the sovereign or the ablest minister to thrust them aside. The material condition of France was one of supreme embarrassment and disorder, only curable by remedies that the political and social condition of the country made it impossible to employ.

This would explain why a change of some sort was inevitable. But why was the change which actually took place, in that direction rather than another ?

Why did not France sink under her economical disorders, as greater empires than France had done ?
Why, instead of sinking and falling asunder, did the
French people advance with a singleness of impulse
unknown before in their history to their own deliverance ? How was it that they overthrew the system
that was crushing them, and purged themselves with
fire and sword of those who administered and maintained it, defying the hopes of the nation ; and then
successfully encountered the giant's task of beating
back reactionary Europe with one arm, and reconstructing the fabric of their own society with the
other ? The answer to this question is found in the
moral and spiritual condition of France. A generation aroused by the social ideas of the eighteenth
century, looking round to survey its own social state,
found itself in the midst of the ruin and disorder of
the disintegrated system of the twelfth century. The
life was gone out of the ancient organisation of
Catholicism and Feudalism, and it seemed as if
nothing but corruption remained. What enabled the
leaders of the nation to discern the horror and despair
of this anarchic dissolution of the worn-out old, and
what inspired them with hope and energy when they
thought of the possible new, was the spiritual preparation that had been in swift progress since the
third decade of the century. The forms and methods
of this preparation were various as the temperaments
that came beneath its influence. But the school of
Voltaire, the school of Rousseau, and the schools of

Quesnay and Montesquieu, different as they were at the roots, all alike energetically familiarised the public mind with a firm belief in human reason, and the idea of the natural rights of man. They impregnated it with a growing enthusiasm for social justice. It is true that we find Voltaire complaining towards the close of his days, of the century being satiated and weary, *un siècle dégoûté*, not knowing well what it wanted. ' The public,' he said, ' has been eighty years at table, and now it drinks a little bad cognac at the end of its meal.' [1] In literature and art this was true ; going deeper than these, the public was eager and sensitive with a freshness far more vital and more fruitful than it had known eighty years back. Sitting down with a keen appetite for taste, erudition, and literary knowledge, men had now risen up from a dazzling and palling board, with a new hunger and thirst after social righteousness. This was the noble faith that saved France; by this sign she was victorious. A people once saturated with a passionate conception of justice is not likely to fall into a Byzantine stage.

Condorcet's peculiarities of political antipathy and preference can hardly be better illustrated than by his view of the two great revolutions in English history. The first was religious, and therefore he hated it ; the second was accompanied by much argument, and had no religion about it, and therefore he extolled it. It is scientific knowledge, he said, that explains why efforts after liberty in un-

---

[1] Letters to Condorcet (1774). *Œuvres*, i. 35.

enlightened centuries are so fleeting, and so deeply
stained by bloodshed. 'Compare these with the
happy efforts of America and France; observe even
in the same century, but at different epochs, the two
revolutions of England fanatical and England
enlightened. We see on the one side contemporaries
of Prynne and Knox, while crying out that they are
fighting for heaven and liberty, cover their unhappy
country with blood in order to cement the tyranny
of the hypocrite Cromwell; on the other, the contemporaries of Boyle and Newton establish with
pacific wisdom the freest constitution in the world.' [1]
It is not wonderful that his own revolution was mis-
understood by one who thus loved English Whigs,
but hated English Republicans; who could forgive
an aristocratic faction grasping power for their order,
but who could not sympathise with a nation rising
and smiting its oppressor, where they smote in the
name of the Lord and of Gideon, nor with a ruler
who used his power with noble simplicity in the
interests of his people, and established in the heart
of the nation a respect for itself such as she has never
known since, simply because this ruler knew nothing
about *principes* or the Rights of Man.

II.

The course of events after 1774 is in its larger
features well known to every reader. Turgot

[1] *Éloge de Franklin*, iii. 422.

nominated Condorcet to be Inspector of Coinage, an offer which Condorcet deprecated in these words : ' It is said of you in certain quarters that money costs you nothing when there is any question of obliging your friends. I should be bitterly ashamed of giving any semblance of foundation to these absurd speeches. I pray you, do nothing for me just now. Though not rich, I am not pressed for money. Entrust to me some important task—the reduction of measures for instance ; then wait till my labours have really earned some reward.' [1] In this patriotic spirit he undertook, along with two other eminent men of science, the task of examining certain projects for canals that engaged the attention of the minister. ' People will tell you,' he wrote, ' that I have got an office worth two hundred and forty pounds. Utterly untrue. We undertook it out of friendship for M. Turgot ; but we refused the payment that was offered.' [2]

Turgot was dismissed (May 1776), and presently Necker was installed in his place. Condorcet had defended with much vigour and some asperity the policy of free internal trade in corn against Necker, who was for the maintenance of the restrictions on commercial intercourse between the different pro- vinces of the kingdom. Consequently, when the new minister came into office, Condorcet wrote to Maurepas resigning his post. ' I have,' he said, ' declared too decidedly what I think about both M. Necker and

[1] *Œuvres*, i. 71.   [2] *Ibid.* i. 73, 74.

his works, to be able to keep any place that depends upon him.' [1] This was not the first taste that Maurepas had had of Condorcet's resolute self-respect. The Duke de la Vrillière, one of the most scandalous persons of the century, was an honorary member of the Academy, and he was the brother-in-law of Maurepas. It was expected from the perpetual secretary that he should compose a eulogy upon the occasion of his death, and Condorcet was warned by friends not to irritate the powerful minister by a slight upon his relation. He was inflexible. ' Would you rather have me persecuted,' he asked, ' for a wrong than for something just and moral ? Think, too, that they will pardon my silence much more readily than they would pardon my words, for my mind is fixed not to betray the truth.' [2]

In 1782 Condorcet was elected into the Academy. His competitor was Bailly, over whom he had a majority of one. The true contest lay less between the two candidates than between D'Alembert and Buffon, who on this occasion are said to have fought one of the greatest battles in the not peaceful history of the Academy. D'Alembert is said to have exclaimed that he was better pleased at winning that victory than he would have been to find out the squaring of the circle.[3] Destiny, which had so pitiful

---

[1] *Œuvres*, i. 296.   [2] *Ibid.* i. 78.

[3] *Ibid.* i. 89. Condorcet had 16 votes, and Bailly 15. ' *Jamais aucune election*,' says La Harpe, who was all for Buffon, ' *n'avait offert ni ce nombre ni ce partage.*'—*Philos. du*

a doom in store for the two candidates of that day, soon closed D'Alembert's share in these struggles of the learned and in all others. He died in the following year, and by his last act testified to his trust in the genèrous character of Condorcet. Having by the benevolence of a lifetime left himself on his death-bed without resources, he confided to his friend's care two old and faithful servants, for whom he was unable to make provision. This charge the philosopher accepted cheerfully, and fulfilled to the end with pious scrupulosity. Even Condorcet's too declamatory manner only adds a certain dignity to the pathetic passage with which he closes the noble *éloge* on his lost friend.[1] Voltaire had been dead these five years, and Turgot, too, was gone. Society offered the survivor no recompense. He found the great world tiresome and frivolous, and he described its pursuits as 'dissipation without pleasure, vanity without meaning, and idleness without repose.' It was perhaps to soften the oppression of these tender regrets that in 1786 Condorcet married.[2]

During the winter of 1788–89, while all France was astir with elections and preparation for elections

---

18*ième siècle*, i. 77. A full account of the election, and of Condorcet's reception, is given in Grimm's *Corr. lit.* xi. 50-56.

[1] *Œuvres*, iii. 109, 110.

[2] His wife, said to be one of the most beautiful women of her time, was twenty-three years younger than himself, and survived until 1822. Cabanis married another sister, and Marshal Grouchy was her brother. Madame Condorcet wrote nothing of her own, except some notes to a translation which she made of Adam Smith's *Theory of Moral Sentiments.*

for the meeting of the States-General that was looked to as the nearing dawn after a long night, Condorcet thought he could best serve the movement by calling the minds of the electors to sides of their duty which they might be in danger of overlooking. One of the subjects on which he felt most strongly, but on which his countrymen have not shown any particular sensibility, was slavery and the slave trade.[1] With terseness and force he appealed to the electors, while they were reclaiming their own rights in the name of justice, not to forget the half-million blacks, whose rights had been still more shamefully torn away from them, and whose need of justice was more urgent than their own. In the same spirit he published a vehement and ingenious protest against the admission of representatives from the St. Domingo plantations to the National Assembly.

Condorcet knew men well enough to be aware of the hazards of political inexperience. Beware of choosing a clever knave, he said, because he will follow his own interest and not yours; but at the same time beware of choosing a man for no better reason than that he is honest, because you need ability quite as much as you need probity. Do not choose a man who has ever taken sides against the liberty of

---

[1] Montesquieu, Raynal, and one or two other writers, had attacked slavery long before, and Condorcet published a very effective piece against it in 1781 (*Réflexions sur l'esclavage des nègres*; *Œuvres*, vii. 63), with an epistle dedicated to the enslaved blacks. About the same time an Abolition Society was formed in France, following the example set in England.

any portion of mankind; nor one whose principles were never known until he found out that he wanted your votes. Be careful not to mistake heat of head for heat of soul; because what you want is not heat but force, not violence but steadfastness. Be careful, too, to separate a man's actions from the accidents of his life; for one may be the enemy or the victim of a tyrant without being the friend of liberty. Do not be carried away by a candidate's solicitations: but, at the same time, make allowance for the existing effervescence of spirits. Prefer those who have decided opinions, to those who are always inventing plans of conciliation; those who are zealous for the rights of man, to those who only profess pity for the misfortunes of the people; those who speak of justice and reason, to those who speak of political interests and of the prosperity of commerce. Distrust those who appeal to sentiment in matters that can be decided by reason; prefer light to eloquence; and pass over those who declare themselves ready to die for liberty, in favour of those who know in what liberty consists.[1]

Though many of these precepts designed to guide the electors in their choice of men are sagacious and admirable, they smack strongly of that absolute and abstract spirit which can never become powerful in politics without danger. It is certain that in the spring of 1789, Condorcet held hereditary monarchy

[1] *Lettres d'un gentilhomme aux messieurs du Tiers État*, ix. 255-259.

to be most suitable to ' the wealth, the population, the extent of France, and to the political system of Europe.' [1] Yet the reasons which he gives for thinking this are not very cogent. It is significant, however, of the little distance which all the most uncompromising and thoughtful revolutionists saw in front of them, that even Condorcet should, so late as the eve of the assembly of the States-General, have talked about attachment to the forms of monarchy and respect for the royal person and prerogative ; and should have represented the notion of the property of the church undergoing any confiscation, as an invention of the enemies of freedom.[2] Before the year was out, the property of the church had undergone confiscation ; before two years had gone he was an ardent republican ; and in less than twelve months after that he had voted the guilt of the king.

It is worth while to cite here a still more pointed example of the want of prevision, so common and so intelligible at that time. Writing in July 1791, he confutes those who asserted that an established and limited monarchy was a safeguard against a usurper, whose power is only limited by his own audacity and address, by pointing out that the extent of France, its divisions into departments, the separation between the various branches of the administration, the

---

[1] *Réflexions sur les pouvoirs et instructions à donner par les provinces à leurs députés aux États-Généraux*, ix. 266.

[2] *Ibid.* ix. 264.

freedom of the press, the multitude of the public prints, were all so many insurmountable barriers against a French Cromwell. 'To anybody who has read with attention the history of the usurpation of Cromwell, it is clear that a single newspaper would have been enough to stop his success. It is clear that if the people of England had known how to read other books beside their Bible, the hypocritical tyrant, unmasked from his first step, would soon have ceased to be dangerous.' Again, is the nation to be cajoled by some ambitious general, gratifying its desire to be an empire-race? 'Is this what is asked by true friends of liberty, those who only seek that reason and right should have empire over men? *What provinces, conquered by a French general, will he despoil to buy our suffrages? Will he promise our soldiers, as the consuls promised the citizens of Rome, the pillage of Spain or of Syria?* No, assuredly; it is because we cannot be an empire-nation that we shall remain a free nation.' [1] How few years between this conclusive reasoning, and the pillage of Italy, the campaign in Syria, the seizure of Spain!

Condorcet was not a member of the assembly in whose formation and composition he had taken so vivid and practical an interest. The first political functions he was invited to undertake were those of a member of the municipality of Paris. In the tremendous drama of which the scenes were now

---

[1] *Réflexions sur les pouvoirs et instructions à donner par les provinces à leurs députés aux États-Généraux*, xii. 228, 229, 234.

opening, the Town-hall of Paris was to prove itself far more truly the centre of movement and action than the Constituent Assembly. The efforts of the Constituent Assembly to build up were tardy and ineffectual.

Politicians of real eminence as reformers possess one of three elements. One class of men is inspired by an intellectual attachment to certain ideas of justice and right reason : another is moved by a deep pity for the hard lot of the mass of every society : while the third, such men as Richelieu, for example, has an instinctive passion for wise and orderly government. The great typical ruler is moved in varying degrees by all three in modern times, when the claims of the poor, the rank and file of the social army, have been raised to the permanent place that. belongs to them. Each of the three types has its own peculiar conditions of success, and there are circumstances in which some one of the three is more able to grapple with the obstacles to order than either of the other two. It soon became very clear that the intellectual quality was not the element likely to quell the tempest that had now arisen.

Condorcet, however, showed himself no pedantic nor fastidious trifler with the tremendous movement which he had contributed to set afoot. The same practical spirit which drove him into the strife guided him in the midst of it. He never wrung his hands, nor wept, nor bewailed the unreason of the multitudes to whom in vain he preached. He did not abandon the cause of the Revolution because his suggestions were often repulsed. ' It would be better,' he said to the Girondins, ' if you cared less for personal matters and attended only to public interests.' Years ago, in his *éloge* on L'Hôpital, he had praised the famous Chancellor for incurring the hostility of both of the two envenomed factions, League and Huguenots, and for disregarding the approbation or disapprobation of the people. ' What operation,' he asked, ' capable of producing any durable good, can be understood by the people ? How should they know to what extent good is possible ? How judge of the means of producing it ? It must ever be easier for a charlatan to mislead the people, than for a man of genius to save it.' [1] Remembering this law, he never lost patience. He was cool and intrepid, if his intrepidity was of the logical sort rather than physical ; and he was steadfast to one or two simple aims, if he was on some occasions too rapid in changing his attitude as to special measures. He was never afraid of the spectre, as the incompetent revolutionist is. On the contrary, he understood its whole internal history ; he knew what had raised it, what passion and what weakness

[1] *Œuvres*, iii. 533. As this was written in 1777, Condorcet was perhaps thinking of Turgot and Necker. Of the latter, his daughter tells us repeatedly, without any consciousness that she is recording a most ignominious trait, that public approbation was the very breath of his nostrils, the thing for which he lived, the thing without which he was wretched.—See vol. i. of Madame de Staël's *Considérations*.

gave to it substance, and he knew that presently reason would banish it and restore men to a right mind. The scientific spirit implanted in such a character as Condorcet's, and made robust by social meditation, builds up an impregnable fortitude in the face of incessant rebuffs and discouragements. Let us then picture Condorcet as surveying the terrific welter from the summer of 1789 to the summer of 1793, from the taking of the Bastille to the fall of the Girondins, with something of the firmness and self-possession of a Roman Cato.

After the flight of the king in June, and his return in what was virtually captivity to Paris, Condorcet was one of the party, very small in numbers and entirely discountenanced by public opinion, then passing through the monarchical and constitutional stage, who boldly gave up the idea of a monarchy and proclaimed the idea of a Republic. In July (1791) he published a piece strongly arguing for a negative answer to the question whether a king is necessary for the preservation of liberty.[1] It was proposed at that time to appoint Condorcet to be governor to the young dauphin. But Condorcet in this piece took such pains to make his sentiments upon royalty known, that in the constitutional frame of mind in which the Assembly then was, the idea

---

[1] *Œuvres*, iii. 227. It was followed by a letter, nominally by a young mechanic, offering to construct an automaton sovereign, like Kempel's chess-player, who would answer all constitutional purposes perfectly.—*Ibid.* iii. 239-241.

had to be abandoned. It was hardly likely that a man should be chosen for such an office, who had just declared the public will to be ' that the uselessness of a king, the needfulness of seeking means of displacing a power founded on illusions, should be one of the first truths offered to his reason; the obligation of concurring in this himself, one of the first of his moral duties; and the desire not to be freed from the yoke of law by an insulting inviolability, the first sentiment of his heart. People are well aware that at this moment the object is much less how to mould a king, than to teach him not to wish to be one.' [1] As all France was then bent on the new constitution, a king included, Condorcet's republican assurance was hardly warranted, and it was by no means well received.

III.

When the Constitution was accepted and the Legislative Assembly came to be chosen, Condorcet proved to have made so good an impression as a municipal officer, that the Parisians returned him for one of their deputies. The Declaration of Pilnitz in August 1791 had mitigated the loyalty that had even withstood the trial of the king's flight. When the Legislative Assembly met, it was found to contain an unmistakable element of republicanism with marked strength. Condorcet was chosen one of the secretaries, and he composed most of those multitudinous

[1] *Œuvres*, xii. 236.

addresses in which this least honoured of all parliamentary chambers tried to prove to the French people that it was actually in existence and at work. Condorcet was officially to the Legislative what Barrère afterwards was to the Convention. But his addresses are turgid, labouring, and not effective for their purpose. They have neither the hard force of Napoleon's proclamations, nor the flowery eloquence of the Anacreon of the Guillotine.

Perhaps, after all, nobody else could have done better. The situation of the Assembly, between a hostile court and a suspicious and distrustful nation, and unable by its very nature to break the bonds, was from the beginning desperate. In December 1791 the Legislative through its secretary informs France of the frankness and loyalty of the king's measures in the face of the menaces of foreign war.[1] Within eight months, when the king's person was in captivity and his power suspended, the same secretary has to avow that from the very beginning the king had treated the Assembly with dissimulation, and had been in virtual league with the national enemies. The documents issued by the Assembly after the violent events of the Tenth of August 1792 are not edifying, and imply in Condorcet, who composed them, a certain want of eye for revolutionary methods. They mark the beginning of that short but most momentous period in the history of the Revolution,

[1] *Déclaration de l'Assemblée Nationale*, Dec. 29, 1791. *Œuvres*, xii. 25.

when formulas, as Carlyle says, had to be stretched out until they cracked—a process truly called, ' especially in times of swift change, one of the sorrowfullest tasks poor humanity has.' You might read the *Exposition of the Motives from which the National Assembly have proclaimed the Convention, and suspended the Executive Power of the King*,[1] without dreaming that it is an account of a revolution that arose out of distrust or contempt for the Assembly ; that had driven the king away from his palace and from power, and had finally annihilated the very chamber that was thus professing to expound its motives for doing what the violence of Paris had really done in defiance of it. The power, in fact, was all outside the chamber, in Danton and the Commune. A few days after this occurred the massacres of prisoners in September—scenes very nearly, if not quite, as bloody and iniquitous as those that attended the suppression of the rebellion by English troops in Ireland six years afterwards.

When the Convention was chosen, the electors of Paris rejected Condorcet. He was elected, however, (Sept. 6) for the department of the Aisne, having among his colleagues in the deputation Tom Paine, and—a much more important personage—the youthful Saint-Just, who was so soon to stupefy the Convention by exclaiming, with mellow voice and face set immovable as bronze : ' An individual has no right to be either virtuous or celebrated in your eyes.

[1] 13th August 1792. *Œuvres*, x. 547.

A free people and a national assembly are not made
to admire anybody.' The electors of the department of the Aisne had unconsciously sent two typical
revolutionists : the man of intellectual ideas, and
the man of passion heated as in the pit. In their
persons the Encyclopædia and the Guillotine met.
Condorcet, who had been extreme in the Legislative,
but found himself a moderate in the Convention,
gave wise counsel as to the true policy towards the
new members : ' Better try to moderate them than
quarrel.' But in this case, not even in their ruin,
were fire and water reconciled.

On the first great question that the Convention
had to decide—the fate of the king—Condorcet voted
on the two main issues that the king was guilty of
conspiring against liberty, and for the punishment
of exile in preference to that of death. On the inter-
mediate issue, whether the decision of the Convention should be final, or should be submitted to the
people for ratification, he voted as a wise man should
hardly have done, in favour of an appeal to the people.
Such an appeal must inevitably have led to violent
and bloody local struggles, and laid France open to
the enemy. It is striking that, though Condorcet
thus voted that the king was guilty, he had previously
laid before the Convention a most careful argument
to show that they were neither morally nor legally
competent to try the king at all. How, he asked,
without violating every principle of jurisprudence,
can you act at the same time as legislators constitut-

ing the crime, as accusers, and as judges ? His proposal was that Louis XVI. should be tried by a tribunal whose jury and judges should be named by the electoral body of the departments.[1] With all respect for Condorcet's anxiety that the conditions of justice should be rigorously observed—for, as he said, ' there is no liberty in a country where positive law is not the single rule of judicial proceedings '— it is difficult to see why the Convention, coming as it did fresh from the electoral bodies, who must have had the question what was to be done with the imprisoned king foremost in their minds, why the members of the Convention should not form as legitimate a tribunal as any body whose composition and authority they had themselves defined and created, and which would be chosen by the very same persons who less than a month before had invested them with their own offices.

It is highly characteristic of Condorcet's tenacity of his own view of the Revolution and of its methods, that on the Saturday (January 19, 1793) when the king's fate was decided against Condorcet's conviction and against his vote—the execution taking place on the Monday morning—he should have appealed to the Convention, at all events to do their best to neutralise the effect of their verdict upon Europe, by instantly initiating a series of humane reforms in the law, among them including the abolition of the

[1] *Opinion sur le jugement de Louis XVI.* November 1792. *Œuvres,* xii. 267-303.

punishment of death. 'The English ministers,' he cried, ' are now seeking to excite that nation against us. Do you suppose that they will venture to continue their calumnious declamations, when you can say to them : " We have abolished the penalty of death, while you still preserve it for the theft of a few shillings. You hand over debtors to the greed or spite of their creditors ; our laws, wiser and more humane, know how to respect poverty and misfortune. Judge between us and you, and see to which of the two peoples the reproach of inhumanity may be addressed with most justice." ? ' [1]

Condorcet, along with Tom Paine, Sieyès, and others, was a member of the first committee for framing a constitution. They laboured assiduously from September to February 1793, when the project was laid upon the table, prefaced by an elaborate dissertation of Condorcet's composition. The time was inauspicious. The animosities between the Girondins and the Mountain were becoming every day more furious. In the midst of this storm, Condorcet—at one moment wounding the Girondins by reproaches against their egotism and personalities, at another exasperating the Mountain by declaring of Robespierre that he had neither an idea in his head nor a feeling in his heart—still pertinaciously kept crying out for the acceptance of his constitution. It was of no avail. The revolution of the second of June came, and swept the Girondins out of the

[1] 19th January 1793. *Œuvres*, xii. 311.

Chamber. Condorcet was not among them, but his political days were numbered. 'What did you do all that time?' somebody once asked of a member of the Convention, during the period which was now beginning and which lasted until Thermidor in 1794. 'I lived,' was the reply. Condorcet was of another temper. He cared as little for his life as Danton or Saint-Just cared for theirs. Instead of cowering down among the men of the Plain or the frogs of the Marsh, he withstood the Mountain to the face.

Hérault de Séchelles, at the head of another committee, brought in a new constitution which was finally adopted and decreed (June 24, 1793). Of this, Sieyès said privately, that it was 'a bad table of contents.' Condorcet denounced it publicly, and declared in so many words that the arrest of the Girondins had destroyed the integrity of the national representation. The Bill he handled with a severity that inflicted keen smarts on the self-love of its designers. A few days later, the capucin Chabot, one of the weak and excitable natures that in ordinary times divert men by the intensity, multiplicity, and brevity of their enthusiasms, but to whom the fiercer air of a revolution is a real poison, rose and in the name of the Committee of General Security called the attention of the Chamber to what he styled a sequel of the Girondist Brissot. This was Condorcet's document criticising the new constitution. 'This man,' said Chabot, 'has sought to raise the department of the Aisne against you, imagining that, because he has happened to sit by the side of a handful of *savants* of the Academy, it is his duty to give laws to the French Republic.'[1] So a decree was passed putting Condorcet under arrest. His name was included in the list of those who were tried before the Revolutionary Tribunal on the Third of October for conspiring against the unity and indivisibility of the Republic. He was condemned in his absence, and declared to be *hors la loi*.

This, then, was the calamitous close of his aspirations from boyhood upwards to be permitted to partake in doing something for the common weal. He had still the work to perform by which posterity will best remember his name, though only a few months intervened between his flight and his cruel end. Friends found a refuge for him in the house of a Madame Vernet, a widow in moderate circumstances, who let lodgings to students. ' Is he an honest and virtuous man ? ' she asked ; ' in that case let him come, and lose not a moment. Even while we talk he may be seized.' The same night Condorcet entrusted his life to her keeping, and for nine months remained in hiding under her roof. When he heard of the execution of the Girondins condemned on the same day with himself, he perceived the risk to which he was subjecting his protectress, and made up his mind to flee. ' I am an outlaw,' he said, ' and if I am discovered you will be dragged to the

---

[1] *Extrait du Moniteur. Œuvres*, xii. 677.

same death.' 'The Convention,' Madame Vernet
answered, with something of the heroism of more
notable women of that time, 'may put you out of
the law; it has not the power to put you out of
humanity. You stay.' This was no speech of the
theatre. The whole household kept vigorous watch
over the prisoner thus generously detained, and month
after month Madame Vernet's humane firmness was
successful in preventing his escape. This time—
his soul grievously burdened by anxiety for the fate
of his wife and child, and by a restless eagerness not
to compromise his benefactress, a bloody death
staring him every moment in the face—Condorcet
spent in the composition, without the aid of a single
book, of his work on the progress of the human mind.
Among the many wonders of an epoch of portents,
this feat of intellectual abstraction is not the least
amazing.

When his task was accomplished, Condorcet felt
with more keenness than ever the deadly peril in
which his presence placed Madame Vernet. He was
aware that to leave her house was to seek death.
He drew up a paper of directions to be given one day
to his little daughter, when she should be of years to
understand and follow them. She is above all things
to banish from her mind every revengeful sentiment
against her father's enemies; to distrust her filial
sensibility, and to make this sacrifice for her father's
own sake. This done, he marched downstairs, and
having by an artful stratagem thrown Madame

Vernet off her guard, he went out at ten o'clock in the morning imperfectly disguised into the street. This was the fifth of April 1794. By three in the afternoon, exhausted by fatigue which his strict confinement made excessive, he reached the house of a friend in the country, and prayed for a night's shelter. His presence excited less pity than alarm. The people gave him refreshment, and he borrowed a little pocket copy of Horace, with which he went forth into the night. He promised himself shelter amid the stone quarries of Clamart.

The door of the house in the rue Servandoni was left on the latch night and day for a whole week. But Madame Vernet's generous hope was in vain; while she still hoped and watched, the end had come. On the evening of the seventh, Condorcet, with one of his legs torn or broken, his garments in rags, with visage gaunt and hunger-stricken, entered an inn in the hamlet of Clamart, and called for an omelette. Asked how many eggs he would have in it, the famishing man answered a dozen. Carpenters, for such he had given himself to be, do not have a dozen eggs in their omelettes. Suspicion was aroused, his hands were not the hands of a workman, and he had no papers to show, but only the pocket Horace. The villagers seized him and hastened to drag him, bound hand and foot, to Bourg-la-Reine, then called for a season Bourg-l'Égalité. On the road he fainted, and they set him on a horse offered by a pitying wayfarer. When they reached the prison, Condorcet, starving, bleeding, way-worn, was flung into his cell. On the morrow, when the gaolers came to seek him, they found him stretched upon the ground, dead and stark. So he perished—of hunger and weariness, say some; of poison ever carried by him in a ring, say others.[1]

An eminent man, who escaped by one accident from the hatchets of the Septembriseurs, and by another from the guillotine of the Terror, while in hiding and in momentary expectation of capture and death, wrote thus in condemnation of suicide, ' the one crime which leaves no possibility of return to virtue.' ' Even at this incomprehensible moment '— the spring of 1793—' when morality, enlightenment, energetic love of country, only render death at the prison-wicket or on the scaffold more inevitable; when it might be allowable to choose among the ways of leaving a life that can no longer be preserved, and to rob tigers in human form of the accursed pleasure of dragging you forth and drinking your blood; yes, on the fatal tumbril itself, with nothing free but voice, I could still cry, *Take care*, to a child that should come too near the wheel: perhaps he may owe his life to me, perhaps the country shall one day owe its salvation to him.' [2]

[1] The abbé Morellet, in his narrative of the death of Condorcet (*Mémoires*, c. xxiv.), says that he died of poison, a mixture of stramonium and opium. He adds that the surgeon described death as due to apoplexy. See Musset-Pathay's *J.-J. Rousseau*, ii. 42.

[2] Dupont de Nemours. *Les Physiocrates*, i. 326.

It has long been the fashion among the followers
of that reaction which Coleridge led and Carlyle
spread and popularised, to dwell exclusively on the
coldness and hardness, the excess of scepticism and
the defect of enthusiasm, that are supposed to have
characterised the eighteenth century. Because the
official religion of the century both in England and
France was lifeless and mechanical, it has been taken
for granted that the level of thought and feeling was
a low one universally ; as if the highest moods of
every era necessarily clothed themselves in religious
forms. The truth is that, working in such natures
as Condorcet's, the principles of the eighteenth
century, its homage to reason and rational methods,
its exaltation of the happiness of men, not excluding
their material well-being, into the highest place, its
passion for justice and law, its large illumination, all
engendered a fervour as truly religious as that of
Catholicism or of Calvinism at their best, while its
sentiment was infinitely less interested and personal.

IV.

The shape of Condorcet's ideas upon history arose
from the twofold necessity which his character imposed upon him, at once of meeting his aspirations
on behalf of mankind, and of satisfying a disciplined
and scientific intelligence. He could not find adequate
gratification in the artificial construction of hypo-
thetical utopias. Conviction was as indispensable

K

as hope ; and distinct grounds for the faith that was in him, as essential as the faith itself. The result of this fact of mental constitution, the intellectual conditions of the time being what they were, was the rise in his mind of the great and central conception of there being a law in the succession of social states, to be ascertained by an examination of the collective phenomena of past history. The merit of this admirable effort, and of the work in which it found expression, is very easily underrated, because the effort was insufficient and merely preparatory, while modern thought has already carried us far beyond it, and at least into sight of the more complete truths to which this effort only pointed the way. Let us remember, however, that it did point the way distinctly and unmistakably. A very brief survey of the state of history as a subject of systematic study enables us to appreciate with precision what service it was that Condorcet rendered, for it carries us back from the present comparatively advanced condition of the science of society to a time before his memorable attempt, when conceptions now become so familiar were not in existence, and when even the most instructed students of human affairs no more felt the need of a scientific theory of the manner in which social effects follow social causes, than the least instructed portion of the literary public feels such a need in our own time. It is difficult after a subject has been separated from the nebulous mass of unclassified knowledge, after it has taken independent shape, and begun to move in lines of its own, to realise the process by which all this was effected, or the way in which before all this the facts concerned presented themselves to the thinker's mind. That we should overcome the difficulty is one of the conditions of our being able to do justice to the great army of the precursors.

Two movements of thought went on in France during the middle of the eighteenth century, that have been comparatively little dwelt upon by historians; their main anxiety has been to justify the foregone conclusion, so gratifying alike to the partisans of the social reaction and to the disciples of modern transcendentalism in its many disguises, that the eighteenth century was almost exclusively negative, critical, and destructive. Each of these two currents was positive, and their influence undeniably constructive, if we consider that it was from their union into a common channel, a work fully accomplished first in the mind of Condorcet, that the notion of the scientific treatment of history and society took its earliest start.

The first of the two movements consisted in the remarkable attempts of Quesnay and his immediate followers to withdraw the organisation of society from the sphere of empiricism, and to substitute for the vulgar conception of arbitrary and artificial institutions as the sole foundation of this organisation, the idea that there is a certain Natural Order, conformity to which in all social arrangements is the essential condition of their being advantageous to the members of the social union. Natural Order in the minds of this school was no metaphysical figment evolved from uninstructed consciousness, but a set of circumstances to be discovered by continuous and methodical observation. It consisted of physical and moral law. Physical law is the regulated course of every physical circumstance in the order evidently most advantageous to the human race. Moral law is the rule of every human action in the moral order, conformed to the physical order evidently most advantageous to the human race. This order is the base of the most perfect government, and the fundamental rule of all positive laws ; for positive laws are only such laws as are required to keep up and maintain the natural order that is evidently most advantageous to the race.[1]

Towards the close of the reign of Louis XIV. the frightful impoverishment of the realm attracted the attention of one or two enlightened observers, and among them of Boisguillebert and Vauban. They had exposed, the former of them with especial force and amplitude, the absurdity of the general system of administration. It seemed to have been devised for the express purpose of paralysing both agriculture and commerce, and exhausting all the sources of the national wealth.[2] But these speculations had been

[1] Quesnay ; *Droit naturel*, ch. v. *Les Physiocrates*, i. 52.
[2] *Économistes financiers du* 18*ième Siècle*. Vauban's *Projet d'une dîme royale* (p. 33), and Boisguillebert's *Factum de la France*, etc. (p. 248 *et seq.*).

mainly fiscal, and pointed little further than to a readjustment of taxation and an improvement in the modes of its collection. The disciples of the New Science, as it was called, the Physiocrats, or believers in the supremacy of Natural Order, went much beyond this, and in theory sought to lay open the whole ground of the social fabric. Practically they dealt with scarcely any but economic circumstances, though some of them mix up with their reasonings upon commerce and agriculture crude and incomplete hints upon forms of government and other questions that belong not to the economical but to the political side of social science.[1] Quesnay's famous *Maxims* open with a declaration in favour of the unity of the sovereign authority, and against the system of counterbalancing forces in government. Almost immediately he passes on to the ground of political economy, and elaborates the conditions of material prosperity in an agricultural realm. Their peculiar distinction in the present connection is the grasp which they had of the principle of there being a natural, and therefore a scientific, order in social conditions; that order being natural in the sense they attached to the term, which from the circumstances of the case is most beneficial to the race. From this point of view they approach the problems of what is now classified as social statics;

[1] De la Rivière, for instance, very notably. Cf. his *Ordre naturel des sociétés politiques. Physiocrates*, ii. 469, 636, etc. See also Baudeau on the superiority of the Economic Monarchy. *Ibid.* pp. 783-791.

and they assume, without consciousness of another aspect being possible, that the society which they are discussing is in a state of equilibrium.

It is evident that with this restriction of the speculative horizon, they were and must remain wholly unable to emerge into the full light of the completely constituted science of society, with laws of movement as well as laws of equilibrium, with definite methods of interpreting past and predicting future states. They could account for and describe the genesis of the social union, as Plato and Aristotle had in different ways been able to do; and they could prescribe some of the conditions of its being maintained in vigour and compactness. Some of them could even see in a vague way the inter-dependence of peoples and the community of the real interests of different nations, each nation, as De la Rivière expressed it, being only a province of the vast kingdom of nature, a branch from the same trunk as the rest.[1] What they could not see was the social evolution; and here too, in the succession of social states, there has been a natural and observable order. In a word, they tried to understand society without the aid of history. Consequently they laid down the truths which they discovered as absolute and fixed, when they were no more than conditional and relative.

Fortunately, inquirers in another field had set a movement afoot that was destined to furnish the

[1] *Ordre nat. des soc. pol.* p. 526.

supplement of their own speculation. This was the remarkable development of the conception of history, which Montesquieu's two memorable books first made conspicuous. Bossuet's well-known discourse on universal history, teeming as it does with religious prejudice, just as Condorcet's sketch teems with prejudice against religion, had perhaps partially introduced the spirit of Universality into the study of history. But it was impossible from the nature of the case for any theologian to know fully what this spirit means ; and it was not until the very middle of the following century that any effective approach was made to that universality which Bossuet did little more than talk about. Then it came not from theology, but from the more hopeful sources of a rational philosophy. Before Montesquieu no single stone of the foundation of scientific history can be said to have been laid. Of course, far earlier writers had sought after the circumstances that brought about a given transaction. Thucydides, for example, had attributed the cause of the Peloponnesian war to the alarm of the Lacedæmonians at the greatness of the power of Athens.[1] It is this sense of the need of explanation, however rudimentary, that distinguishes the great historian from the chronicler, even from a superior chronicler like Livy, who in his account of so great an event as the Second Punic War plunges straightway into narrative of what happened, without concern why it

[1] Bk. i. 23.

happened. Tacitus had begun his *Histories* with remarks upon the condition of Rome, the feeling of the various armies, the attitude of the provinces, so that, as he says, ' *non modo casus eventusque rerum, qui plerumque fortuiti sunt, sed ratio etiam causæque noscantur.*' [1] But these and the like instances in historical literature were only political explanations, more or less adequate, of particular transactions; they were no more than the sagacious remarks of men with statesmanlike minds, upon the origin of some single set of circumstances.

The rise from this to the high degree of generality that marks the speculations of Montesquieu, empirical as they are, was as great as the rise from the mere maxims of worldly wisdom to the widest principles of ethical philosophy. Polybius, indeed, in the remarkable chapters with which his *Histories* open, uses expressions that are so modern as almost to startle us. ' People who study history,' he says, ' in separate and detached portions, without reference to one another, and suppose that from them they acquire a knowledge of the whole, are like a man who in looking on the severed members of what had once been an animated and comely creature, should think that this was enough to give him an idea of its beauty and force when alive. The empire of Rome was what by its extent in Italy, Africa, Asia, Greece, brought history into the condition of being organic ($\sigma\omega\mu\alpha\tau\sigma\epsilon\iota\delta\eta\varsigma$).' His object was to examine the general and collective

[1] *Hist.* i. 4.

ordering of events; when it came into existence; whence it had its source; how it had this special completion and fulfilment—the universal empire of Rome.[1] Striking as this is, there is not in it any real trace of the abstract conception of social history. Polybius recognises the unity of history, so far as that could be understood in the second century before Christ, but he treats his subject in the concrete, describing the chain of events without attempting to seek their law. It was Montesquieu who first applied the comparative method to social institutions; who first considered physical conditions in connection with the laws of a country; who first perceived and illustrated how that natural order which the Physiocrats only considered in relation to the phenomena of wealth and its production, really extended over its political phenomena as well; who first set the example of viewing a great number of social facts all over the world in groups and classes; and who first definitely and systematically inquired into the causes of a set of complex historical events and institutions, as being both discoverable and intelligible. This was a marked advance upon both of the ideas, by one or other of which men had previously been content to explain to themselves the course of circumstances in the world; either the inscrutable decrees of a non-human providence, or the fortuitous vagaries of an eyeless destiny.

It was Turgot, however, who completed the

[1] Polyb. *Hist.* I. iii. 4; iv. 3, 7.

historical conception of Montesquieu, in a piece
written in 1750, two years after the appearance of
the *Esprit des lois*, and in one or two other fragmentary compositions of about the same time, not
the less remarkable because the writer was only
twenty-three years old. Vico in Italy had insisted
on the doctrine that the course of human affairs is
in a cycle, and that they move in a constant and
self-repeating orbit.[1] Turgot, on the contrary, with
more wisdom, at the opening of his subject is careful
to distinguish the ever-varying spectacle of the succession of men from generation to generation, from
the circle of identical revolutions in which the
phenomena of nature are enclosed. In the one
case time only restores at each instant the image
of what it has just caused to disappear ; in the
other, the reason and the passions are ever incessantly
producing new events. ' All the ages are linked
together by a succession of causes and effects which
bind the state of the world to all the states that have
gone before. The multiplied signs of speech and
writing, in supplying men with the means of an
assured possession of their thoughts and of com-
municating them to one another, have formed a
common treasure that one generation transmits to
another, as an inheritance constantly augmented by

[1] The well-known words of Thucydides may contain the
germ of the same idea, when he speaks of the future as being
likely to represent again, after the fashion of human things, 'if
not the very image, yet the near resemblance of the past.'   Bk.
i. 22. 4.

the discoveries of each generation ; and the human race, looked at from its origin, appears in the eyes of the philosopher one immense whole, which, just as in the case of each individual, has its infancy and its growth.' [1]

Pascal and others in ancient and modern times [2] had compared in casual and unfruitful remarks the history of the race to the history of the individual, but Turgot was able in some sort to see the full meaning and extent of the analogy, as well as the limitations proper to it, and to draw from it some of the larger principles which the idea involved. The first proposition in the passage just quoted, that a chain of causes and effects unites each age with every other age that has gone before, is one of the most memorable sentences in the history of thought. And Turgot not only saw that there is a relation of cause and effect between successive states of society ; he had glimpses into some of the conditions of that relation. To a generation that stands on loftier heights his attempts seem rudimentary and strangely simple, but it was these attempts that cut the steps for our ascent. How is it, he asked, for instance, that the succession of social states is not uniform ? that they follow with unequal step along the track marked out for them ? He found the answer in the

[1] *Discours en Sorbonne. Œuvres de Turgot*, ii. 597. (Ed. of 1844.)
[2] Cf. Sir G. C. Lewis's *Methods of Observation in Politics*, ii. 439, note.

inequality of natural advantages, and he was able to discern the necessity of including in these advantages the presence, apparently accidental, in some communities and not in others, of men of especial genius or capacity in some important direction.[1] Again, he saw that just as in one way natural advantages accelerate the progress of a society, in another natural obstacles also accelerate it, by stimulating men to the efforts necessary to overcome them : *le besoin perfectionne l'instrument.*[2] The importance of following the march of the human mind over all the grooves along which it travels to further knowledge, was fully present to him, and he dwells repeatedly on the constant play going on between discoveries in one science and those in another. In no writer is there a fuller and more distinct sense of the essential unity and integrity of the history of mankind, nor of the multitude of the mansions into which this vast house is divided, and the many keys which he must possess that would open and enter in.

Even in empirical explanations Turgot shows a breadth and accuracy of vision truly surprising, considering his own youth and the youth of his subject. The reader will be able to appreciate this, and to discern at the same time the arbitrary nature of Montesquieu's method, if he will contrast, for example, the remarks of this writer upon polygamy with the far wider and more sagacious explanation of the

---

[1] *Œuvres de Turgot,* ii. 599, 645, etc.
[2] *Ibid.* ii. 601.

circumstances of such an institution given by Turgot.[1] Unfortunately, he has left us only short and fragmentary pieces, but they suggest more than many large and complete works. That they had a very powerful and direct influence upon Condorcet there is no doubt, as well from the similarity of general conception between him and Turgot, as from the nearly perfect identity of leading passages in their writings. Let us add that in Turgot's fragments we have what is unhappily not a characteristic of Condorcet, the peculiar satisfaction and delight in scientific history of a style that states a fact in such phrases as serve also to reveal its origin, bearings, significance, in which every successive piece of description is so worded as to be self-evidently a link in the chain of explanation, an ordered term in a series of social conditions.

Before returning to Condorcet we ought to glance at the remarkable piece, written in 1784, in which Kant propounded his idea of a universal or cosmo-political history, which, contemplating the agency of the human will upon a large scale, should unfold to our view a regular stream of tendency in the great succession of events.[2] The will, metaphysically

[1] *Esprit des lois*, xvi. cc. 2-4. And *Discours sur l'histoire universelle*, in Turgot's Works, ii. 640, 641. For a further account of Turgot's speculations, see article "Turgot" in the present volume.

[2] *Idea of a Universal History on a Cosmo-Political Plan.* It was translated by De Quincey, and is to be found in vol. xiii. of his collected works, pp. 133-152.

considered, Kant said, is free, but its manifestations, that is to say, human actions, ' are as much under the control of universal laws of nature as any other physical phenomena.'

The very same course of incidents, which taken separately and individually would have seemed perplexed and incoherent, ' yet viewed in their connection and as the action of the human *species* and not of independent beings, never fail to observe a steady and continuous, though slow, development of certain great predispositions in our nature.' As it is impossible to presume in the human race any *rational* purpose of its own, we must seek to observe some *natural* purpose in the current of human actions. Thus a history of creatures with no plan of their own, may yet admit a systematic form as a history of creatures blindly pursuing a plan of nature. Now we know that all predispositions are destined to develop themselves according to their final purpose. Man's rational predispositions are destined to develop themselves in the species and not in the individual. History, then, is the progress of the development of all the tendencies laid in man by nature. The method of development is the antagonism of these tendencies in the social state, and its source the *unsocial sociality* of man—a tendency to enter the social state, combined with a perpetual resistance to that tendency, which is ever threatening to dissolve it. The play of these two tendencies unfolds talents of every kind, and by gradual increase of light a preparation is made for such a mode of thinking as is capable of ' exalting a social concert that had been *pathologically* extorted from the mere necessities of situation, into a *moral* union founded on the reasonable choice.' Hence the highest problem for man is the establishment of a universal civil society, founded on the empire of political justice ; and ' the history of the human species as a whole may be regarded as the unravelling of a hidden plan of nature for accomplishing a perfect state of civil constitution for society in its internal relations (and, as the condition of that, in its external relations also), as the sole state of society in which the tendencies of human nature can be all and fully developed.' Nor is this all. We shall not only be able to unravel the intricate web of past affairs, but shall also find a clue for the guidance of future statesmen in the art of political prediction. Nay more, this clue ' will open a consolatory prospect into futurity, in which at a remote distance we shall observe the human species seated upon an eminence won by infinite toil, where all the germs are unfolded that nature has implanted within it, and its destination on this earth accomplished.'

That this conception involves an assumption about tendencies and final purposes which reverses the true method of history, and moreover reduces what ought to be a scientific inquiry to be a foregone justification of nature or providence, should not prevent us from appreciating its signal merits in insisting on a systematic presentation of the collective activity of the race, and in pointing out, however cursorily, the use of such an elucidation of the past in furnishing the grounds of practical guidance in dealing with the future and in preparing it. Considering the brevity of this little tract, its pregnancy and suggestiveness have not often been equalled. We have seen enough of it here to enable us to realise the differences between this and the French school. We miss the wholesome objectivity resulting from the stage which had been reached in France by the physical sciences. Condorcet's series of *éloges* shows unmistakably how deep an impression the history of physical discovery had made upon him, and how clearly he understood the value of its methods. The peculiar study which their composition had occasioned him is of itself almost enough to account for the fact that a conception that had long been preparing in the superior minds of the time, should fully develop itself in him rather than in anybody else.

V.

The Physiocrats had introduced the idea of there being a natural order in social circumstances, that order being natural which is most advantageous to mankind. Turgot had declared that one age is bound to another by a chain of causation. Condorcet fused these two conceptions. He viewed the history of the ages as a whole, and found in their succession a natural order ; an order that, when uninterrupted and undisturbed, tended to accumulate untold advantages upon the human race ; that was every day becoming more plain to the vision of men, and therefore every day more and more assured from disturbance by ignorant prejudice and sinister interests. There is an order at once among the circumstances of a given generation, and among the successive sets of circumstances in successive generations. ' If we consider the development of human faculties in its results, so far as they relate to the individuals who exist at the same time on a given space, and if we follow that development from generation to generation, then we have before us the picture of the progress of the human mind. This progress is subject to the same general laws that are to be observed in the development of the faculties of individuals, for it is the result of that development, considered at the same time in a great number of individuals united in society. But the result that presents itself at any one instant depends upon that which was offered by the instants preceding ; in turn it influences the result in times still to follow.'

This picture will be historical, inasmuch as being subject to perpetual variations it is formed by the observation, in due order, of different human societies in different epochs through which they have passed. It will expose the order of the various changes, the influence exercised by each period over the next, and thus will show in the modifications impressed upon

L

the race, ever renewing itself in the immensity of the ages, the track that it has followed, and the exact steps that it has taken towards truth and happiness. Such observation of what man has been and of what he is, will then lead us to means proper for assuring and accelerating the fresh progress that his nature allows us to anticipate still further.[1]

Thus Condorcet's purpose was not to justify nature, as it had been with Kant, but to search in the past for rational grounds of a belief in the splendour of men's future destinies. His view of the character of the relations among the circumstances of the social union, either at a given moment or in a succession of periods, was both accurate and far-sighted. When he came actually to execute his own great idea, and to specify the manner in which those relations arose and operated, he instantly diverged from the right path. Progress in his mind is exclusively produced by improvement in intelligence. It is the necessary result of man's activity in the face of that disproportion ever existing between what he knows and what he desires and feels the necessity to know.[2] Hence the most fatal of the errors of Condorcet's sketch. He measures only the contributions made by nations and eras to what we know : leaving out of sight their failures and successes in the elevation of moral standards and ideals, and in the purification of human passions.

---

[1] *Tableau des progrès de l'esprit humain. Œuvres*, vi. 12, 13.
[2] *Œuvres*, vi. 21.

One seeks in vain in Condorcet's sketch for any account of the natural history of western morals, or for any sign of consciousness on his part that the difference in ethical discipline and feeling between the most ferocious of primitive tribes and the most enlightened eighteenth-century Frenchmen, was a result of evolution that needed historical explanation, quite as much as the difference between the astrolatry of one age and the astronomy of another. We find no recognition of the propriety of recounting the various steps of that long process by which, to use Kant's pregnant phrase, the relations born of pathological necessity were metamorphosed into those of moral union. The grave and lofty feeling, for example, which inspired the last words of the *Tableau* —whence came it ? Of what long-drawn chain of causes in the past was it the last effect ? It is not enough to refer us generally to previous advances in knowledge and intellectual emancipation, because even supposing the successive modifications of our moral sensibilities to be fundamentally due to the progress of intellectual enlightenment, we still want to know in the first place something about the influences that harness one process to the other, and in the second place, something about the particular directions these modifications of moral constitution have taken.

If this is one very radical omission in Condorcet's scheme, his angry and vehement aversion for the various religions of the world (with perhaps one

exception) is a sin of commission still more damaging
to its completeness. An unfavourable view of the
influences upon human development of the Christian
belief, even in its least corrupt forms, was not
untenable. Nay, he was at liberty to go further
than this, and to depict religion as a natural
infirmity of the human mind in its immature stages,
just as there are specific disorders incident in childhood to the human body. Even on this theory, he
was bound to handle it with the same gravity that
he would have expected to find in a pathological
treatise by a physician. Who would write of the
sweating sickness with indignation, or describe
zymotic diseases with resentment? Condorcet's
pertinacious anger against theology is just as
irrational as this would be, from the scientific point
of view which he pretends to have assumed.

From the earliest times to the latest it is all one
story according to Condorcet. He can speak with
respect of philosophies even when, as in the case of
the Scotch school of the eighteenth century, he
dislikes and condemns them.[1] Of religion his contempt and hatred only vary slightly in degree.
Barbarous tribes have sorcerers, trading on the gross
superstitions of their dupes : so in other guise and
with different names have civilised nations to-day.
As other arts progressed, superstition, too, became
less rude ; priestly families kept all knowledge in
their own hands, and thus preserved their hypo-

[1] *Œuvres*, vi. 186.

critical and tyrannical assumptions from detection. They disclosed nothing to the people without supernatural admixture, the better to maintain their personal pretensions. They had two doctrines, one for themselves, and the other for the people. Sometimes, as they were divided into several orders, each of them reserved to itself certain mysteries. Thus all the inferior orders were at once rogues and dupes, and the great system of hypocrisy was only known in all its completeness to a few adepts. Christianity belonged to the same class. Its priests, we must admit, ' in spite of their knaveries and their vices, were enthusiasts ready to perish for their doctrines.' In vain did Julian endeavour to deliver the empire from the scourge. Its triumph was the signal for the incurable decay of all art and knowledge. The church may seem to have done some good in things where her interests did not happen to clash with the interests of Europe, as in helping to abolish slavery, for instance ; but after all ' circumstances and manners ' would have produced the result necessarily and of themselves. Morality, which was taught by the priests only, contained those universal principles that have been unknown to no sect ; but it created a host of purely religious duties and imaginary sins. These duties were more rigorously enjoined than those of nature, and actions that were indifferent, legitimate, or even virtuous, were more severely rebuked and punished than real crimes. Yet, on the other hand, a moment of repentance, consecrated by the absolution of a priest, opened the gates of heaven to the worst miscreants.[1]

It is obvious that Condorcet was unfitted by his temper, and the school to which he most belonged, from accepting religion as a fact in the history of the human mind that must have some positive explanation. To look at it in this way as the creation of a handful of selfish impostors in each community, was to show a radical incompetence to carry out the scheme that had been so scientifically projected. The picture is ruined by the angry caricature of what ought to have been one of the most important figures in it. Never perhaps was there so thorough an inversion of the true view of the comparative elevation of different parts of human character, as is implied in Condorcet's strange hint that Cromwell's satellites would have been much better men if they had carried instead of the Bible at their saddle - bows some merry book of the stamp of Voltaire's *Pucelle*.[2]

Apart from the misreading of history in explaining religion by the folly of the many and the frauds of a few, Condorcet's interpretation involved the profoundest infidelity to his own doctrine of the intrinsic purity and exaltation of human nature. This doctrine ought in all reason to have led him to

[1] *Œuvres*, vi. pp. 35, 55, 101, 102, 111, 117, 118, etc.
[2] See Condorcet's vindication of the *Pucelle* in his *Life of Voltaire*. *Œuvres*, iv. 88, 89. See also Comte's *Phil. pos.* v. 450.

look for the secret of the popular acceptance of beliefs that to him seemed most outrageous, in some possibly finer side which they might possess for others, appealing not to the lower but to the higher qualities of a nature with instincts of perfection. Take his account of Purgatory. The priests, he says, drew up so minute and comprehensive a table of sins that nobody could hope to escape from censure. Here you come upon one of the most lucrative branches of the sacerdotal trafficking ; people were taught to imagine a hell of limited duration, which the priests only had the power to abridge ; and this grace they sold, first to the living, then to the kinsmen and friends of the dead.[1] Now it was surely more worthy of a belief in the natural depravity than in the natural perfectibility of the sons of Adam, thus to assume without parley or proviso a base mercenariness on the one hand, and grovelling terror on the other, as the origin of a doctrine which was obviously susceptible of a kinder explanation. Would it not have been more consistent with belief in human goodness to refer the doctrine to a merciful and affectionate and truly humanising anxiety to assuage the horrors of what is perhaps the most frightful idea that has ever corroded human character, the idea of eternal punishment ? We could in part have pardoned Condorcet if he had striven to invent ever so fanciful origins for opinions and belief in his solicitude for the credit of humanity. As it is, he

[1] *Œuvres*, vi. 118.

distorts the history of religion only to humanity's discredit. How, if the people were always predisposed to virtue, were priests, sprung of the same people and bred in the same traditions, so invariably and incurably devoted to baseness and hypocrisy? Was the nature of a priest absolutely devoid of what physicians call recuperative force, restoring him to a sound mind, in spite of professional perversion? In fine, if man had been so grossly enslaved in moral nature from the beginning of the world down to the year 1789 or thereabouts, how was it possible that notwithstanding the admitted slowness of civilising processes, he should suddenly spring forth the very perfectible and nearly perfected being that Condorcet passionately imagined him to be? [1]

It has already been hinted that there was one partial exception to Condorcet's animosity against religion. This was Mahometanism. Towards this his attitude is fully appreciative, though of course he deplores the superstitions that mixed themselves

---

[1] As Comte says in his remarks on Condorcet (*Phil. pos.* iv. 185-193): '*Le progrès total finalement accompli ne peut être sans doute que le résultat général de l'accumulation spontanée des divers progrès partiels successivement réalisés depuis l'origine de la civilisation, en vertu de la marche successivement lente et graduelle de la nature humaine*'; so that Condorcet's picture presents a standing miracle, '*où l'on s'est même interdit d'abord la ressource vulgaire de la Providence.*' Comte's criticism, however, seems to leave out of sight what full justice Condorcet did to the various partial advances in the intellectual order.

up with the Arabian prophet's efforts for purification.
After the seven vials of fiery wrath have been poured
out upon the creed of Palestine, it is refreshing to
find the creed of Arabia almost patronised and
praised. The writer who could not have found in
his heart to think Gregory the Great or Hildebrand
other than a mercenary impostor, nor Cromwell
other than an ambitious hypocrite, admits with
exquisite blandness of Mahomet that he had the
art of employing all the means of subjugating men
avec adresse, mais avec grandeur.[1] Another reason,
no doubt, besides his hatred of the church, lay at
the bottom of Condorcet's tolerance or more towards
Mahometanism. The Arabian superstition was not
fatal to knowledge ; Arabian activity in algebra,
chemistry, optics, and astronomy atoned in Condorcet's eyes for the Koran.

It is fair to add further, that Condorcet showed
a more just appreciation of the effects of Protestantism upon western development than has been common
among French thinkers. He recognises that men
who had learnt, however imperfectly, to submit their
religious prejudices to rational examination, would
naturally be likely to extend the process to political
prejudices also. Moreover, if the reformed churches
refused to render to reason all its rights, still they
agreed that its prison should be less narrow ; the
chain was not broken, but it ceased to be either so
heavy or so short as it had been. And in countries

[1] *Œuvres,* vi. 120-123.

where what was by the dominant sect insolently styled tolerance, succeeded in establishing itself, it was possible to maintain the tolerated doctrines with a more or less complete freedom. So there arose in Europe a sort of freedom of thought, not for men, but for Christians ; and, ' if we except France, it is only for Christians that it exists anywhere else at the present day,' a limitation which has now fortunately ceased to be altogether exact.

If we have smiled at the ease with which what is rank craftiness in a Christian, is toned down into address in a Mahometan, we may be amused too at the leniency that describes some of the propagandist methods of the eighteenth century. Condorcet becomes rapturous as he tells with what admixture of the wisdom of the serpent the humane philosophers of his century ' covered the truth with a veil that prevented it from hurting too weak sight, and left the pleasure of conjecturing it ; caressing prejudices with address, to deal them the more certain blows ; scarcely ever threatening them, nor ever more than one at once, nor even one in its integrity ; sometimes consoling the enemies of reason by pretending to desire no more than a half-tolerance in religion and half-liberty in politics ; conciliating despotism while they combated the absurdities of religion, and religion when they rose against despotism ; attacking these two scourges in their principle, even when they seemed only to bear ill-will to revolting or ridiculous abuses, and striking these poisonous trees in their

very roots, while they appeared to be doing no more
than pruning crooked branches.'[1] Imagine the holy
rage with which such acts would have been attacked,
if Condorcet had happened to be writing about the
Jesuits. Unfortunately, the serene composure of the
historical conscience was as unknown to him as it is
always to orthodox apologists. It is to be said,
moreover, that he had less excuse for being without
it, for he rested on the goodness of men, and not, as
theologians rest, on their defects.

One or two detached remarks are suggested by
Condorcet's picture, that it may be worth while
to make. He is fully alive, for example, to the
importance to mankind of the appearance among
them of one of those men of creative genius, like
Archimedes or like Newton, whose lives constitute
an epoch in human history. Their very existence he
saw to be among the greatest benefits conferred on
the race by Nature. He hardly seems to have been
struck, on the other hand, with the appalling and
incessant waste of these benefits ; with the number
of men of Newtonian capacity who are born into the
world only to chronicle small beer ; with the hosts
of high souls who labour and flit away like shadows,
perishing in the accomplishment of minor and subordinate ends. We may suspect that the notion of
all this immeasurable profusion of priceless treasures,
its position as one of the laws of the condition of
man on the globe, would be unspeakably hard of

[1] *Œuvres,* vi. 187-189.

endurance to one holding Condorcet's peculiar form of optimism.

Again, it would be worth while to examine some of the acute and ingenious hints which Condorcet throws out by the way. It would be interesting to consider, as he suggests, the influence upon the progress of the human mind of the change from writing on such subjects as science, philosophy, and jurisprudence in Latin, to the usual language of each country. That change rendered the sciences more popular, but it increased the trouble of the scientific men in following the general march of knowledge. It caused a book to be read in one country by more men of inferior competence, but less read throughout Europe by men of superior light. And though it relieves men who have no leisure for extensive study from the trouble of learning Latin, it imposes upon profounder persons the necessity of learning a variety of modern languages.[1]

VI.

Our expectations for the future, Condorcet held, may be reduced to these three points : the destruction of inequality among nations ; the progress of equality among the people of any given nation ; and, finally, the substantial perfecting (*perfectionnement réel*) of man.

I. With reference to the first of these aspirations, it will be brought about by the abandonment among

[1] *Œuvres*, vi. 163.

European peoples of their commercial monopolies, their treacherous practices, their mischievous and extravagant proselytising, and their sanguinary contempt for those of another colour or another creed. Vast countries, now a prey to barbarism and violence, will present in one region numerous populations only waiting to receive the means and instruments of civilisation from us, and as soon as they find brothers in the Europeans, will joyfully become their friends and pupils ; and in another region, nations enslaved under the yoke of despots or conquerors, crying aloud for liberators. In yet other regions, it is true, there are tribes almost savage, cut off by the harshness of their climate from a perfected civilisation, or else conquering hordes, ignorant of every law but violence and every trade but brigandage. The progress of these last two descriptions of people will naturally be more tardy, and attended by more storm and convulsion. It is possible even that, reduced in number, in proportion as they see themselves repulsed by civilised nations, they will end by insensibly disappearing.[1] It is perhaps a little hard to expect Esquimaux or the barbaric marauders of the sandy expanses of Central Asia insensibly to disappear, lest by their cheerless presence they should destroy the unity and harmony of the transformation scene in the grand drama of Perfectibility.

II. The principal causes of the inequality that unfortunately exists among the people of the same

[1] *Œuvres*, pp. 239-244.

community are three : inequality in wealth ; inequality of condition between the man whose means
of subsistence are both assured and transmissible,
and him for whom these means depend upon the
duration of his working life ; thirdly, inequality
of instruction. How are we to establish a continual tendency in these three sources of inequality to
diminish in activity and power ? To lessen, though
not to demolish, inequalities in wealth, it will be
necessary for all artificial restrictions and exclusive
advantages to be removed from fiscal or other legal
arrangements, by which property is either acquired
or accumulated : and among social changes tending
in this direction will be the banishment by public
opinion of an avaricious or mercenary spirit from
marriage. Again, inequality between permanent and
precarious incomes will be radically modified by the
development of the application of the calculation of
probabilities to life. The extension of annuities and
insurance will not only benefit many individuals, but
will benefit society at large by putting an end to that
periodical ruin of a large number of families, which is
such an ever-renewing source of misery and degradation. Another means to the same end will be found
in discovering, by the same doctrine of probabilities,
some other equally solid base for credit instead of a
large capital, and for rendering the progress of
industry and the activity of commerce more independent of the existence of great capitalists. Something approaching to equality of instruction, even for

those who can only spare a few of their early years
for study, and in after times only a few hours of
leisure, will become more attainable by improved
selection of subjects, and improved methods of
teaching them. The dwellers in one country will
cease to be distinguished by the use of a rude or of a
refined dialect ; and this, it may be said in passing,
was sometimes thought to be the result of the school
system in the United States. One portion of them
will no longer be dependent upon any other for
guidance in the smallest affairs. We cannot obliterate
nor ignore natural differences of capacity, but after
public instruction has been properly developed, ' the
difference will be between men of superior enlightenment, and men of an upright character who feel the
value of light without being dazzled by it ; between
talent or genius, and that good sense which knows
how to appreciate and to enjoy both.' [1]

III. What are the changes that we may expect
from the substantial perfecting of human nature and
society ? The progress of agricultural science will
make the same land more productive, and the same
labour more efficient. Nay, who shall predict what
the art of converting elementary substances into
food for our use may one day become ? The constant
tendency of population to advance to the limits of
the means of subsistence thus amplified will be
checked by a rising consciousness in men, that if
they have obligations in respect of creatures still

[1] *Œuvres,* pp. 244-251.

unborn, these obligations consist in giving them, not existence but happiness, in adding to the well-being of the family, and not cumbering the earth with useless and unfortunate beings. This changed view upon population will partly follow from the substitution of rational ideas for those prejudices which have penetrated morals with an austerity that is corrupting and degrading.[1] The movement will be further aided by one of the most important steps in human progress—the destruction, namely, of the prejudices that have established inequality of rights between the two sexes, and which are so mischievous even to the sex that seems to be most favoured. We seek in vain for any justification of such an inequality in difference of physical organisation, in force of intelligence, or in moral sensibility. It has no other origin than abuse of strength, and it is to no purpose that attempts are made to excuse it by sophisms.[2]

Among other improvements under our third head will be the attainment of greater perfection in language, leading at once to increased accuracy and increased concision. Laws and institutions, following the progress of knowledge, will be constantly undergoing modifications tending to identify individual

[1] *Œuvres*, pp. 257, 258.
[2] Condorcet, we know, thought the indissolubility of marriage a monstrously bad thing, but the grounds which he gives for his thinking so would certainly lead to the infinite dissolubility of society. See a passage in the *Fragment on the Tenth Epoch*, vi. 523-526. See also some curious words in a letter to Turgot, i. 221, 222.

with collective interests. Wars will grow less frequent with the extinction of those ideas of hereditary and dynastic rights, that have occasioned so
many bloody contests. The art of learning will be
facilitated by the institution of a Universal Language ;
and the art of teaching by resort to Technical Methods,
or systems which unite in orderly arrangement a
great number of different objects, so that their
relations are perceived at a single glance.[1]

Finally, progress in medicine, the use of more
wholesome food and healthy houses, the diminution
of the two most active causes of deterioration, namely,
misery and excessive wealth, must prolong the average
duration of life, as well as raise the tone of health
while it lasts. The force of transmissible diseases
will be gradually weakened, until their quality of
transmission vanishes.

The rapidity and the necessary incompleteness
with which Condorcet threw out in isolated hints his
ideas of the future state of society, impart to his
conception a certain mechanical aspect, which conveys
an incorrect impression of his notion of the sources
whence social change must flow. His admirable,
careful remarks upon the moral training of children
prove him to have been as far removed as possible
from any of those theories of the formation of
character which merely prescribe the imposition of
moulds and casts from without, instead of carefully

[1] *Œuvres*, pp. 269-272.

M

tending the many spontaneous and sensitive processes of growth within.

With machinery and organisation Condorcet did not greatly concern himself; probably too little rather than too much. The central idea of all his aspirations was to procure the emancipation of reason, free and ample room for its exercise, and improved competence among men in the use of it. The subjugation of the modern intelligence beneath the disembodied fancies of the grotesque and sombre imagination of the Middle Ages, did not offend him more than the idea of any fixed organisation of the spiritual power, or any final and settled and universally accepted solution of belief and order would have done. With De Maistre and Comte the problem was the organised and systematic reconstruction of an anarchic society. With Condorcet it was how to persuade men to exert the individual reason methodically and independently, not without co-operation, but without anything like official or other subordination. His cardinal belief and precept was, as with Socrates, that the βίος ἀνεξέταστος is not to be lived by man. As we have seen, the freedom of the reason was so dear to him, that he counted it an abuse for a parent to instil his own convictions into the defenceless minds of his young children. This was the natural outcome of Condorcet's mode of viewing history as the record of intellectual emancipation, while to Comte its deepest interest was as a record of moral and emotional cultivation. If we

value in one type of thinker the intellectual con-
scientiousness, which refrains from perplexing men
by propounding problems unless the solution can be
set forth also, perhaps we owe no less honour in the
thinker of another type to that intellectual self-denial
which makes him very careful lest the too rigid pro-
jection of his own specific conclusions should by any
means obstruct the access of a single ray of fertilising
light. This religious scrupulosity, which made him
abhor all interference with the freedom and openness
of the understanding as the worst kind of sacrilege,
was Condorcet's eminent distinction. If, as some
think, the world will gradually transform its fear or
love of unknowable gods into a devout reverence for
those who have stirred in men a sense of the dignity
of their own nature and of its large and multitudinous
possibilities, then will his name not fail of deep and
perpetual recollection.

THE
CHAMPION OF SOCIAL REACTION.

I.

OWING to causes lying tolerably near the surface,
the remarkable Catholic reaction that took place in
France at the beginning of the nineteenth century,
has never received in England the attention it
deserves ; not only for its striking interest as an
episode in the history of European thought, but also
for its peculiarly forcible and complete presentation
of those ideas with which what is called the modern
spirit is supposed to be engaged in deadly war. For
one thing, the Protestantism of England strips a
genuinely Catholic movement of speculation of the
pressing and practical importance which belongs to
it in a country where nearly all spiritual sentiment
that has received any impression of religion at all,
unavoidably runs in Catholic forms. With us the
theological reaction against the ideas of the eighteenth
century was not and could not be other than
Protestant. The defence and reinstatement of
Christianity in each case was conducted, as might

have been expected, with reference to the dominant
creed and system of the country. If Coleridge had
been a Catholic, his works thus newly coloured by
an alien creed would have been read by a small
sect only, instead of exercising, as they did, a wide
influence over the whole nation, reaching people
through those usual conduits of press and pulpit,
by which the products of philosophic thought are
conveyed to other than philosophic minds. As
naturally in France, hostility to all those influences
which were believed to have brought about the
Revolution; to sensationalism in metaphysics; to
atheism in what should have been theology; to the
notion of sovereignty of peoples in politics, inevitably
sought a rallying-point in a renewed allegiance
to the prodigious spiritual system that had fostered
the germs of order and social feeling in Europe, and
whose name remains even now as the most permanent symbol and exemplar of stable organisation.
Another reason for English indifference to this movement is the rapidity with which here, as elsewhere, dust gathers thickly round the memory of
the champions of lost causes. Some of the most
excellent of human characteristics — intensity of
belief, and a fervid anxiety to realise aspirations
—unite with some of the least excellent of them,
to make us too habitually forget that, as Mill has so
excellently said, the best adherents of a fallen standard
in philosophy, in religion, in politics, are usually next
in all good qualities of understanding and sentiment

to the best of those who lead the van of the force that triumphs. Men are not so ânxious as they should be, considering the infinite diversity of effort that goes to the advancement of mankind, to pick up the fragments of truth and positive contribution, that nothing be lost, and as a consequence the writings of antagonists with whom we are believed to have nothing in common, lie unexamined and disregarded.

In the case of the group of writers who, after a century of criticism, ventured once more with an intrepid confidence—differing fundamentally from the tone of preceding apologists in the Protestant camp, who were nearly as critical as the men they refuted —to vindicate not the bare outlines of Christian faith, but the entire scheme, in its extreme manifestation, of the most ancient of all Christian organisations, this apathy is very much to be regretted on several grounds. In the first place, it is impossible to see intelligently to the bottom of the momentous spirit of ultramontanism, which is so deep a difficulty of continental Europe, and, touching us in Ireland, is perhaps already one of our own deepest difficulties,—without comprehending in its best shape the theory on which ultramontanism rests. And this theory it is impossible to seize thoroughly, without some knowledge of the ideas of its most efficient defenders in its earlier years. Secondly, it is among these ideas that we have to look for the representation in their most direct, logical, uncom-

promising, and unmistakable form of those theological
ways of regarding life and prescribing right conduct,
whose more or less rapidly accelerated destruction
is the first condition of the further elevation of
humanity, as well in power of understanding as in
morals and spirituality. In all contests of this kind
there is the greatest and most obvious advantage in
being able to see your enemy full against the light.
Thirdly, in one or two respects, the Catholic re-
actionaries at the beginning of the nineteenth century
insisted very strongly on principles of society which
the general thought of the century before had almost
entirely dropped out of sight, and which we who, in
spite of many differences, still sail down the same
great current, and are propelled by the same tide,
are accustomed almost equally either to leave in the
background of speculation, or else deliberately to
deny and suppress. Such we may account the
importance which they attach to organisation, and
the value they set upon a common spiritual faith
and doctrine as a social basis. That the form which
the recognition of these principles is destined to
assume, will at all correspond to their hopes and
anticipations, is one of the most unlikely things
possible. This, however, need not detract from the
worth for our purpose of their exposition of the
principles themselves. Again, the visible traces of
the impression made by the writings of this school
on the influential founder of the earliest Positivist
system, are sufficiently deep and important to make

some knowledge of them of the highest historical interest, both to those who accept and to those who detest the system.

At the beginning of the nineteenth century, there were three chief schools of thought, the Sensational, the Catholic, and the Eclectic ; or as it may be put in other terms, the Materialist, the Theological, and the Spiritualist. The first looked for the sources of knowledge, the sanction of morals, the inspiring fountain and standard of æsthetics, to the outside of men, to matter, and the impressions made by matter on the corporeal senses. The second looked to divine revelation, authority and the traditions of the church. The third, steering a middle course, looked partly within and partly without, relied partly on the senses, partly on revelation and history, but still more on a certain internal consciousness of a direct and immediate kind, which is the supreme and reconciling judge of the reports alike of the senses, of history, of divine revelation.[1] Each of these schools had many exponents. The three most conspicuous champions of revived Catholicism were De Maistre, De Bonald, and Chateaubriand. The last of them, the author of the *Génie du Christianisme*, was effective in France because he is so deeply sentimental, but he was too little trained in speculation, and too little equipped with knowledge, to be fairly taken as the best intellectual representative of their way of thinking. De

[1] See Damiron's *La Philosophie en France au XIXième siècle*. Introduction to vol. i. (Fifth edition.)

Bonald was of much heavier calibre. He really thought, while Chateaubriand only felt, and the *Législation primitive* and the *Pensées sur divers sujets* contain much that an enemy of the school will find it worth while to read, in spite of an artificial, and, so far as a foreigner may judge, a detestable style.

De Maistre was the greatest of the three, and deserves better than either of the others to stand as the type of the school. His style is so wonderfully lucid, that, notwithstanding the mystical, or, as he said, the illuminist side of his mind, we can never be in doubt about his meaning, and this is not by any means the case with De Bonald. To say nothing of his immensely superior natural capacity, De Maistre's extensive reading in the literature of his foes was a source of strength, that might indeed have been thought indispensable, if only other persons had not attacked the same people as he did, without knowing much, or anything at all, at first hand about them. Then he goes over the whole field of allied subjects, which we have a right to expect to have handled by anybody with a systematic view of the origin of knowledge, the meaning of ethics, the elements of social order and progressiveness, the government and scheme of the universe. Above all, his writings are penetrated with the air of reality and life, that comes of actual participation in the affairs of the world with which social philosophers have to deal. Lamennais had in many respects a finer mind than De Maistre, but the conclusions in

which he was finally landed, no less than his liberal
aims, prevent him from being an example of the truly
Catholic reaction.   He obviously represented the
Revolution, or the critical spirit, within the Catholic
limits, while De Maistre's ruling idea was, in his own
trenchant phrase, ' *absolument tuer l'esprit du dix-
huitième siècle.*'   On all these accounts he appears
to be the fittest expositor of those conceptions which
the anarchy that closed the eighteenth century provoked into systematic existence.

There can be little doubt that the effective
way in which De Maistre propounded and vindicated
his theory made a deep impression on the mind of
Comte.   Very early in his career he declared : ' De
Maistre has for me the peculiar property of helping
me to estimate the philosophic capacity of people,
by the repute in which they hold him.'   Among his
other reasons at that time for thinking well of Guizot
was that, notwithstanding Guizot's transcendent
Protestantism, he complied with the test of appreciating De Maistre.[1]   Comte's rapidly assimilative intelligence perceived that here at last there was a
definite, consistent, and intelligible scheme for the
reorganisation of European society, with him the
great end of philosophic endeavour.   Its principle of
the division of the spiritual and temporal powers,
and of the relation that ought to subsist between
the two, was the base of Comte's own scheme.   In
general form the plans of social reconstruction are

[1] Littré, *Auguste Comte et la phil. posit.* p. 152.

identical; in substance, it need scarcely be said, the differences are fundamental. The temporal power, according to Comte's design, is to reside with industrial chiefs, and the spiritual power to rest upon a doctrine scientifically established. De Maistre, on the other hand, believed that the old authority of kings and Christian pontiffs was divine, and any attempt to supersede it in either case would have seemed to him as desperate as impious.

II.

Joseph de Maistre was born at Chambéry in the year 1754.[1] His family was the younger branch of a stock in Languedoc, which about the beginning of the seventeenth century divided itself into two, one remaining in France, the other establishing itself in Piedmont. It is not wonderful that the descendants of the latter, settled in a country of small extent and little political importance, placed a high value on their kinship with an ancient line in the powerful kingdom of France. Joseph de Maistre himself was always particularly anxious to cultivate close relations with his French kinsfolk, partly from the old aristocratic feeling of blood, and partly from his intellectual appreciation of the gifts of the French mind, and its

[1] The facts of De Maistre's life I have drawn from a very meagre biography by his son, Count Rodolphe de Maistre, supplemented by two volumes of *Lettres et opuscules* (Fourth edition; Paris, Vaton. 1865), and a volume of his *Diplomatic Correspondence*, edited by M. Albert Blanc.

vast influence as an universal propagating power.
His father held a high office in the government of
Savoy, and enjoyed so eminent a reputation that on
his death both the Senate and the King of Sardinia
deliberately recorded their appreciation of his loss
as a public calamity. His mother is said to have
been a woman of lofty and devout character, and her
influence over her eldest son was exceptionally strong
and tender. He used to declare in after life that he
was as docile in her hands as the youngest of his
sisters. Among other marks of his affectionate
submission to parental authority, we are told that
during the whole time of his residence at Turin,
where he followed a course of law, he never read a
single book without previously writing to Chambéry
to one or other of his parents for their sanction. Such
traditions linger in families, and when he came to
have children of his own, they too read nothing of
which their father had not been asked to express his
approbation. De Maistre's early education was
directed by the Jesuits ; and as might have been
expected from the generous susceptibility of his
temper, he never ceased to think of them with warm
esteem. To the end of his life he remembered the
gloom that fell upon the household, though he was
not nine years old at the time, when the news arrived
of the edict of 1764, abolishing the Society in the
kingdom of France. One element of his education he
commemorates in a letter to his favourite daughter.
' Let your brother,' he says, ' work hard at the French

poets. Let him learn them by heart, especially the
incomparable Racine ; never mind whether he under-
stands him yet or not. I didn't understand him
when my mother used to come repeating his verses
by my bedside, and lulled me to sleep with her fine
voice to the sound of that inimitable music. I knew
hundreds of lines long before I knew how to read ;
and it is thus that my ears, accustomed betimes to
this ambrosia, have never since been able to endure
any sourer draught.'

After his law studies at the University of Turin,
then highly renowned for its jurisconsults, the young
De Maistre went through the successive stages of an
official career, performing various duties in the public
administration, and possessing among other honours
a seat in the Senate, over which his father presided.
He led a tranquil life at Chambéry, then, as at all
other times, an ardent reader and student. Unaided
he taught himself five languages. English he
mastered so perfectly, that though he could not
follow it when spoken, he could read a book in that
tongue with as much ease as if it had been in his own.
To Greek and German he did not apply himself until
afterwards, and he never acquired the same pro-
ficiency in them as in English, French, Italian, Latin,
and Spanish. To be ignorant of German then, it
will be remembered, was not what it would be now,
to be without one of the literary senses.

Like nearly every other great soldier of reaction,
he showed in his early life a decided inclination for

new ideas.   The truth that the wildest extravagances
of youthful aspiration are a better omen of a vigorous
and enlightened manhood than the decorous and
ignoble faith in the perfection of existing arrangements, was not belied in the case of De Maistre.
His intelligence was of too hard and exact a kind to
inspire him with the exalted schemes that present
themselves to those more nobly imaginative minds
who dream dreams and see visions.   He projected
no Savoyard emigration to the banks of the Sus-
quehanna or Delaware, to found millennial societies
and pantisocratic unions.   These generous madnesses
belong to men of more poetic temper.   Still, in
spite of the deadening influences of officialism and
relations with a court, De Maistre had far too
vigorous and active a character to subside without
resistance into the unfruitful ways of obstruction
and social complacency.   It is one of the most
certain marks of a superior spirit, that the impulses
earliest awakened by its first fresh contact with the
facts of the outer world, are those that quicken a
desire for the improvement of society, the increase
of the happiness of men, the amelioration of human
destiny.   With this unwritten condition of human
nature De Maistre, like other men of his mental
calibre, complied.   He incurred the suspicion and
ill-will of most of those by whom he was immediately
surrounded, by belonging to a Reform Lodge at
Chambéry.   The association was one of a perfectly
harmless character, but being an association, it

diffused a tarnishing vapour of social disaffection
and insurgency over the names of all who ventured
to belong to it, and De Maistre was pointed out to
the Sardinian court as a man, with leanings towards
new things, and therefore one of whom it were well
to beware. There was little ground for apprehension. When the menacing sounds of the approaching
hurricane in France grew heavy in the air, the little
lodge at Chambéry voluntarily dissolved itself, and
De Maistre was deputed to convey to the king, Victor
Amadeo III., the honourable assurance of its members
that they had assembled for the last time.

In 1786, at the age of thirty-two, De Maistre had
married, and when the storm burst that destroyed
all the hopes of his life, he was the father of two
children. In one of his gay letters to a venerable
lady who was on intimate terms with them both, he
has left a picture of his wife, which is all the more
interesting for what it reveals of his own character.
' The contrast between us two is the very strangest
in the world. For me, as you may have found out,
I am the *pococurante* senator, and above all things
very free in saying what I think. She, on the contrary, will take care that it is noon before allowing
that the sun has risen, for fear of committing herself.
She knows what must be done or what must not be
done on the tenth of October 1808, at ten o'clock in
the morning, to avoid some inconvenience which
otherwise would come to pass at midnight between
the fifteenth and sixteenth of March 1810. " But,

my dear husband, you pay attention to nothing;
you believe that nobody is thinking of any harm.
Now I know, I have been told, I have guessed, I
foresee, I warn you," etc. " Come now, my dear,
leave me alone. You are only wasting your time :
I foresee that I shall never foresee things : that's
your business." She is the supplement to me, and
hence when I am separated from her, as I am now, I
suffer absurdly from being obliged to think about
my own affairs ; I would rather have to chop wood
all day. . . . My children ought to kiss her very
steps ; for my part, I have no gift for education.
She has such a gift, that I look upon it as nothing
less than the eighth endowment of the Holy Ghost ;
I mean a certain fond persecution by which it is
given her to torment her children from morning to
night to do something, not to do something, to learn
—and yet without for a moment losing their tender
affection for her. How can she manage it ? I cannot
make it out.' She was laughingly called by himself
and her friends, Madame Prudence.. It is certain
that few women have found more necessity for the
qualities implied in this creditable nickname.

They had not been married many years before
they were overtaken by irreparable disaster. The
French Revolution broke out, and Savoy was invaded
by the troops of the new Republic. Count De Maistre,
with his wife and children, fled from Chambéry across
the Alps to Aosta. ' Ma chère amie,' he said to his
wife, by the side of a great rock which he never

N

afterwards forgot, ' the step that we are taking to-day is irrevocable ; it decides our lot for life ' ; and the presentiment was true. Soon the *Loi des Allobroges* was promulgated, which enjoined upon all who had left their homes in Savoy to return instantly, under pain of confiscation of all their property. It was the very depth of winter. Madame de Maistre was in the ninth month of her pregnancy. She knew that her husband would endure anything rather than expose her to the risks of a journey in such a season. So, urged by a desire to save something from the wreck of their fortune by compliance with the French decree, she seized the opportunity of her husband's absence at Turin, and started for Savoy without acquainting him with her design. She crossed the Great St. Bernard in the beginning of January on the back of a mule, accompanied by her two little children wrapped in blankets. The Count, on his return to Aosta two or three days afterwards, forthwith set off in her steps, in the trembling expectation of finding her dead or dying in some Alpine hovel. But the favour of fate and a stout heart brought her safe to Chambéry, where shortly afterwards she was joined by her husband. The authorities vainly tendered him the oath, vainly bade him inscribe his name on the register of citizens ; and when they asked him for a contribution to support the war, he replied curtly that he did not give money to kill his brothers in the service of the King of Sardinia. As soon as his wife was delivered of their third child, whom he was destined not to see again for nearly twenty years, he quitted her side, abandoned his property and his country, and took refuge at Lausanne, where in time his wife and his two eldest children once more came to him.

Gibbon tells us how a swarm of emigrants, escaping from the public ruin, was attracted by the vicinity, the manners, and the language of Lausanne. ' They are entitled to our pity,' he reflected, ' and they may claim our esteem, but they cannot in their present state of mind and fortune contribute much to our amusement. Instead of looking down as calm and idle spectators on the theatre of Europe, our domestic harmony is somewhat embittered by the infusion of party spirit.' Gibbon died in London almost at the very moment when De Maistre arrived at Lausanne, but his account of things remained true, and political feuds continued to run as high as ever. Among the people with whom De Maistre was thrown was Madame de Staël. ' As we had not been to the same school,' he says, ' either in theology or in politics, we had some scenes, enough to make one die of laughter ; still without quarrelling. Her father, who was then alive, was the friend and relative of people that I love with all my heart, and that I would not vex for all the world. So I allowed the *émigrés* who surrounded us to cry out as they would, without ever drawing the sword.' De Maistre thought he never came across a head so completely turned wrong as Madame de Staël's, the infallible consequence,

as he took it to be, of modern philosophy operating
upon a woman's nature. He once said of her:
' Ah! if Madame de Staël had been Catholic, she
would have been adorable, instead of famous.' We
can believe that his position among the French
émigrés was not particularly congenial. For though
they hated the Revolution, they had all drunk of
the waters of the eighteenth-century philosophy, and
De Maistre hated this philosophy worse than he
hated the Revolution itself. Then again, they would
naturally vapour about the necessities of strong
government. ' Yes,' said the Savoyard exile, ' but
be quite sure that, to make the monarchy strong, you
must rest it on the laws, avoiding everything arbitrary,
too frequent commissions, and all ministerial jobberies.'
We may well believe how unsavoury this rational and
just talk was to people who meant by strong government a system that should restore to them their old
prerogatives of anti-social oppression and selfish corruption. The order that De Maistre vindicated was
a very different thing from the deadly and depraving order that was the object of the prayers of
incorrigible royalists around him.

After staying three years at Lausanne, De Maistre
went to Turin, but shortly afterwards the Sardinian
king, at the end of a long struggle, was forced to
bend to the power of the French, then in the
full tide of success. Bonaparte's brilliant Italian
campaign needs no words here. The French entered
Turin, and De Maistre, being an *émigré*, had to leave

it. Furnished with a false passport, and undergoing
a thousand hardships and dangers, he made his way,
once more in the depth of a severe winter (1797),
to Venice. He went part of the way down the Po
in a small trading ship, crowded with ladies, priests,
monks, soldiers, and a bishop. There was only one
small fire on board, at which all the cooking had to
be done, and where the unhappy passengers had to
keep themselves warm as they could. At night they
were confined each to a space about three planks
broad, separated from neighbours by pieces of canvas
hanging from a rope above. Each bank of the river
was lined by military posts—the left by the Austrians,
and the right by the French ; and the danger of being
fired into was constantly present to aggravate the
misery of overcrowding, scanty food, and bitter cold.
Even this wretchedness was surpassed by the hardships that confronted the exiles at Venice. The
physical distress endured here by De Maistre and his
unfortunate family exceeded that of any other period
of their wanderings. He was cut off from the court,
and from all his relations and friends, and reduced
for the means of existence to a few fragments of
silver plate that had somehow been saved from the
universal wreck. This slender resource grew less day
by day, and when it was exhausted the prospect was
a blank. The student of De Maistre's philosophy
may see in what crushing personal anguish some of
its most sinister growths had their roots. When the
cares of beggary come suddenly upon a man in middle

life, they burn deep. Alone, and starving for a
cause that is dear to him, he might encounter
grim fate with a fortitude in which there should
be many elevating and consoling elements. But the
destiny is intolerably hard which condemns a man of
humane mould, as De Maistre certainly was, to look
helplessly on the physical pains of a tender woman
and famishing little ones. The hour of bereavement
has its bitterness, but the bitterness is gradually
suffused with soft reminiscence. The grip of beggary
leaves a mark on such a character as De Maistre's
that no prosperity of after days effaces. The seeming
inhumanity of his theory of life, that is so revolting
to comfortable people like M. Villemain, was in truth
the only explanation of his own cruel sufferings in
which he could find any solace. It was not that
he hated mankind, but his destiny looked as if
God hated him, and this was a horrible moral complexity out of which he could only extricate himself
by a theory in which pain and torment seem to stand
out as the main facts in human existence.

To him, indeed, prosperity never came. Hope
smiled on him momentarily, but, in his own words :
' It was only a flash in the night.' While he was
in Venice, the armies of Austria and Russia recon-
quered the north of Italy, and Charles Emanuel IV.,
in the natural anticipation that the allies would
at once restore his dominions, hastened forward.
Austria, however, as De Maistre had seen long
before, was indifferent, or even absolutely hostile,

to Sardinian interests, and she successfully opposed Charles Emanuel's restoration. The king received, at Florence, the news of the perfidy of his nominal ally, but not until after he had made arrangements for rewarding the fidelity of some of his most loyal adherents.

It was from Florence that De Maistre accepted the king's nomination to the chief place in the government of the island of Sardinia. Through the short time of his administration here, he was overwhelmed with vexations only a little more endurable than the physical distresses that had weighed him down at Venice. During the war, justice had been administered in grossly irregular fashion. Hence, people had taken the law into their own hands, and retaliation had completed the round of wrong-doing. The taxes were collected with difficulty. The higher class exhibited an invincible repugnance to paying their debts. Some of these difficulties in the way of firm and orderly government were insuperable, and De Maistre vexed his soul in an unequal and only partially successful contest. In after years, amid the miseries of his life in Russia, he wrote to his brother thus : ' Sometimes in moments of solitude that I multiply as much as I possibly can, I throw my head back on the cushion of my sofa, and there with my four walls around me, far from all that is dear to me, confronted by a sombre and impenetrable future, I recall the days when in a little town that you know well '—he meant Cagliari—' with my head resting on

another sofa, and only seeing around our own exclusive circle (good heavens, what an impertinence !)
little men and little things, I used to ask myself :
" Am I then condemned to live and die in this place,
like a limpet on a rock ? " I suffered bitterly ; my
head was overloaded, wearied, flattened, by the
enormous weight of Nothing.'

Presently a worse thing befell him. In 1802
he received an order from the king to proceed to
St. Petersburg as envoy extraordinary and minister
plenipotentiary at the court of Russia. Even from
this bitter proof of devotion to his sovereign he
did not shrink. He had to tear himself from
his wife and children, without any certainty when
the cruel separation would end ; to take up new
functions which the circumstances of the time
rendered unspeakably difficult ; while the petty
importance of the power he represented, and its
mendicant attitude in Europe, robbed his position
of the public distinction and dignity that may
richly console a man for private sacrifice. It is a
kind destiny that veils their future from mortal
men. Fifteen years passed before De Maistre's exile
came to a close. From 1802 to 1817 he did not quit
the inhospitable latitudes of northern Russia.

His letters during this desolate period furnish
a striking picture of his manner of life and
his mental state. We see in them his most
prominent characteristics. Not even the pain-
fulness of the writer's situation ever clouds his

intrepid and vigorous spirit. Lively and gallant
sallies of humour to his female friends, sagacious
judgments on the position of Europe to political
people, bits of learned criticism for erudite people,
tender and playful chat with his two daughters,
all these alternate delightfully with one another.
Whether he is writing to his little girl whom he has
never known, or to the King of Sardinia, or to some
author who sends him a book, or to a minister who
has found fault with his diplomacy, there is in all
alike the same constant and remarkable play of a
bright and penetrating intellectual light, coloured
by a humour that is now and then sardonic, but
more often genial and lambent. There is a certain
semi-latent quality of hardness lying at the bottom
of De Maistre's style, both in his letters and in his
more elaborate compositions. His writings seem to
recall the flavour and bouquet of some of the fortify-
ing and stimulating wines of Burgundy, from which
time and warmth have not yet drawn out a certain
native roughness that lingers on the palate. This
hardness, if one must give the quality a name that
only imperfectly describes it, sprang not from any
original want of impressionableness or sensibility of
nature, but partly from the relentless buffetings he
had to endure at the hands of fortune, and partly
from the preponderance that had been given to the
rational side of his mind by long habits of sedulous
and accurate study. Few men knew so perfectly
as he knew how to be touching without ceasing to be

masculine, or how to go down into the dark pits of human life without forgetting the broad sunlight, or how to keep habitually close to visible and palpable fact, while eagerly addicted to speculation. His contemplations were perhaps somewhat too near the ground; they led him into none of those sublimer regions of subtle feeling where the rarest human spirits have loved to travel; we do not think of his mind among those who have gone

> Voyaging through strange seas of thought alone.

If this kind of temper, strong, keen, frank, and a little hard and mordant, brought him too near a mischievous disbelief in the dignity of men and their lives, at least it kept him well away from morbid weakness in ethics, and from beating the winds in metaphysics. But of this we shall see more in considering his public pieces, than can be gathered from his letters.

The discomforts of De Maistre's life at St. Petersburg were extreme. The dignity of his official style and title was an aggravation of the exceeding straitness of his means. The ruined master could do little to mitigate the ruin of his servant. He had to keep up the appearance of an ambassador on the salary of a clerk. 'This is the second winter,' he writes to his brother in 1810, 'that I have gone through without a pelisse, which is exactly like going without a shirt at Cagliari. When I come from court a very sorry lackey throws a common cloak over my shoulders.' The climate suited him better than he had expected ; and in one letter he vows that he was the only living being in Russia who had passed two winters without fur boots and a fur hat. It was considered indispensable that he should keep a couple of servants ; so, for his second, De Maistre was obliged to put up with a thief, whom he rescued under the shelter of ambassadorial privilege from the hands of justice, on condition that he would turn honest. The Austrian ambassador, with whom he was on good terms, would often call to take him out to some entertainment. 'His fine servants mount my staircase groping their way in the dark, and we descend preceded by a servant carrying *luminare minus quam ut præesset nocti.*' 'I am certain,' he adds pleasantly, 'that they make songs about me in their Austrian patois. Poor souls ! it is well they can amuse themselves.'

Sometimes he was reduced so far as to share the soup of his valet, for lack of richer and more independent fare. Then he was constantly fretted by enemies at home, who disliked his trenchant diplomacy, and distrusted the strength and independence of a mind that was too vigorous to please the old-fashioned ministers of the Sardinian court. These chagrins he took as a wise man should. They disturbed him less than his separation from his family. 'Six hundred leagues away from you all,' he writes to his brother, 'the thoughts of my family, the reminiscences of childhood, transport me with sadness.'

Visions of his mother's saintly face haunted his
chamber ; almost gloomier still was the recollection
of old intimates with whom he had played, lived,
argued, and worked for years, and yet who now no
longer bore him in mind. There are not many
glimpses of this melancholy in the letters meant for
the eye of his beloved *trinité féminine*, as he playfully
called his wife and two daughters. '*A quoi bon vous
attrister*,' he asked bravely, '*sans raison et sans
profit ?*' Occasionally he cannot help letting out to
them how far his mind is removed from composure.
'Every day as I return home I find my house as
desolate as if it were yesterday you left me. In
society the same fancy pursues me, and scarcely ever
quits me.' Music, as might be surmised in so sensitive a nature, drove him almost beside himself with
its mysterious power of intensifying the dominant
emotion. 'Whenever by any chance I hear the
harpsichord,' he says, 'melancholy seizes me. The
sound of the violin gives me such a heavy heart,
that I am fain to leave the company and hasten home.'
He tossed in his bed at night, thinking he heard the
sound of weeping at Turin, making a thousand efforts
to picture to himself the looks of that 'orphan child
of a living father' whom he had never known, wondering if ever he should know her, and battling with a
myriad of black phantoms that seemed to rustle in
his curtains. 'But you, M. de Chevalier,' he said
apologetically to the correspondent to whom he told
these dismal things, 'you are a father, you know the

cruel dreams of a waking man; if you were not of
the profession I would not allow my pen to write
you this jeremiad.' As De Maistre was accustomed
to think himself happy if he got three hours' sound
sleep in the night, these sombre and terrible vigils
were ample enough to excuse him if he had allowed
them to overshadow all other things. But the vigour
of his intellect was too strenuous, and his curiosity
and interest in every object of knowledge too inextinguishable. 'After all,' he said, ' the only thing
to do is to put on a good face, and to march to the
place of torture with a few friends to console you
on the way. This is the charming image under
which I picture my present situation. Mark you,'
he added, ' I always count books among one's consoling friends.'

In one of the most gay and charming of his letters,
apologising to a lady for the remissness of his correspondence, he explains that diplomacy and books
occupy every moment. ' You will admit, madam,
there is no possibility of one's shutting up books
entirely. Nay, more than ever, I feel myself burning
with the feverish thirst for knowledge. I have
had an access of it that I cannot describe to you.
The most curious books literally run after me,
and hurry to place themselves in my hands. As
soon as diplomacy gives me a moment of breathing-
time I rush headlong to that favourite pasture, to that
ambrosia of which the mind can never have enough—

Et voilà ce qui fait que votre ami est muet.'

He thinks himself happy if, by refusing invitations
to dinner, he can pass a whole day without stirring
from his house. ' I read, I write, I study ; for after
all one must know something.' In his hours of
depression he fancied that he only read and worked,
not for the sake of the knowledge, but to stupefy
and tire himself out, if that were possible.

As a student De Maistre was indefatigable. He
never belonged to the languid band who hope to
learn difficult things by easy methods. The only
way, he warned his son, is to shut your door, to say
that you are not within, and to work. ' Since they
have set themselves to teach us how we ought to
learn the dead languages, you can find nobody who
knows them ; and it is amusing enough that people
who don't know them should be so obstinately bent
on demonstrating the vices of the methods employed
by us who do know them.' He was one of the
wise and laborious students who do not read without
a pen in their hands. He never shrank from the
useful toil of transcribing abundantly, from all the
books he read, everything that could by any possibility eventually be of service to him in his inquiries.
His notebooks were enormous. As soon as one of
them was filled, he carefully made up an index of its
contents, numbered it, and placed it on a shelf with
its unforgotten predecessors. In one place he
accidentally mentions that he had some thirty of
these folios over the head of his writing-table.

' If I am a pedant at home,' he said, ' at least I am

as little as possible a pedant out of doors.' In the
evening he would occasionally seek the society of
ladies, by way of recovering some of the native gaiety
of heart that had hitherto kept him alive. 'I blow
on this spark,' to use his own words, 'just as an old
woman blows among the ashes to get a light for her
lamp.' A student and a thinker, De Maistre was
also a man of the world, and he may be added to the
long list of writers who have shown that to take an
active part in public affairs, and mix in society, gives
a peculiar life, reality, and force to both scholarship
and speculation. It was computed at that time that
the author of a philosophic piece could not safely
count upon more than a hundred and fifty readers
in Russia ; and hence, we might be sure, even if we
had not De Maistre's word for it, that away from
his own house he left his philosophy behind. The
vehemence of his convictions did not prevent him
from being socially tolerant to others who hated
them. 'If I had the good fortune to be among his
acquaintances,' he wrote of a heretical assailant,
' he would see that among the people with convictions it would be hard to find one so free from
prejudice as I am. I have many friends among
the Protestants, and now that their system is
tottering, they are all the dearer to me.' In spite of
his scanty means, his shabby valet, his threadbare
cloak, and his low diplomatic position, the fire
and honesty of his character combined with his
known ability to place him high in the esteem of the

society of St. Petersburg. His fidelity, devotion,
and fortitude, mellowed by many years and by
meditative habits, and tinged perhaps by the patrician
consciousness of birth, formed in him a modest
dignity that men respected. They perceived it to
be no artificial assumption, but the outward image
of a high and self-respecting spirit. His brother
diplomatists, even the representatives of France,
appear to have treated him with marked consideration. His letters prove him to have been a favourite
among ladies. The Emperor Alexander showed him
considerable kindness. He conferred on his brother,
Xavier de Maistre, a post in one of the public museums,
while to the Sardinian envoy's son he gave a commission in the Russian service.

The first departure of this son for the campaign of
1807 occasioned some of the most charming passages
in De Maistre's letters, both to the young soldier
himself and to others. For though without a touch
of morbid expansiveness, he never denied himself
the solace of opening his heart to a trusted friend,
and a just reserve with strangers did not hinder a
humane and manly confidence with intimates. ' This
morning,' he wrote to his stripling, soon after he had
joined the army, ' I felt a tightening at my heart
when a pet dog came running in and jumped upon
your bed, where he finds you no more. He soon
perceived his mistake, and said clearly enough, after
his own fashion : *I am mistaken ; where can he be
then ?* As for me I have felt all that you will feel, if

ever you pursue this mighty trade of being a father.'
And then he begs of his son, if he should find himself
with a tape line in his hand, that he will take his
exact measure and forward it. Soon came the news
of the battle of Friedland, and the unhappy father
thought he read the fate of his son in the face of
every acquaintance he met. And so it was in later
campaigns, as De Maistre records in correspondence
that glows with tender and healthy solicitude. All
this is worth dwelling upon, for two reasons if no
more. First, because De Maistre has been too much
regarded and spoken of as a man of cold sensibility,
and little moved by the hardships that fill the destiny
of our race. And, again, because his own keen
acquaintance with mental anguish helps us to understand the zeal with which he attempts to reconcile
the blind cruelty and pain and torture endured by
mortals with the benignity and wisdom of the immortal. ' After all,' he used to say, ' there are only
two real evils—remorse and disease.' It is interesting and suggestive to recall how a later publicist
viewed the ills that dwarf our lives. ' If I were asked
to class human miseries,' said Tocqueville, ' I would
do so in this order : first, Disease ; second, Death ;
third, Doubt.' At a later date, he altered the order,
and deliberately declared doubt to be the most in-
supportable of all evils, worse than death itself.
But Tocqueville was an aristocrat, as Guizot once
told him, who accepted his defeat. He stood on the
brink of the torrent of democracy, and shivered.

De Maistre was an aristocrat too, but he was incapable of knowing what doubt or hesitation meant. He never dreamt that his cause was lost, and he mocked and defied the Revolution to the end. We easily see how natures of this sort, ardent, impetuous, unflinching, find themselves in the triumphant paths that lead to remorse at their close, and how they thus come to feel remorse rather than doubt as the consummate agony of the human mind.

Having had this glimpse of De Maistre's character away from his writings, we need not linger long over the remaining events of his life. In 1814 his wife and two daughters joined him in the Russian capital. Two years later an outburst of religious fanaticism caused the sudden expulsion of the Jesuits from Russia, to De Maistre's infinite mortification. Several conversions had taken place from the Orthodox to the Western faith, and these inflamed the Orthodox party, headed by the Prince de Galitzin, the minister of public worship, with theological fury. De Maistre, whose intense attachment to his own creed was well known, fell under suspicion of having connived at these conversions, and the Emperor himself went so far as to question him. 'I told him,' De Maistre says, 'that I had never changed the faith of any of his subjects, but that if any of them had by chance made me a sharer of their confidence, neither honour nor conscience would have allowed me to tell them that they were wrong.' This kind of dialogue between a sovereign and an ambassador implied a situation plainly unfavourable to effective diplomacy. The envoy obtained his recall, and after twenty-five years' absence returned to his native country (1817). On his way home De Maistre passed a few days in Paris, and thus, for the first and last time, one of the most eminent of modern French writers found himself on French soil.

The king accorded De Maistre an honourable reception, conferred upon him a high office and a small sum of money, and lent his ear to other counsellors. The philosopher, though insisting on declaring his political opinions, then, as ever, un-waveringly anti-revolutionary, threw himself mainly upon the literary composition that had been his solace in yet more evil days than these. It was at this time that he gave to the world the supreme fruit of nearly half a century of study, meditation, and contact with the world, in *Du Pape, Les Soirées de Saint-Pétersbourg,* and *L'Église gallicane.* Their author did not live long to enjoy the vast discussion they occasioned, nor the reputation they have since conferred upon his name. He died in February 1821 after such a life as we have seen.

III.

It is not at all surprising that they upon whom the revolutionary deluge came, should have looked with indiscriminating horror and affright on all the influences which in their view had united first to

gather up, and then to release the destructive flood.
The eighteenth century to men like De Maistre seemed
an infamous parenthesis, mysteriously interposed
between the glorious age of Bossuet and Fénelon,
and that yet brighter era for faith and the church
which was still to come in the good time of Divine
Providence. The philosophy of the eighteenth century, he says on more than one occasion, will form
one of the most shameful epochs of the human
mind : it never praised even good men except for
what was bad in them. He looked upon the gods
whom that century had worshipped as the direct
authors of the bloodshed and ruin in which their
epoch had closed. The memory of mild and humane
philosophers was covered with the kind of black
execration that prophets of old had hurled at Baal
or Moloch ; Locke and Hume, Voltaire and Rousseau,
were habitually spoken of as very scourges of God.
From this temper two consequences naturally flowed.
In the first place, while it lasted there was no hope
of an honest philosophic discussion of the great
questions that divide speculative minds. Moderation
and impartiality were virtues of almost superhuman
difficulty for controversialists who had made up their
minds that it was their opponents who had erected
the guillotine, confiscated the sacred property of the
church, slaughtered and banished her children, and
filled the land with terror and confusion. It is hard
amid the smoking ruins of the homestead to do full
justice to the theoretical arguments of the authors

of the conflagration. Hence De Maistre, though intimately acquainted with the works of his foes in the letter, was prevented by the vehemence of his antipathy to the effects he attributed to them, from having any just critical estimate of their value and true spirit. ' I do not know one of these men,' he says of the philosophers of the eighteenth century, ' to whom the sacred title of honest man is quite suitable.' They are all wanting in probity. Their very names ' *me déchirent la bouche.*' To admire Voltaire is the sign of a corrupt soul ; and if anybody is drawn to the works of Voltaire, then be sure that God does not love such an one. The divine anathema is written on the very face of this arch-blasphemer ; on his shameless brow ; in the two extinct craters still sparkling with sensuality and hate ; in that frightful *rictus* running from ear to ear ; in those lips tightened by cruel malice, like a spring ready to fly back and launch forth blasphemy and sarcasm ; he plunges into the mud, rolls in it, drinks of it ; he surrenders his imagination to the enthusiasm of hell, which lends him all its forces ; Paris crowned him, Sodom would have banished him.[1] Locke, again, did not understand himself. His distinguishing characteristics are feebleness and precipitancy of judgment. Vagueness and irresolution reign in his expressions as they do in his thoughts. He constantly exhibits that most decisive sign of mediocrity—he passes close by the greatest questions without perceiving them. In the

[1] *Soirées de Saint-Pétersbourg* (8th ed., 1862), vol. i. pp. 238-243.

study of philosophy, contempt for Locke is the
beginning of knowledge.[1] Condillac was even more
vigilantly than anybody else on his guard against his
own conscience. But Hume was perhaps the most
dangerous and the most guilty of all those mournful
writers who will for ever accuse the eighteenth century
before posterity—the one who employed the most
talent with the most coolness to do most harm.[2] To
Bacon De Maistre paid the compliment of composing
a long refutation of his main ideas, in which Bacon's
blindness, presumption, profanity, and scientific
charlatanry are denounced in vehement terms, and
treated as the natural outcome of a low morality.

De Maistre believed that his opponents were even
worse citizens than they were bad philosophers, and
it was his horror of them in the former capacity that
made him so bitter and resentful against them in
the latter. He could think of no more fitting image
for opinions that he did not happen to believe than
counterfeit money, 'which is struck in the first
instance by great criminals, and is afterwards passed
on by honest folk who perpetuate the crime without
knowing what they do.' A philosopher of the highest
class, we may be sure, does not permit himself to be
drawn down from the true object of his meditations
by these sinister emotions. But De Maistre belonged
emphatically to minds of the second order, whose
eagerness to find truth is never intense and pure

---

[1] *Soirées de Saint-Pétersbourg, 6ième entretien,* i. 397-442.
[2] *Ibid.* (8th ed., 1862), vol. i. p. 403.

enough to raise them above perturbing antipathies to persons. His whole attitude was fatal to his claim to be heard as a truth-seeker. He was not only persuaded of the general justice of the orthodox system, but he refused to believe that it was capable of being improved or supplemented by anything which a temperate and fair examination of other doctrines might peradventure be found to yield. With De Maistre there was no peradventure. Again, no speculative mind of the highest order ever mistakes, or ever moves systematically apart from, the main current of the social movement of its time. It is implied in the very definition of a thinker of supreme quality that he should detect, and be in a certain accord with, the most forward and central of the ruling tendencies of his epoch. The years that have elapsed since De Maistre was driven to attempt to explain the world to himself, have sufficed to show that the central conditions at that time for the permanent reorganisation of the society that had just been so violently rent in pieces, were assuredly not theological, military, nor ultramontane, but the opposite of all these.

There was a second consequence of the conditions of the time. The catastrophe of Europe affected the matter as well as the manner of contemporary speculation. The French Revolution has become to us no more than a term in a historic series. To some of the best of those who were confronted on every side by its tumult and agitation, it was the prevailing of the gates of hell, the moral disruption of the universe, the absolute and total surrender of the world to them that plough iniquity and sow wickedness. Even under ordinary circumstances few men have gone through life without encountering some triumphant iniquity, some gross and prolonged cruelty, which makes them wonder how heaven should allow such things to be. If we remember the aspect which the Revolution wore in the eyes of those who, seeing it, yet did not understand, we can imagine what dimensions this eternal enigma must have assumed in their sight. It was inevitable that the first problem to press on men with resistless urgency should be the ancient question of the method of the Creator's temporal government. What is the law of the distribution of good and evil fortune ? How can we vindicate with regard to the conditions of this life, the different destinies that fall to men ? How can we defend the moral ordering of a world in which the wicked and godless constantly triumph, while the virtuous and upright who retain their integrity, are as frequently buffeted and put to shame ?

This tremendous question has never been presented with such sublimity of expression, such noble simplicity and force of thought, as in the majestic and touching legend of Job. But its completeness, as a presentation of the human tragedy, is impaired by the excessive prosperity that is finally supposed to reward the patient hero for his fortitude. Job received twice as much as he had before, and his latter end was blessed more than his beginning. In the chronicles of actual

history men fare not so. There is a terribly logical
finish about some of the dealings of fate, and in life
the working of a curse is seldom stayed by any
dramatic necessity for a smooth consummation.
Destiny is no artist. The facts that confront us are
relentless. No statement of the case is adequate
which maintains, by ever so delicate an implication,
that in the long run somehow it is well in temporal
things with the just, and ill with the unjust. Until
we have firmly looked in the face the grim truth that
temporal rewards and punishments do not follow
the possession or the want of spiritual or moral
virtue, so long we are still ignorant what that enigma
is, which speculative men, from the author of the
book of Job downwards, have striven to resolve. We
can readily imagine the fullness with which the
question would grow up in the mind of a royalist and
Catholic exile at the end of the eighteenth century.

Nothing can be more clearly put than De Maistre's
answers to the question that the circumstances of
the time placed before him. What is the law of the
distribution of good and evil fortune in this life ? Is
it a moral law ? Do prosperity and adversity fall
respectively to the just and the unjust, either individually or collectively ? Has the ancient covenant
been faithfully kept, that whoso hearkens diligently
to the divine voice, and observes all the command-
ments to do them, shall be blessed in his basket and
his store and in all the work of his hand ? Or is
God a God that hideth himself ?

De Maistre perceived that the optimistic conception of the Deity as benign, merciful, infinitely
forgiving, was far from covering the facts.   So
he insisted on seeing in human destiny the ever-
present hand of a stern and terrible judge, administer-
ing a Draconian code with blind severity.   God
created men under conditions that left them free
to choose between good and evil.   All the physical
evil that exists in the world is a penalty for the
moral evil that has resulted from the abuse by
men of this freedom of choice.   For these physical
calamities the Deity is only responsible in the way
in which a criminal judge is responsible for a hanging.
Men cannot blame the judge for the gallows; the
fault is their own in committing those offences for
which hanging is prescribed beforehand as the penalty.
These curses that dominate human life are not the
result of the cruelty of the divine ruler, but of the
folly and wickedness of mankind, who, seeing the
better course, yet deliberately choose the worse.
The order of the world is overthrown by the iniquities
of men; it is we who have provoked the exercise
of the divine justice, and called down the tokens of
his vengeance.   The misery and disaster that surround us like a cloak are the penalty of our crimes
and the price of our expiation.   As the divine St.
Thomas has said : *Deus est auctor mali quod est poena,
non autem mali quod est culpa.*   There is a certain
quantity of wrong done over the face of the world ;
therefore the great Judge exacts a proportionate

quantity of punishment. The total amount of evil
suffered makes nice equation with the total amount
of evil done; the extent of human suffering tallies
precisely with the extent of human guilt. Of course
you must take original sin into account, 'which
explains all, and without which you can explain
nothing.' 'In virtue of this primitive degradation
we are subject to all sorts of physical sufferings *in
general*; just as in virtue of this same degradation
we are subject to all sorts of vices *in general*. This
original malady therefore [which is the correlative
of original sin] has no other name. It is only the
capacity of suffering all evils, as original sin is only
the capacity of committing all crimes.' [1] Hence all
calamity is either the punishment of sins actually
committed by the sufferers, or else it is the general
penalty exacted for general sinfulness. Sometimes
an innocent being is stricken, and a guilty being
appears to escape. But is it not the same in the
transactions of earthly tribunals ? And yet we do
not say that they are conducted without regard to
justice and righteousness. 'When God punishes any
society for the crimes that it has committed, he does
justice as we do justice to ourselves in these sorts
of circumstance. A city revolts; it massacres the
representatives of the sovereign; it shuts its gates
against him; it defends itself against his arms; it
is taken. The prince has it dismantled and deprived
of all its privileges; nobody will find fault with this

[1] *Soirées,* i. 76.

decision on the ground that there are innocent persons shut up in the city.'[1]

De Maistre's deity is thus a colossal Septembriseur, enthroned high in the peaceful heavens, demanding ever-renewed holocausts in the name of the public safety.

It is true, as a general rule, that the objects that men have worshipped have improved in morality and wisdom as men themselves have improved. The quiet gods, without effort of their own, have grown holier and purer by the agitations and toil which civilise their worshippers. In other words, the same influences that elevate and widen our sense of human duty give corresponding height and nobleness to our ideas of the divine character. The history of the civilisation of the earth is the history of the civilisation of Olympus also. It will be seen that the deity

---

[1] De Maistre found a curiously characteristic kind of support for this view in the fact that evils are called *fléaux*: flails are things to beat with : so evils must be things with which men are beaten ; and as we should not be beaten if we did not deserve it, *argal*, suffering is a merited punishment. Apart from that common infirmity which leads people, after they have discovered an analogy between two things, to argue from the properties of the one to those of the other, as if, instead of being analogous, they were identical, De Maistre was particularly fond of inferring moral truths from etymologies. He has an argument for the deterioration of man, drawn from the fact that the Romans expressed in the same word, *supplicium*, the two ideas of prayer and punishment (*Soirées*, 2ième *entretien*, i. p. 108). His profundity as an etymologist may be gathered from his analysis of *cadaver: ca*-ro, *da*-ta, *ver*-mibus. There are many others of the same quality.

whom De Maistre sets up is below the moral level of
the time in respect of Punishment.   In intellectual
matters he vehemently proclaimed the superiority of
the tenth or the twelfth over the eighteenth century,
but it is surely carrying admiration for those loyal
times indecently far, to seek in the vindictive sackings
of revolted towns, and the miscellaneous butcheries
of men, women, and babes, which then marked the
vengeance of outraged sovereignty, the most apt
parallel and analogy for the systematic administration of human society by its Creator.   Such
punishment can no longer be regarded as moral in
any deep or permanent sense; it implies a gross, harsh,
and revengeful character in the executioner, that
is eminently perplexing and incredible to those who
expect to find an idea of justice in the government of the world, at least not materially below
what is attained in the clumsy efforts of uninspired
publicists.

In mere point of administration, the criminal code
that De Maistre put into the hands of the Supreme
Being works in a more arbitrary and capricious
manner than any device of an Italian Bourbon.   As
Voltaire asks—

> *Lisbonne, qui n'est plus, eut-elle plus de vices*
> *Que Londres, que Paris, plongés dans les délices?*
> *Lisbonne est abîmée, et l'on danse à Paris.*

Stay, De Maistre replies, look at Paris thirty years
later, not dancing, but red with blood.   This kind
of thing is often said, even now ; but it is time to

abandon the prostitution of the name of Justice
to a process which brings Louis XVI. to the block,
and consigns De Maistre to poverty and exile, because
Louis XIV., the Regent, and Louis XV. had been
profligate men or injudicious rulers. The reader may
remember how the unhappy Emperor Maurice, as his
five innocent sons were in turn murdered before his
eyes, at each stroke piously ejaculated : ' Thou art
just, O Lord ! and thy judgments are righteous.' [1]
Any name would befit this kind of transaction better
than that which, in the dealings of men with one
another, we reserve for the honourable anxiety that
he should reap who has sown, that the reward should
be to him who has toiled for it, and the pain to him
who has deliberately incurred it. What is gained by
attributing to the divine government a method
tainted with every quality that could vitiate the
enactment of penalties by a temporal sovereign ?

  We need not labour this part of the discussion.
Though conducted with much brilliance and vigour
by De Maistre, it is not his most important or remarkable contribution to thought. Before passing on to
that, it is worth while to make one remark. It will
be inferred from De Maistre's general position that
he was no friend to physical science. Just as moderns
see in the advance of the methods and boundaries
of physical knowledge the most direct and sure
means of displacing the unfruitful subjective methods
of old, and so of renovating the entire field of human

------

[1] Gibbon, c. xlvi. vol. v. p. 385.

thought and activity, so did De Maistre see, as his
school has seen since, that here was the stronghold
of his foes. ' Ah, how dearly,' he exclaimed, ' has
man paid for the natural sciences ! ' Not but that
Providence designed that man should know something about them; only it must be in due order.
The ancients were not permitted to attain to much,
or even any, sound knowledge of physics, indisput-
ably above us as they were in force of mind, a fact
shown by the superiority of their languages which
ought to silence for ever the voice of our modern
pride. Why did the ancients remain so ignorant of
natural science ? Because they were not Christian.
' When all Europe was Christian, when the priests
were the universal teachers, when all the establish-
ments of Europe were Christianised, when theology
had taken its place at the head of all instruction,
and the other faculties were ranged around her like
maids of honour round their queen, the human race
being thus prepared, then the natural sciences were
given to it.' Science must be kept in its place, for
it resembles fire which, when confined in the grates
prepared for it, is the most useful and powerful of
man's servants; scattered about anyhow, it is the
most terrible of scourges. Whence the marked
supremacy of the seventeenth century, especially in
France ? From the happy accord of religion, science,
and chivalry, and from the supremacy conceded to
the first. The more perfect theology is in a country,
the more fruitful it is in true science; and that is

why Christian nations have surpassed all others in
the sciences, and that is why the Indians and Chinese
will never reach us, so long as we remain respectively
as we are. The more theology is cultivated, honoured,
and supreme, then, other things being equal, the more
perfect will human science be : that is to say, it will
have the greater force and expansion, and will be
the more free from every mischievous and perilous
connection.[1]

Little would be gained here by serious criticism of
a view of this kind from a positive point. How little,
the reader will understand from De Maistre's own
explanations of his principles of Proof and Evidence.
' They have called to witness against Moses,' he says,
' history, chronology, astronomy, geology. The objections have disappeared before true science ; but those
were profoundly wise who despised them before any
inquiry, or who only examined them in order to
discover a refutation, but without ever doubting
that there was one. Even a mathematical objection
ought to be despised, for though it may be a demonstrated truth, still you will never be able to demonstrate that it contradicts a truth that has been
demonstrated before.' His final formula he boldly
announced in these words : ' *Que toutes les fois qu'une
proposition sera prouvée par le genre de preuve qui
lui appartient, l'objection quelconque, MÊME INSOLUBLE,
ne doit plus être écoutée.*' Suppose, for example, that
by a consensus of testimony it were perfectly proved

[1] See the *Examen de la philosophie de Bacon*, vol. ii. pp. 58 *et seq.*

that Archimedes set fire to the fleet of Marcellus by
a burning-glass ; then all the objections of geometry
disappear. Prove if you can, and if you choose, that
by certain laws a glass, in order to be capable of
setting fire to the Roman fleet, must have been as
big as the whole city of Syracuse, and ask me what
answer I have to make to that. ' *J'ai à vous répondre
qu'Archimède brûla la flotte romaine avec un miroir
ardent.*'

The interesting thing about such opinions as these
is not the exact height and depth of their falseness,
but the considerations which could recommend them
to a man of so much knowledge, both of books and
of the outer facts of life, and of so much natural acuteness as De Maistre. Persons who have accustomed
themselves to ascertained methods of proof, are apt
to look on a man who vows that if a thing has been
declared true by some authority whom he respects,
then that constitutes proof to him, either as the
victim of a preposterous and barely credible infatuation, or else as a flat impostor. Yet De Maistre was no
ignorant monk. He had no selfish or official interest
in taking away the keys of knowledge. The true
reasons for his detestation of the eighteenth-century
philosophers, science, and literature, are simple
enough. Like every wise man, he felt that the end
of all philosophy and science is emphatically social,
the construction and maintenance and improvement
of a fabric under which the communities of men may
find shelter, and may secure all the conditions for

P

living their lives with dignity and service. Then he
held that no truth can be harmful to society. If he
found any system of opinions, any given attitude of
the mind, injurious to tranquillity and the public
order, he instantly concluded that, however plausible
they might seem when tested by logic and demonstra-
tion, they were fundamentally untrue and deceptive.
What is logic, compared with eternal salvation in the
next world, and the practice of virtue in this ? The
recommendation of such a mind as De Maistre's is
the intensity of its appreciation of order and social
happiness. The obvious weakness of such a mind,
and the curse inherent in its influence, is that it over-
looks the prime condition of all ; that social order can
never be established on a durable basis so long as the
discoveries of scientific truth in all its departments
are suppressed, or incorrectly appreciated, or socially
misapplied. De Maistre did not perceive that the
cause which he supported was no longer the cause of
peace and tranquillity and right living, but was in a
state of absolute decomposition, and therefore was
the cause of disorder and blind wrong living. Of
this we shall now see more.

IV.

When the waters of the deluge of 1789 began to
abate, the best minds soon satisfied themselves that
the event which Bonaparte's restoration of order
enabled them to look back upon with a certain tran-

quillity had been neither more nor less than a new
irruption of barbarians into the European world.
The monarchy, the nobles, and the church, with all
the ideas that gave each of them life and power,
had fallen before atheists and Jacobins, as the ancient
empire of Rome had fallen before Huns and Goths,
Vandals and Lombards.   The leaders of the Revolution had succeeded one another, as Attila had come
after Alaric, and Genseric had been followed by
Odoacer.   The problem that presented itself was
not new in the history of western civilisation ; the
same dissolution of old bonds that perplexed the
foremost men at the beginning of the nineteenth
century, had distracted their predecessors from the
fifth to the eighth, though their conditions and
circumstances were widely different.   The practical
question in both cases was the same—how to establish
a stable social order which, resting on principles that
should command the assent of all, might secure the
co-operation of all for its harmonious and efficient
maintenance, and might offer a firm basis for the
highest and best life that the moral and intellectual
state of the time allowed.   Two courses were open,
or seemed to be open, in this gigantic enterprise of
reconstructing a society.   One of them was to treat
the case of the eighteenth century as if it were not
merely similar to, but exactly identical with, the
case of the fifth, and as if exactly the same forces
that had knit western Europe together into a com-
pact civilisation a thousand years before, would

again suffice for a second consolidation. Christianity, rising with the zeal and strength of youth out of the ruins of the Empire, and feudalism by the need of self-preservation imposing a form upon the unshapen associations of the barbarians, had between them compacted the foundations and reared the fabric of mediæval life. Why, many men asked themselves, should not Christian and feudal ideas repeat their glorious achievement, and be the means of reorganising the system which a blind rebellion against them had thrown into deplorable and fatal confusion? Let the century that had come to such an end be regarded as a mysteriously intercalated episode, and no more, in the long drama of faith and sovereign order. Let it pass as a sombre and pestilent stream, whose fountains no man should discover, whose waters had for a season mingled with the mightier current of the divinely allotted destiny of the race, and had then gathered themselves apart and flowed off, to end as they had begun, in the stagnation and barrenness of the desert. Philosophers and men of letters, astronomers and chemists, atheists and republicans, had shown that they were only powerful to destroy, as Goths and Vandals had been. They had shown that they were impotent, as Goths and Vandals had been, in building up again. Let men turn their faces, then, once more to that system by which in the ancient times Europe had been delivered from a relapse into eternal night.

The second course was very different from this.

The minds to whom it commended itself were cast in
a different mould, and drew their inspiration from
other traditions. In their view the system which
the church had been the main agency in organising,
had fallen quite as much from its own irremediable
weakness as from the direct onslaughts of assailants
within and without. The barbarians had rushed in,
it was true, in 1793 ; but this time it was the church
and feudalism that were in the position of the old
empire on whose ruins they had built. What had
once restored order and belief to the West, was now
in its own turn overtaken by decay and dissolution.
To look to them to unite these new barbarians in a
stable and vigorous civilisation, because they had
organised Europe of old, was as infatuated as it would
have been to expect the later emperors to equal the
exploits of the Republic and their greatest predecessors in the purple.   To despise philosophers and
men of science was only to play over again in a new
dress the very part which Julian had enacted in the
face of nascent Christianity.   The eighteenth century,
instead of being the home of malaria that the Catholic
and Royalist party represented, was in truth the
seed-ground of a new and better future.   Its ideas
were to furnish the material and the implements by
which should be repaired the breaches and chasms
in European order that had been made alike
by despots and Jacobins, by priests and atheists,
by aristocrats and sans-culottes. Amidst all the
demolition upon which its leading minds had been

so zealously bent, they had been animated by the
warmest love of social justice, of human freedom,
of equal rights, and by the most fervent and sincere
longing to make a nobler happiness more universally
attainable by all the children of men. It was to these
great principles that we ought eagerly to turn, to
liberty, to equality, to brotherhood, if we wished to
achieve before the new invaders a work of civilisation
and social reconstruction, such as Catholicism and
feudalism had achieved for the multitudinous invaders
of old.

Such was the difference that divided opinion when
men took heart to survey the appalling scene of
moral desolation that the cataclysm of 1793 had
left behind. We may admire the courage of either
school. For if the conscience of the Liberals was
oppressed by the sanguinary tragedy in which
freedom, brotherhood, justice had been consummated,
the Catholic and the Royalist were just as sorely
burdened with the weight of kingly baseness and
priestly hypocrisies. If the one had some difficulty
in interpreting Jacobinism and the Terror, the other
was still more severely pressed to interpret the fact,
the origin, the meaning of the Revolution ; if the
Liberal had Marat and Hébert, the Royalist had
Louis XV., and the Catholic had Dubois and De
Rohan. Each school could intrepidly hurl back the
taunts of its enemy, and neither of them did full
justice to the strong side of the other. Yet we who
are, in England at all events, removed a little aside

from the centre of this dire battle, may perceive that
at that time both of the contending hosts fought
under honourable banners, and could inscribe upon
their shields an intelligible device. Indeed, unless
the modern Liberal admits the strength inherent
in the cause of his enemies, it is impossible for him
to explain to himself the duration and obstinacy
of the conflict, the slow advance and occasional
repulse of the host in which he has enlisted, and the
tardy progress that Liberalism has made in the
stupendous reconstruction which the Revolution has
forced the modern political thinker to meditate upon,
and the modern statesman to extend and control.

De Maistre, from those general ideas as to the
method of the government of the world, of which
we have already seen something, had formed what
he conceived to be a perfectly satisfactory way of
accounting for the eighteenth century and its terrific
climax. The will of man is left free ; he acts contrary to the will of God ; and then God exacts the
shedding of blood as the penalty. So much for the
past. The only hope of the future lay in an immediate
return to the system that God himself had established, and in the restoration of the spiritual power
that had presided over the reconstruction of Europe
in darker and more chaotic times than even these.
Though, perhaps, he nowhere expresses himself on
this point in a distinct formula, De Maistre was
firmly impressed with the idea of historic unity and
continuity. He looked upon the history of the West

in its integrity, and was entirely free from anything
like the disastrous kind of misconception that makes
the English Protestant treat the long period between
St. Paul and Martin Luther as a howling waste, or
that makes some Americans omit from all account
the still longer period of human effort from the
crucifixion of Christ to the Declaration of Independence. The rise of the vast structure of western
civilisation during and after the dissolution of the
Empire, presented itself to his mind as a single and
uniform process, though marked in portions by
temporary, casual, parenthetical interruptions, due
to depraved will and disordered pride. All the
dangers to which this civilisation had been exposed
in its infancy and growth were before his eyes. First,
there were the heresies with which the subtle and
debased ingenuity of the Greeks had stained and
distorted the great but simple mysteries of the faith.
Then came the hordes of invaders from the North,
sweeping with irresistible force over regions that the
weakness or cowardice of the wearers of the purple
left defenceless before them. Before the northern
tribes had settled in their possessions, and had full
time to assimilate the faith and the institutions which
they found there, the growing organisation was
menaced by a more deadly peril in the incessant and
steady advance of the bloody and fanatical tribes
from the East. And in this way De Maistre's mind
continued the picture down to the latest days of
all, when men had arisen who, denying God and

mocking at Christ, were bent on the destruction of the very foundations of society, and had nothing better to offer the human race than a miserable return to a state of nature.

As he thus reproduced this long drama, one benign and central figure was ever present, changeless in the midst of ceaseless change; laboriously building up with preterhuman patience and preterhuman sagacity, when other powers, one after another in evil succession, were madly raging to destroy and to pull down; thinking only of the great interests of order and civilisation, of which it had been constituted the eternal protector, and showing its divine origin and inspiration alike by its unfailing wisdom and its unfailing benevolence. It is the Sovereign Pontiff who thus stands forth throughout the history of Europe, as the great Demiurgus of universal civilisation. If the Pope had filled only such a position as the Patriarch held at Constantinople, or if there had been no Pope and Christianity had depended exclusively on the East for its propagation, with no great spiritual organ in the West, what would have become of western development? It was the energy and resolution of the Pontiffs that resisted the heresies of the East, and preserved to the Christian religion that plainness and intelligibility, without which it would never have made a way to the rude understanding and simple hearts of the barbarians from the North. It was their wise patriotism that protected Italy against Greek oppression, and by acting

the part of mayors of the palace to the decrepit
Eastern emperors, it was they who contrived to
preserve the independence and maintain the fabric of
society until the appearance of the Carlovingians, in
whom, with the rapid instinct of true statesmen, they
at once recognised the founders of a new Empire of
the West. If the Popes, again, had possessed over
the Eastern Empire the same authority they had
over the Western, they would have repulsed not only
the Saracens, but the Turks too, and none of the evils
which these nations have inflicted on us would ever
have taken place.[1]   Even as it was, when the Saracens
threatened the West, the Popes were the chief agents
in organising resistance, and giving spirit and animation to the defenders of Europe.   Their alert vision
saw that to crush for ever that formidable enemy,
it was not enough to defend ourselves against
his assaults ; we must attack him at home.   The
Crusades, vulgarly treated as the wars of a blind and
superstitious piety, were in truth wars of high policy.
From the Council of Clermont down to the famous
day of Lepanto, the hand and spirit of the Pontiff
were to be traced in every part of the tremendous
struggle that prevented Europe from being handed
over to the tyranny, ignorance, and barbarism that

[1] De Maistre forgot or underestimated the services of Leo the
Isaurian whose repulse of the Caliph's forces at Constantinople
(A.D. 717) was perhaps as important for Europe as the more
renowned victory of Charles Martel.   But then Leo was an
Iconoclast and heretic. Cf. Finlay's *Byzantine Empire*, pp.
22, 23.

have always been the inevitable fruits of Mahometan conquest, and had already stamped out civilisation in Asia Minor and Palestine and Greece, once the very garden of the universe.

This admirable and politic heroism of the Popes in the face of foes pressing from without, De Maistre found more than equalled by their wisdom, courage, and activity in organising and developing the elements of a civilised system within. The maxim of old societies had been that which Lucan puts into the mouth of Cæsar—*humanum paucis vivit genus.* A vast population of slaves had been one of the inevitable social conditions of the period : the Popes never rested from their endeavours to banish servitude from among Christian nations. Women in old societies had filled a mean and degraded place : it was reserved for the new spiritual power to rescue the race from that vicious circle in which men had debased the nature of women, and women had given back all the weakness and perversity they had received from men, and to perceive that ' the most effectual way of perfecting the man is to ennoble and exalt the woman.'

The organisation of the priesthood, again, was a masterpiece of practical wisdom. Such an order, removed from the fierce or selfish interests of ordinary life by the holy regulation of celibacy, and by the austere discipline of the church, was indispensable in the midst of such a society as that which it was the function of the church to guide. Who but the

members of an order thus set apart, acting in strict
subordination to the central power, and so presenting
a front of unbroken spiritual unity, could have held
their way among tumultuous tribes, half-barbarous
nobles, and proud and unruly kings, protesting against
wrong, passionately inculcating new and higher ideas
of right, denouncing the darkness of the false gods,
calling on all men to worship the cross and adore the
mysteries of the true God ? Compare now the impotency of the Protestant missionary, squatting in
gross comfort with wife and babes among the savages
he has come to convert, preaching a disputatious
doctrine, wrangling openly with the rival sent by
some other sect—compare this impotency with the
success that follows the devoted sons of the church,
impressing their proselytes with the mysterious virtue
of their continence, the self-denial of their lives, the
unity of their dogma and their rites ; and then
recognise the wisdom of these great churchmen who
created a priesthood after this manner in the days
when every priest was as the missionary is now.

Finally, it was the occupants of the holy chair
who prepared, softened, one might almost say
sweetened, the occupants of thrones ; it was to
them that Providence had confided the education of
the sovereigns of Europe. The Popes brought up
the youth of the European monarchy ; they made it
precisely in the same way in which Fénelon made
the Duke of Burgundy. In each case the task consisted in eradicating from a fine character an element

of ferocity that would have ruined all. 'Everything
that constrains a man strengthens him. He cannot
obey without perfecting himself; and by the mere
fact of overcoming himself he is better. Any man
will vanquish the most violent passion at thirty,
because at five or six you have taught him of his
own will to give up a plaything or a sweetmeat.
That came to pass to the monarchy, which happens
to an individual who has been well brought up. The
continued efforts of the church, directed by the
Sovereign Pontiff, did what had never been seen
before, and what will never be seen again, where
that authority is not recognised. Insensibly, without
threats or laws or battles, without violence and without resistance, the great European charter was proclaimed, not on paper nor by the voice of public
criers; but in all European hearts, then all Catholic.
Kings surrender the power of judging by themselves,
and nations in return declare kings infallible and
inviolable. Such is the fundamental law of the
European monarchy, and it is the work of the Popes.'[1]

All this, however, is only the external development of De Maistre's central idea, the historical
corroboration of a truth to which he conducts us in
the first instance by general considerations. Assuming, what it is less and less characteristic of the present
century at any rate to deny, that Christianity was
the only actual force by which the regeneration of
Europe could be effected after the decline of the

[1] *Du Pape*, bk. iii. ch. iv. p. 298 (ed. 1866).

Roman civilisation, he insists that, as he again and
again expresses it, 'without the Pope there is no
veritable Christianity.' In saying that without the
Pope there is no true Christianity, what he considered
himself as having established was, that unless there
be some supreme and independent possessor of
authority to settle doctrine, to regulate discipline,
to give authentic counsel, to apply accepted principles
to disputed cases, then there can be no such thing as
a religious system which shall have power to bind the
members of a vast and not homogeneous body in the
salutary bonds of a common civilisation, or to guide
and inform an universal conscience. In each individual state everybody admits the absolute necessity
of having some sovereign power that shall make,
declare, and administer the laws, and from whose
action in any one of these aspects there shall be no
appeal; a power that shall be strong enough to
protect the rights and enforce the duties it has
authoritatively proclaimed and enjoined. In free
England, as in despotic Turkey, the privileges and
obligations that the law tolerates or imposes, and all
the benefits their existence confers on the community,
are the creatures and conditions of a supreme
authority from which there is no appeal, whether
the instrument by which this authority makes its
will known be an act of parliament or a ukase.
This conception of temporal sovereignty, especially
familiarised to a later generation by the teaching of
Austin, was carried by De Maistre into discussions

upon the limits of the Papal power with great ingenuity and force, and, if we accept the premisses,
with great success.

It should be said here, that throughout his book
on the Pope, De Maistre talks of Christianity exclusively as a statesman or a publicist would talk about
it; not theologically nor spiritually, but politically
and socially. The question with which he concerns
himself is the utilisation of Christianity as a force to
shape and organise a system of civilised societies; a
study of the conditions under which this utilisation
had taken place in the earlier centuries of the era;
and a deduction from them of the conditions under
which we might ensure a repetition of the process in
changed modern circumstance. In the eighteenth
century men were accustomed to ask of Christianity,
as Protestants always ask of so much of Catholicism
as they have dropped, whether or no it is true. But
after the Revolution the question changed, and
became an inquiry whether and how Christianity
could contribute to the reconstruction of society.
People asked less how true it was, than how strong
it was; less how many unquestioned dogmas, than
how much social weight it had, or could develop;
less as to the precise amount and form of belief that
would save a soul, than as to the way in which it
might be expected to assist the European community.

It was the strength of this temper in him that
led to his extraordinary detestation of and contempt
for the Greeks. Their turn for pure speculation

excited all his anger. In a curious chapter, he exhausts invective in denouncing them.[1] The sarcasm of Sallust delights him, that the actions of Greece were very fine, *verum aliquanto minores quam fama feruntur.* Their military glory was only a flash of about a hundred and fourteen years from Marathon; compare this with the prolonged splendour of Rome, France, and England. In philosophy they displayed decent talent, but even here their true merit is to have brought the wisdom of Asia into Europe, for they invented nothing. Greece was the home of syllogism and of unreason. 'Read Plato : at every page you will draw a striking distinction. As often as he is Greek, he wearies you. He is only great, sublime, penetrating, when he is a theologian ; in other words, when he is announcing positive and everlasting dogmas, free from all quibble, and which are so clearly marked with the eastern cast, that not to perceive it one must never have had a glimpse of Asia. . . . There was in him a sophist and a theologian, or, if you choose, a Greek and a Chaldean.' The Athenians could never pardon one of their great leaders, all of whom fell victims in one shape or another to a temper frivolous as that of a child, ferocious as that of men,—' *espèce de moutons enragés, toujours menés par la nature, et toujours par nature dévorant leurs bergers.*' As for their oratory, ' the tribune of Athens would have been the disgrace of mankind if Phocion and men like him, by occasionally

[1] *Du Pape,* bk. iv. ch. vii.

ascending it before drinking the hemlock, or setting
out for their place of exile, had not in some sort
balanced such a mass of loquacity, extravagance, and
cruelty.' [1]

It is very important to remember this constant
solicitude for ideas that should work well, in connection with the book of De Maistre's that has had
most influence in Europe, by supplying a base for
the theories of ultramontanism. Unless we perceive
very clearly that throughout his ardent speculation
on the Papal power his mind was bent upon enforcing
the practical solution of a pressing social problem, we
easily misunderstand him and underrate what he had
to say. A charge has been forcibly urged against
him by an eminent English critic, for example, that

[1] A remark of Finlay's is worth quoting here. 'The
Greeks,' he says, 'had at times only a secondary share in the
ecclesiastical controversies in the Eastern Church, though the
circumstance of these controversies having been carried on in
the Greek language has made the natives of Western Europe
attribute them to a philosophic, speculative, and polemic spirit,
inherent in the Hellenic mind. A very slight examination of
history is sufficient to prove that several of the heresies which
disturbed the Eastern Church had their origin in the more profound religious ideas of the oriental nations, and that many of
the opinions called heretical were in a great measure expressions
of the mental nationality of the Syrians, Armenians, Egyptians,
and Persians, and had no conception whatever with the Greek
mind.'—*Byzantine Empire, from* 716 *to* 1057, p. 262.

The same writer (p. 263) remarks that 'the religious
or theological portion of Popery, as a section of the Christian
Church, is really Greek ; and it is only the ecclesiastical,
political, and theoretic peculiarities of the fabric which can be
considered as the work of the Latin Church.

Q

he has confounded supremacy with infallibility, than
which, as the writer truly says, no two ideas can be
more perfectly distinct, one being superiority of force,
and the other incapacity of error.[1] De Maistre made
logical blunders in abundance quite as bad as this,
but he was too acute, I think, deliberately to erect so
elaborate a structure upon a confusion so obvious,
that must have stared him in the face from the first
page of his work to the last. If we look upon his
book as a mere general defence of the Papacy, designed
to explore and fortify all it: pretensions one by
one, we should have great right to complain against
having two claims so essentially divergent, treated
as though they were the same thing, or could be
held in their places by the same supports. But let
us regard the treatise on the Pope not as meant to
convince freethinkers or Protestants that divine grace
inspires every decree of the Holy Father, though that
would have been the right view of it if it had been
written fifty years earlier. It was composed within
the first twenty years of the nineteenth century, when
the universe, to men of De Maistre's stamp, seemed
once more without form and void. His object, as he
tells us more than once, was to find a way of restoring
a religion and a morality in Europe ; of giving to
truth the forces demanded for the conquests she
was meditating ; of strengthening the thrones of
sovereigns, and of gently calming that general ferment-

[1] Sir J. Fitzjames Stephen in the *Saturday Review*, Sept. 9,
1865, p. 334.

ation of spirit threatening mightier evils than any that had yet overwhelmed society. From this point of view we shall see that the distinction between supremacy and infallibility was not worth recognising.

Practically, he says, ' infallibility is only a consequence of supremacy, or rather it is absolutely the same thing under two different names. . . . In effect it is the same thing, *in practice*, not to be subject to error, and not to be liable to be accused of it. Thus, even if we should agree that no divine promise was made to the Pope, he would not be less infallible or deemed so, as the final tribunal ; for every judgment from which you cannot appeal is and must be (*est et doit être*) held for just in every human association, under any imaginable form of government ; and every true statesman will understand me perfectly, when I say that the point is to ascertain not only if the Sovereign Pontiff is, but if he must be, infallible.' [1] In another place he says distinctly enough that the infallibility of the church has two aspects ; in one of them it is the object of divine promise, in the other it is a human implication, and that in the latter aspect infallibility is supposed in the church, just ' as we are absolutely bound to suppose it, even in temporal sovereignties (where it does not really exist), under pain of seeing society dissolved.' The church only demands what other sovereignties demand, though she has the immense superiority over them of having her claim backed by direct

[1] *Du Pape*, bk. i. ch. i. p. 17.

promise from heaven.[1] Take away the dogma, if
you will, he says, and only consider the thing politically, which is exactly what he really does all through
the book. The Pope, from this point of view, asks
for no other infallibility than that which is attributed
to all sovereigns.[2] Without either vindicating or
surrendering the supernatural side of the Papal
claim, he only insists upon the political, social, or
human side of it, as an inseparable quality of an
admitted supremacy.[3] In short, from beginning to
end of this speculation, from which the best kind of
ultramontanism has drawn its defence, he evinces
a deprecatory anxiety—a rare humour with De
Maistre—not to fight on the issue of the dogma
of infallibility over which Protestants and unbelievers
have won an infinite number of cheap victories ; that
he leaves as a theme more fitted for the disputations
of theologians.   My position, he seems to keep saying,

[1] *Du Pape*, bk. i. ch. xix. pp. 124, 125.
[2] *Ibid.* bk. i. ch. xvi. p. 111.
[3] ' *Il n'y a point de souveraineté qui pour le bonheur des
hommes, et pour le sien surtout, ne soit bornée de quelque manière,
mais dans l'intérieur de ces bornes, placées comme il plaît à Dieu,
elle est toujours et partout absolue et tenue pour infaillible.   Et
quand je parle de l'exercice légitime de la souveraineté, je
n'entends point ou je ne dis point l'exercice* juste, *ce qui produirait
une amphibologie dangereuse, à moins que par ce dernier mot on
ne veuille dire que tout ce qu'elle opine dans son cercle est* juste ou
tenu pour tel, *ce qui est la vérité.   C'est ainsi qu'un tribunal
suprême, tant qu'il ne sort pas de ses attributions, est toujours
juste ;* car c'est la même chose DANS LA PRATIQUE, d'être
infaillible, ou de se tromper sans appel.'—*Ibid.* bk. ii. ch. xi.
p. 212 (footnote).

is that if the Pope is spiritually supreme, then he is
virtually and practically *as if he were* infallible, just
in the same sense in which the English Parliament
and monarch, and the Russian Czar, are as if they
were infallible. But let us not argue so much about
this, which is only secondary. The main question
is whether without the Pope there can be a true
Christianity, ' that is to say, a Christianity, active,
powerful, converting, regenerating, conquering, perfecting.'

De Maistre was probably conducted to his theory
by an analogy, which he tacitly leaned upon more
strongly than it could well bear, between temporal
organisation and spiritual organisation. In inchoate
communities, the momentary self-interest and the
promptly stirred passions of men would rend the
growing society in pieces, unless they were restrained
by the strong hand of law in some shape or other,
written or unwritten, and administered by an authority, either physically too strong to be resisted, or else
set up by the common consent seeking to further the
general convenience. To divide this authority, so
that none should know where to look for a sovereign
decree, nor be able to ascertain the commands of
sovereign law ; to embody it in the persons of many
discordant expounders, each assuming oracular
weight and equal sanction ; to leave individuals to
administer and interpret it for themselves, and to
decide among themselves its application to their own
cases ; what would this be but a deliberate prepara-

tion for anarchy and dissolution ? For it is one of
the clear conditions of the efficacy of the social union,
that every member of it should be able to know for
certain the terms on which he belongs to it, the
compliances which it will insist upon in him, and the
compliances which it will in turn permit him to insist
upon in others, and therefore it is indispensable that
there should be some definite and admitted centre
where this very essential knowledge should be
accessible.

Some such reflections as these must have been at
the bottom of De Maistre's defiant apology for the
Papal supremacy, or at any rate they may serve to
bring before our minds with greater clearness the
kind of foundations on which his scheme rested.
For law substitute Christianity, for social union
spiritual union, for legal obligations the obligations
of the faith. Instead of individuals bound together
by allegiance to common political institutions, conceive communities united in the bonds of religious
brotherhood into a sort of universal republic, under
the moderate supremacy of a supreme spiritual power.
As a matter of fact, it was the intervention of this
spiritual power that restrained the anarchy, internal
and external, of the ferocious and imperfectly organised
sovereignties figuring in the early history of modern
Europe. And as a matter of theory, what could be
more rational and defensible than such an intervention
made systematic, with its rightfulness and disinterestedness universally recognised ? Grant Chris-

tianity as the spiritual basis of the life and action
of modern communities; supporting both the
organised structure of each of them, and the inter-
dependent system composed of them all; accepted
by the individual members of each, and by the
integral bodies forming the whole. But who shall
declare what the Christian doctrine is, and how its
maxims bear upon special cases, and what oracles
they announce in particular sets of circumstance?
Amid the turbulence of popular passion, in face of
the crushing despotism of an insensate tyrant, between
the furious hatred of jealous nations or the violent
ambition of rival sovereigns, what likelihood would
there be of either party to the contention yielding
tranquilly and promptly to any presentation of
Christian teaching made by the other, or by some
suspected neutral as a decisive authority between
them? Obviously there must be some supreme and
indisputable interpreter, before whose final decree
the tyrant should quail, the flood of popular lawlessness flow back within its accustomed banks, and contending sovereigns or jealous nations fraternally
embrace. Again, in those questions of faith and
discipline which the ill-exercised ingenuity of men
is for ever raising and pressing upon the attention
of Christendom, it is just as obvious that there must
be some tribunal to pronounce an authoritative judgment. Otherwise, each nation is torn into sects;
and amid the throng of sects where is unity? 'To
maintain that a crowd of independent churches form

a church, one and universal, is to maintain in
other terms that all the political governments of
Europe only form a single government, one and
universal.' There could no more be a kingdom of
France without a king, nor an empire of Russia without an emperor, than there could be one universal
church without an acknowledged head. That this
head must be the successor of St. Peter, is declared
alike by the voice of tradition, the explicit testimony
of the early writers, the repeated utterances of later
theologians of all schools, and that general sentiment
which presses itself upon every conscientious reader
of religious history.

The argument, he contends, that the voice of the
church is to be sought in general councils, is absurd.
To maintain that a council has any other function
than to assure and certify the Pope, when he chooses
to strengthen his judgment or to satisfy his doubts, is
to destroy visible unity. Suppose there to be an equal
division of votes, as happened in the famous case
of Fénelon, and might as well happen in a general
council, the doubt would after all be solved by the
final vote of the Pope. And 'what is doubtful for
twenty selected men is doubtful for the whole human
race. Those who suppose that by multiplying the
deliberating voices doubt is lessened, must have very
little knowledge of men, and can never have sat in a
deliberative body.' Again, supposing there to present
itself one of those questions of divine metaphysics
that it is absolutely necessary to refer to the decision

of the supreme tribunal.   Then our interest is not that
it should be decided in such or such a manner, but
that it should be decided without delay and without
appeal.   Besides, the world is now grown too vast
for general councils, which seem to be made only
for the youth of Christianity.   In fine, why pursue
futile or mischievous discussions as to whether the
Pope is above the Council or the Council above the
Pope?   In ordinary questions in which a king is
conscious of sufficient light, he decides them himself,
while the others in which he is not conscious of this
light, he transfers to the States-General presided over
by himself, but he is equally sovereign in either case.
So with the Pope and the Council.   Let us be content
to know, in the words of Thomassin,[1] that ' the Pope
in the midst of his Council is above himself, and that
the Council decapitated of its chief is below him.'

The vigour with which De Maistre sums up all
these pleas for supremacy is very remarkable ; and

[1] Thomassin, the eminent French theologian, flourished from
the middle to the end of the seventeenth century.   The aim of
his writings generally was to reconcile conflicting opinions on
discipline or doctrine by exhibiting a true sense in all.   In this
spirit he wrote on the Pope and the Councils, and on the never-
ending question of Grace.   Among other things, he insisted
that all languages could be traced to the Hebrew.   He wrote a
defence of the edict in which Louis XIV. revoked the Edict of
Nantes, contending that it was less harsh than some of the
decrees of Theodosius and Justinian, which the holiest fathers
of the church had not scrupled to approve—an argument which
would now be thought somewhat too dangerous for common
use, as cutting both ways.   Gibbon made use of his *Discipline
de l'Église* in the twentieth chapter, and elsewhere.

to the crowd of enemies and indifferents, and especially to the statesmen who are among them, he appeals with admirable energy. ' What do you want, then ? Do you mean that the nations should live without any religion, and do you not begin to perceive that a religion there must be ?　And does not Christianity, not only by its intrinsic worth but because it is in possession, strike you as preferable to every other ? Have you been better contented with other attempts in this way ? Peradventure the twelve apostles might please you better than the Theophilanthropists and Martinists ? Does the Sermon on the Mount seem to you a passable code of morals ? And if the entire people were to regulate their conduct on this model, should you be content ? I fancy that I hear you reply affirmatively. Well, since the only object now is to maintain this religion for which you thus declare your preference, how could you have, I do not say the stupidity, but the cruelty, to turn it into a democracy, and to place this precious deposit in the hands of the rabble ?

' You attach too much importance to the dogmatic part of this religion. By what strange contradiction would you desire to agitate the universe for some academic quibble, for miserable wranglings about mere words (these are your own terms) ? Is it so then that men are led ? Will you call the Bishop of Quebec and the Bishop of Luçon to interpret a line of the Catechism ? That believers should quarrel about infallibility is what I know, for I see it ; but that statesmen should quarrel in the same way about this great privilege, is what I shall never be able to conceive. . . . That all the bishops in the world should be convoked to determine a divine truth necessary to salvation — nothing more natural, if such a method is indispensable ; for no effort, no trouble, ought to be spared for so exalted an aim. But if the only point is the establishment of one opinion in the place of another, then the travelling expenses of even one single Infallible are sheer waste. If you want to spare the two most valuable things on earth, time and money, make all haste to write to Rome, in order to procure thence a lawful decision which shall declare the unlawful doubt. Nothing more is needed ; policy asks no more.' [1]

De Maistre has been surpassed by no thinker that we know of as a defender of the old order. If anybody could rationalise the idea of supernatural intervention in human affairs, the idea of a Papal supremacy, the idea of a spiritual unity, De Maistre's acuteness and intellectual vigour, and, above all, his keen sense of the urgent social need of such a thing being done, would assuredly have enabled him to do it. In 1817, when he wrote the work in which this task is attempted, the hopelessness of such an achievement was less obvious than it is now. The Bourbons had been restored. The Revolution lay in a deep slumber that many persons excusably took for

[1] *Du Pape*, bk. i. ch. xvii. p. 117.

extinction. Legitimacy and the spiritual system that was its ally in the face of the Revolution, though mostly its rival or foe when they were left alone together, seemed to be restored to the fullness of their power. Many years have elapsed since then, and each year has seen a progressive decay in the principles that were then triumphant. It was not, therefore, without reason that De Maistre warned people against believing ' *que la colonne est replacée, parce qu'elle est relevée.*' The solution which he so elaborately recommended to Europe has shown itself desperate and impossible. Catholicism may long remain a vital creed to millions of men, a deep source of spiritual consolation and refreshment, and a bright lamp in perplexities of conduct and morals ; but resting on dogmas which cannot by any amount of compromise be incorporated with the daily increasing mass of knowledge, assuming as the condition of its existence forms of the theological hypothesis which all the preponderating influences of contemporary thought concur directly or indirectly in discrediting, upheld by an organisation which its history for several centuries has exposed to the distrust and hatred of men as the sworn enemy of mental freedom and growth, the pretensions of Catholicism to renovate society are among the most pitiable and impotent that ever devout, high-minded, and benevolent persons deluded themselves into maintaining or accepting. Over the modern invader it is as powerless as paganism was over the invaders of old. The

barbarians of industrialism, grasping chiefs and
mutinous men, give no ear to priest or pontiff, who
speak only dead words, who confront modern issue;
with blind eyes, and who stretch out a palsied hand
to help. Christianity, according to Lessing's well
known saying, has been tried and failed ; the religion
of Christ remains to be tried.   One would prefer to
qualify the first clause, by admitting how much
Christianity has done for Europe even with its old
organisation, and to restrict the charge of failure
within the limits of the modern time.   Whether it
changed forms and with new supplements the teach
ing of its founder is destined to be the chief inspirer
of the social and human sentiment that seems to be
the only spiritual bond capable of uniting men
together again in a common and effective faith, is
question which it is unnecessary to discuss her
' *They talk about the first centuries of Christianity,*' said
De Maistre, ' *I would not be sure that they are over yet*
Perhaps not ; only if the first centuries are not yet
over, it is certain that the Christianity of the futur
will have to be so different from the Christianity
the past, as to demand or deserve another name.

Even if Christianity, itself renewed, could succes
fully encounter the achievement of renewing societ
De Maistre's ideal of a spiritual power controllir
the temporal power, and conciliating peoples wi
their rulers by persuasion and a coercion only mor
appears to have little chance of being realised.   T
separation of the two powers is sealed, with a cor

pleteness that is increasingly visible. The principles
on which the process of the emancipation of politics
is being so rapidly carried on, demonstrate that the
most marked tendencies of modern civilisation are
strongly hostile to a renewal of a connection whether
of virtual subordination or nominal equality, that
has laid such enormous burdens on the consciences
and understandings of men. If the church has the
uppermost hand, except in primitive times, it impairs
freedom; if the state is supreme, it impairs
spirituality. The free church in the free state is an
idea that every day more fully recommends itself to
the public opinion of Europe, and the sovereignty of
the Pope, like that of all other spiritual potentates,
can only be exercised over those who choose of their
own accord to submit to it; a sovereignty of a kind
that De Maistre thought not much above anarchy.

To conclude, De Maistre's mind was of the highest
type of those who fill the air with the arbitrary
assumptions of theology, and the abstractions of the
metaphysical stage of thought. At every point you
meet the peremptorily declared volition of a divine
being, or the ontological property of a natural object.
The French Revolution is explained by the will of
God; and the kings reign because they have the
esprit royal. Every truth is absolute, not relative;
every explanation is universal, not historic. These
differences in method and point of view amply explain
his arrival at conclusions that seem so monstrous to
men who look upon all knowledge as relative, and

insist that the only possible road to true opinion lies away from volitions and abstractions in the positive generalisations of experience.   There can be no more satisfactory proof of the rapidity with which we are leaving these ancient methods, and the social results they produced, than the willingness with which every rightly instructed mind now admits how indispensable were the first, and how beneficial the second.   Those can best appreciate De Maistre and his school, what excellence lay in their aspirations, what wisdom in their system, who know most clearly why their aspirations were hopeless, and what makes their system an anachronism.

ROBESPIERRE.

I.

A FRENCH writer has recently published a careful and interesting volume on the famous events that ended in the overthrow of Robespierre and the close of the Reign of Terror.[1] These events are known in the historic calendar as the Revolution of Thermidor in the Year II. After the fall of the monarchy, the Convention decided that the year should begin with the autumnal equinox, and that the enumeration should date from the birth of the Republic. The Year I. opens on September 22, 1792; the Year II. opens on the same day of 1793. The month of Thermidor begins on July 19. The memorable Ninth Thermidor therefore corresponds to July 27, 1794. This has commonly been taken as the date of the commencement of a counter-revolution, and in one sense it was so. Comte, however, and others have preferred to fix the reaction at the execution of Danton (April 5, 1794), or Robespierre's official

[1] *La Révolution de Thermidor.* Par Ch. d'Héricault. Paris: Didier, 1876.

R

proclamation of Deism in the Festival of the Supreme
Being (May 7, 1794).

M. d'Héricault does not belong to the school of
writers who treat the course of history as a great high-
road, following a firmly traced line, and set with plain
and ineffaceable landmarks. The French Revolution
has nearly always been handled in this way, alike by
those who think it fruitful in blessings, and by their
adversaries, who pronounce it a curse inflicted by the
wrath of heaven. Historians have looked at the
Revolution as a plain landsman looks at the sea. To
the landsman the ocean seems one huge immeasurable flood, obeying a simple law of ebb and flow, and
offering to the navigator a single uniform force. Yet
in truth we know that the oceanic movement is the
product of many forces ; the seeming uniformity
covers the energy of a hundred currents and counter-
currents ; the sea-floor is not even, nor the same, but
is subject to untold conditions of elevation and
subsidence ; the sea is not one mass, but many
masses moving along definite lines of their own. It
is the same with the great tides of history. Wise
men shrink from summing them up in single propositions. That the French Revolution led to an
immense augmentation of happiness, both for the
French and for mankind, can only be denied by the
Pope. That it secured its beneficent results un-
tempered by any mixture of evil, can only be maintained by men as mad as Doctor Pangloss. The
Greek poetess Corinna said to the youthful Pindar,

when he had interwoven all the gods and goddesses
in the Theban mythology into a single hymn, that
we should sow with the hand and not with the sack.
Corinna's monition to the singer is proper to the
interpreter of historical truth : he should cull with
the hand, and not sweep in with the scythe. It is
doubtless mere pedantry to abstain from the widest
conception of the sum of a great movement. A
clear, definite, and stable idea of the meaning in the
history of human progress of such vast groups of
events as the Reformation or the Revolution, is indispensable for any one to whom history is a serious
study of society. It is just as important, however,
not to forget that they were really groups of events,
and not in either case a single uniform movement.
The World-Epos is after all only a file of the morning
paper in a state of glorification. A sensible man
learns, in everyday life, to abstain from praising and
blaming character by wholesale ; he becomes content
to say of this trait that it is good, and of that act
that it was bad. So in history, we become unwilling
to join or to admire those who insist upon trans-
ferring their sentiment upon the whole to their
judgment upon each part. We seek to be allowed
to retain a decided opinion as to the final value to
mankind of a long series of transactions, and yet not
to commit ourselves to set the same estimate on each
transaction in particular, still less on each person
associated with it. Why shall we not prize the
general results of the Reformation, without being

obliged to defend John of Leyden and the Munster Anabaptists ?

M. d'Héricault's volume naturally suggests such reflections as these. Of all the men of the Revolution, Robespierre has suffered most from the audacious idolatry of some writers, and the splenetic impatience of others. M. Louis Blanc and M. Ernest Hamel talk of him as an angel or a prophet, and the Ninth Thermidor is a red day indeed in their martyrology. Michelet and M. d'Héricault treat him as a mixture of Cagliostro and Caligula, both a charlatan and a miscreant. We are reminded of the commencement of an address of the French Senate to the first Bonaparte : ' Sire,' they began, ' the desire for perfection is one of the worst maladies that can afflict the human mind.' This bold aphorism touches one of the roots of the judgments we pass both upon men and events. It is because people so irrationally think fit to insist upon perfection, that Robespierre's admirers would fain deny he ever had a fault, and the tacit adoption of the same impracticable standard makes it easier for Robespierre's wholesale detractors to deny that he had a single virtue or performed a single service. The point of view is essentially unfit for history. The real subject of history is the improvement of social arrangements, and no conspicuous actor in public affairs since the world began saw the true direction of improvement with an absolutely unerring eye from the beginning of his career to the end. It is folly for the historian, as it is for the statesman, to strain after the imaginative unity of the dramatic creator. Social progress is an affair of many small pieces and slow accretions, and the interest of historic study lies in tracing, amid the immense turmoil of events and through the confusion of voices, the devious course of the sacred torch, as it shifts from bearer to bearer. And it is not the bearers who are most interesting, but the torch.

In the old Flemish town of Arras, known in the diplomatic history of the fifteenth century by a couple of important treaties, and famous in the industrial history of the Middle Ages for its pre-eminence in the manufacture of the most splendid kind of tapestry hangings, Maximilian Robespierre was born in May 1758. He was therefore no more than five-and-thirty years old when he came to his ghastly end in 1794. His father was a lawyer, and, though the surname of the family had the prefix of nobility, they belonged to the middle class. When this decorative prefix became dangerous, Maximilian Derobespierre dropped it. His great rival, Danton, was less prudent or less fortunate, and one of the charges made against him was that he had styled himself Monsieur D'Anton.

Robespierre's youth was embittered by sharp misfortune. His mother died when he was only seven years old, and his father had so little courage under the blow that he threw up his practice, deserted his children, and died in purposeless wanderings through

Germany. Friendly kinsfolk charged themselves
with the maintenance of the four orphans.
Maximilian was sent to the school of the town,
whence he proceeded with a sizarship to the college
of Louis-le-Grand in Paris. He was an apt and
studious pupil, but austere, and disposed to the
sombre cast of spirits that is common enough where
a lad of some sensibility and much self-esteem finds
himself stamped with a badge of social inferiority.
Robespierre's worshippers love to dwell on his fondness for birds : with the universal passion of mankind
for legends of the saints, they tell how the untimely
death of a favourite pigeon afflicted him with anguish
so poignant that, even sixty long years after, it made
his sister's heart ache to look back upon the pain
of that tragic moment. Always a sentimentalist,
Robespierre was from boyhood a devout enthusiast
for the high priest of the sentimental tribe.
Rousseau was then passing the last squalid days of
his life among the meadows and woods at Ermenon-
ville. Robespierre, who could not have been more
than twenty at the time, for Rousseau died in the
summer of 1778, is said to have gone on a reverential
pilgrimage in search of an oracle from the lonely
sage, as Boswell and Gibbon and a hundred others
had gone before him. Rousseau was wont to use his
real adorers as ill as he used his imaginary enemies.
Robespierre may well have shared the discouragement of the enthusiastic father who informed
Rousseau that he was about to bring up his son on

the principles of *Emilius*. ' Then so much the worse,'
cried the perverse philosopher, ' both for you and
your son.' If he had been endowed with second
sight, he would have thought at least as rude a presage
due to this last and most ill-starred of a whole generation of neophytes.

In 1781 Robespierre returned to Arras, and amid
the welcome of his relatives and the good hopes of
friends began the practice of an advocate. For eight
years he led an active and seemly life. He was not
wholly pure from that indiscretion of the young
appetite about which the world is mute, but whose
better ordering and governance would give a diviner
brightness to the earth. Still, if he did not escape
the ordeal of youth, Robespierre was frugal, laborious,
and persevering. His domestic amiability made him
the delight of his sister, and his zealous self-sacrifice
for the education and advancement in life of his
younger brother was afterwards repaid by Augustin
Robespierre's devotion through all the fierce and
horrible hours of Thermidor. Though cold in temperament, extremely reserved in manners, and fond of
industrious seclusion, Robespierre did not disdain the
social diversions of the town. He was a member of
a reunion of Rosati, who sang madrigals and admired
one another's bad verses. Those who love the ironical
surprises of fate, may picture the young man who was
doomed to play so terrible a part in terrible affairs,
going through the harmless follies of a ceremonial
reception by the Rosati, taking three deep breaths

over a rose, solemnly fastening the emblem to his
coat, emptying a glass of rose-red wine at a draught
to the good health of the company, and finally recit-
ing couplets that Voltaire would have found almost
as detestable as the Law of Prairial or the Festival
of the Supreme Being. More laudable efforts of
ambition were prize essays, in which Robespierre
has the merit of taking the right side in important
questions. He protested against the inhumanity of
laws inflicting civil infamy upon the innocent
family of a convicted criminal. And he protested
against the still more wicked cruelty that reduced
unfortunate children born out of wedlock to something like the status of the mediæval serf. Robespierre's compositions at this time do not rise above
the ordinary level of declaiming mediocrity, but they
promised a manhood of benignity and enlightenment.
To compose prize essays on political reforms was
better than to ignore or to oppose political reform.
But the course of events afterwards owed their least
desirable bias to the fact that such compositions were
the nearest approach to political training that so
many of the revolutionary leaders underwent. One
is inclined to apply to practical politics Arthur Young's
sensible remark about the endeavour of the French
to improve the quality of their wool : ' A cultivator
at the head of a sheep-farm of 3000 or 4000 acres,
would in a few years do more for their wools than all
the academicians and philosophers will effect in ten
centuries.'

In his profession he distinguished himself in one
or two causes of local celebrity. An innovating
citizen had been ordered by the authorities to remove
a lightning-conductor from his house within three
days, as being a mischievous practical paradox, as
well as a danger and an annoyance to his neighbours.
Robespierre pleaded the innovator's case on appeal,
and won it. He defended a poor woman who had
been wrongfully accused by a monk belonging to
the powerful corporation of a great neighbouring
abbey. The young advocate did not even shrink
from manfully arguing a case against the august
Bishop of Arras himself. His independence did him
no harm. The Bishop afterwards appointed him to
the post of judge or legal assessor in the episcopal
court. This tribunal was a remnant of what had
once been the sovereign authority and jurisdiction
of the Bishops of Arras. That a court with the power
of life and death should thus exist by the side of a
proper corporation of civil magistrates, is an illustration of the inextricable labyrinth of the French law
and its administration on the eve of the Revolution.
Robespierre did not hold his office long. Every one
has heard the striking story, how the young judge,
whose name was within half a dozen years to take
a place in the popular mind of France and of Europe
with the bloodiest monsters of myth or history,
resigned his post in a fit of remorse after condemning
a murderer to be executed. ' He is a criminal, no
doubt,' Robespierre kept groaning in reply to the

consolations of his sister, for women are apt to be more positive creatures than men : ' a criminal, no doubt ; but to put a man to death ! '

Among Robespierre's associates in the festive mummeries of the Rosati was a young officer of Engineers, who was destined to be his colleague in the dread Committee of Public Safety, and to leave an important name in French history. In the garrison at Arras, Carnot was quartered,—that iron head, whose genius for the administrative organisation of war achieved even greater things for the new Republic than the genius of Louvois had achieved for the old monarchy. Carnot surpassed not only Louvois, but perhaps all other names save one in modern military history, by uniting to the most powerful gifts for organisation, both the strategic talent that planned the momentous campaign of 1794, and the splendid personal energy and skill that prolonged the defence of Antwerp against the allied army in 1814. Partisans dream of the unrivalled future of peace, glory, and freedom that would have fallen to the lot of France, if only the gods had brought about a hearty union between the military genius of Carnot and the political genius of Robespierre. So, no doubt, after the restoration of Charles II. in England, there were good men who thought that all would have gone very differently, if only the genius of the great creator of the Ironsides had taken counsel with the genius of Venner, the Fifth-Monarchy Man, and Feak, the Anabaptist prophet.

The time was now come when such men as Robespierre were to be tried with fire, when they were to drink the cup of fury, and the dregs of the cup of trembling. Sibyls and prophets have already spoken their inexorable decree, as Goethe has said, on the day that first gives the man to the world ; no time and no might can break the stamped mould of his character; only as life wears on, do all its aforeshapen lines come into light. He is launched into a sea of external conditions as independent of his own will as the temperament with which he confronts them. It is action that tries, and variation of circumstances. The leaden chains of use bind many an ugly unsuspected prisoner in the soul; and when the habit of their lives has been sundered, the most immaculate are capable of antics beyond prevision. A great crisis of the world was prepared for Robespierre and those others, his allies or his destroyers, who with him came like the lightning and went like the wind.

At the end of 1788 the King of France found himself forced to summon the States-General. It was the first assembly since 1614. On the memorable Fourth of May 1789, Robespierre appeared at Versailles as one of the representatives of the third estate of his native province of Artois. The excitement and enthusiasm of the elections to this renowned assembly, the immense demands and boundless expectations they disclosed, would have warned a cool observer of events, if in the heated air a cool observer

could have been found, that the hour had struck for
the fulfilment of those grim apprehensions of revolution that had risen in the minds of many shrewd men,
good and bad, in the course of the previous half-
century. No cardinal event in history ever comes
wholly unforeseen. The antecedent causes are so
wide-reaching, many, and continuous, that their
direction is always sure to strike the eye of one or
more observers in all its significance. Louis the
Fifteenth, whose invincible weariness and heavy
disgust veiled a penetrating discernment, measured
accurately the scope of the conflict between the
crown and the parlements : but, said he, things as
they are will last my time. Under the roof of his
own palace at Versailles, in the apartment of Madame
de Pompadour's famous physician, one of Quesnay's
economic disciples had cried out, ' The realm is in
a sore way ; it will never be cured without a great
internal commotion ; but woe to those who have to
do with it ; into such work the French go with no
slack hand.' Rousseau, in a passage in the *Confessions*, not only divines a speedy convulsion, but with
striking practical sagacity enumerates the political
and social causes that were unavoidably drawing
France to the edge of the abyss. Lord Chesterfield,
so different a man from Rousseau, declared as early
as 1752, that he saw in France every symptom history
had taught him to regard as the forerunner of deep
change ; before the end of the century, so his prediction ran, both the trade of king and the trade

of priest in France would be shorn of half their glory.
D'Argenson in the same year declared a revolution
inevitable, and with a curious precision of anticipation
assured himself that, if once the necessity arose of
convoking the States-General, they would not assemble
in vain : *qu'on y prenne garde! ils seraient fort
sérieux!* Oliver Goldsmith, idly wandering through
France, towards 1755, discerned in the mutinous
attitude of the judicial corporations, that the genius
of freedom was entering the kingdom in disguise,
and that a succession of three weak monarchs would
end in the emancipation of the people of France.
The most touching of all these presentiments is to
be found in a private letter of the great Empress,
the mother of Marie Antoinette herself. Maria
Theresa describes the ruined state of the French
monarchy, and only prays that if it be doomed to
ruin, at least the blame may not fall upon her daughter.
The Empress had not learnt that when the giants of
social force are advancing from the sombre shadow
of the past, our poor prayers are of no more avail
than the unbodied visions of a dream.

The old popular assembly of the realm was not
resorted to before every means of dispensing with so
drastic a remedy had been tried. Historians sometimes write as if Turgot were the only able and reforming minister of the century. Heaven forbid that
we should put any other minister on a level with that
high and beneficent figure. But Turgot was not the
first statesman, both able and patriotic, who had

been disgraced for want of compliance with the
conditions of success at court; he was only the last
of a series. Chauvelin, a man of vigour and capacity,
was dismissed with ignominy in 1736. Machault, a
reformer, at once courageous and wise, shared the
same fate twenty years later; and in his case revolution was as cruel and as heedless as reaction, for, at
the age of ninety-one, the old man was dragged,
blind and deaf, before the Revolutionary Tribunal
and thence despatched to the guillotine. Between
Chauvelin and Machault, the elder D'Argenson, who
was greater than either of them, had been raised to
power, and as speedily hurled down from it (1747),
for no better reason than that his manners were
uncouth, and that he would not waste his time in
frivolities that were the breath of life in the great
gallery at Versailles and on the smooth-shaven lawns
of Fontainebleau.

Not only had wise counsellors been tried; con-
sultative assemblies had been tried as well. Necker
had been dismissed in 1781, after publishing the
memorable *Report* that first initiated the nation in
the elements of financial knowledge. The disorder
waxed greater, and the monarchy drew nearer to
bankruptcy each year. The only nineteenth-century
parallel to the state of things in France under Louis
the Sixteenth is to be sought in the state of things
in Egypt or in Turkey. Louis the Fourteenth had
left a debt of between two and three thousand millions
of livres, but this had been wiped out by the heroic

operations of Law; operations, by the way, that
have never yet been scientifically criticised. But
the debt soon grew again, by foolish wars, by the
prodigality of the court, and by the rapacity of the
nobles. It amounted in 1789 to something like two
hundred and forty millions sterling; and it is interesting to notice that this was exactly the sum of the
public debt of Great Britain at the same time. The
year's excess of expenditure over receipts in 1774
was about fifty millions of livres: in 1787 it was one
hundred and forty millions, or according to a different
computation even two hundred millions. The
material case was not at all desperate, if only the
court had been less infatuated, and the spirit of the
privileged orders had been less blind. The fatality
of the situation lay in the characters of a handful of
men and women. For France was abundant in
resources, and even at this moment was far from
unprosperous, in spite of the incredible trammels of
law and custom. An able financier, with the support
of a popular chamber and the assent of the sovereign,
could have had no difficulty in restoring the public
credit. But the conditions, simple as they might
seem to a patriot or to posterity, were unattainable
so long as power remained with a caste that were
anything we please, only not patriots. An Assembly
of Notables was brought together, but it was only
the phantasm of national representation. Yet the
situation was so serious that even this body, arbitrary
of origin as it was, still was willing to accept vital

reforms. The privileged order, who were then the worst conservative party in Europe, immediately persuaded the magisterial corporation to resist the Notables. The judicial corporation or Parlement of Paris had been suppressed under Louis the Fifteenth, and unfortunately revived again at the accession of his grandson. By the inconvenient constitution of the French government, the assent of that body was indispensable to fiscal legislation, on the ground that such legislation was part of the general police of the realm. The king's minister, now Loménie de Brienne, devised a new judicial constitution. But the church-men, the nobles, and the lawyers all united in pro-testations against the blow. The common people are not always the best judges of a remedy for the evils under which they are the worst sufferers, and they broke out in disorder both in Paris and the provinces. They discerned an attack upon their local independence. Nobody would accept office in the new courts, and the administration of justice was at a standstill. A loan was thrown upon the market, but the public could not be persuaded to take it up. It was impossible to collect the taxes. The interest on the national debt was unpaid, and the fundholder was dismayed and exasperated by an announcement that only two-fifths would be discharged in cash. A very large part of the national debt was held in the form of annuities for lives, and men who had invested their savings on the credit of the government, saw themselves left without a provision. The total

number of fundholders cannot be ascertained with
any precision, but it must have been very considerable, especially in Paris and the other large cities.
Add to these all the civil litigants in the kingdom,
who had portions of their property virtually seques-
trated by the suspension of the courts into which the
property had been taken. The resentment of this
immense body of defrauded public creditors and
injured private suitors explains the alienation of the
middle class from the monarchy. In the convulsions
of our own time, the moneyed interests have been on
one side, and the population without money on the
other. But in the first and greatest convulsions,
those who had nothing to lose found their animosities
shared by those who had had something to lose, and
had lost it.

Deliberative assemblies, then, had been tried, and
ministers had been tried; both had failed, and no
other device was left, except one that was destructive to absolute monarchy. Louis the Sixteenth
was in 1789 in much the same case as that of the
King of England in 1640. Charles had done his best
to raise money without any parliament for twelve
years: he had lost patience with the Short Parliament; finally, he was driven without choice or
alternative to face as he best could the stout resolution and the wise patriotism of the Long Parliament.
Men sometimes wonder how it was that Louis, when
he came to find the National Assembly unmanageable,
and discovering how rapidly he was drifting towards

S

the thunders of the revolutionary cataract, did not break up a Chamber over which neither the court, nor even a minister so popular as Necker, had the least control. It is a question whether the sword would not have broken in his hand. Even supposing, however, that the army would have consented to a violent movement against the Assembly, the king would still have been left in the same desperate straits from which he had looked to the States-General to extricate him. He might perhaps have dispersed the Assembly; he could not disperse debt and deficit. Those monsters would have haunted him implacably. There was no new formula of exorcism, nor any untried enchantment. The success of violent designs against the National Assembly, had success been possible, could, after all, have been followed by no other consummation than the relapse of France into the anarchy of Poland, or the sullen decrepitude of Turkey.

This will seem no better than fatalism. But, in truth, there are two popular ways of reading the history of events between 1789 and 1794, and each of them seems as bad as the other. According to one, whatever happened in the Revolution was good and admirable, because it happened. According to the other, something good and admirable was always attainable, and, if only bad men had not interposed, always ready to happen. Of course the only sensible view is that many of the revolutionary solutions were detestable, but no other solution was within reach. This is undoubtedly the best of possible worlds ; if the best is not so good as we could wish, that is the fault of the possibilities. Such a doctrine is neither fatalism nor optimism, but an honest recognition of long chains of cause and effect in human things.

The great gathering of chosen men was first called States-General ; then it called itself National Assembly ; it is commonly known in history as the Constituent Assembly. The name is of ironical association, for the constitution which it framed after much travail endured for no more than a few months. Its deliberations lasted from May 1789 until September 1791. Among its members were three principal groups. There was, first, a band of blind adherents of the old system of government with all or most of its abuses. Second, there was a Centre of timid and one-eyed men, who were for transforming the old absolutist system into something that should resemble the constitution of our own country. Finally, there was a Left, with some differences of shade, but all agreeing in the necessity of a thorough remodelling of every institution and most of the usages of the country. ' Silence, you thirty votes ! ' cried Mirabeau one day, when he was interrupted by the dissents of the Mountain. This was the original measure of the party that, in the twinkling of an eye, was to wield the destinies of France. In our own time we have wondered at the rapidity with which a Chamber that was one day on

the point of bringing back the grand-nephew of Louis
the Sixteenth, found itself a little later voting the
Republic that has since been ratified by the nation,
and has at this moment the ardent good wishes of
every enlightened politician in Europe. In the same
way it is startling to think that within three years
of the beheading of Louis the Sixteenth, there was
probably not one serious republican in the representative assembly of France. Yet it is always so. We
might make just the same remark of the House of
Commons at Westminster in 1640, and of the Assembly
of Massachusetts or of New York as late as 1770.
The final flash of a long unconscious train of thought
or intent is ever a shock. It is a mistake to set
these swift changes down to political levity rather
than to quickness of political intuition. It was the
king's attempt at flight in the summer of 1791 that
first created a republican party. It was this unhappy exploit, and no theoretical preferences, that
awoke France to the necessity of choosing between
the sacrifice of monarchy and the restoration of
territorial aristocracy.

Political intuition was never one of Robespierre's
conspicuous gifts. But he had a doctrine that for a
certain time served the same purpose. Rousseau
had kindled in him a fervid democratic enthusiasm,
and had penetrated his mind with the principle of
the Sovereignty of the People. This famous dogma
contained implicitly within it the more indisputable
and the better truth that a society ought to be

disorder of monarchy and feudalism, he had accepted
the counter principle that the people can do no
wrong, and nobody of sense now doubts that in their
first great act the people of Paris did what was right.
Six days after the fall of the Bastille, the Centre
were for issuing a proclamation denouncing popular
violence and ordering rigorous vigilance. Robespierre was then so little known in the Assembly that
even his name was usually misspelt in the journals.
From his obscure bench on the Mountain he cried
out with bitter vehemence against the proposed proclamation :—'Revolt! But this revolt is liberty.
The battle is not at its end. To-morrow, it may be,

the shameful designs against us will be renewed;
and who will there be then to repulse them, if
beforehand we declare the very men to be rebels,
who have rushed to arms for our protection and
safety ? ' This was the cardinal truth of the situation. Everybody knows Mirabeau's saying about
Robespierre :—' That man will go far : he believes
every word that he says ! ' This is much, but it is
only half. It is not only that the man of power
believes what he says ; what he believes must fit in
with the facts and the demands of the time. Now
Robespierre's firmness of conviction happened at this
stage to be rightly matched by his clearness of sight.

It is true that a passionate mob, its unearthly
admixture of laughter with fury, of vacancy with
deadly concentration, is as terrible as an uncouth
antediluvian, or the unfamiliar monsters of the sea,
or one of the giant plants that make men shudder
with mysterious fear. The history of our own
country in the eighteenth century tells of the riots
against meeting-houses in Doctor Sacheverell's time,
and the riots against Papists and their abettors in Lord
George Gordon's time, and Church-and-King riots in
Doctor Priestley's time. It would be too daring, therefore, to maintain that the rabble of the poor are sure
to have any more unerring political judgment than
the rabble of the opulent. But, in France in 1789,
Robespierre was justified in saying that revolt meant
liberty. If there had been no revolt in July, the
court party would have had time to mature their

infatuated designs of violence against the Assembly. In October these designs had come to life again. The royalists at Versailles had exultant banquets, at which, in the presence of the queen, they drank confusion to all patriots, and trampled the new emblem of freedom passionately underfoot. The news of this odious folly soon travelled to Paris. Its significance was speedily understood by a populace whose wits were sharpened by famine. Thousands of fire-eyed women and men tramped intrepidly out towards Versailles. If they had done less, the Assembly would have been dispersed or arbitrarily decimated, even though such a measure would certainly have left the government in desperation.

At that dreadful moment of the Sixth of October, amid the slaughter of guards and the frantic yells of hatred against the queen, it is no wonder that some were found to urge the king to flee to Metz. If he had accepted the advice, the course of the Revolution would have been different; but its march would have been just as irresistible, for revolution lay in the force of a hundred combined circumstances. Louis, however, rejected these counsels, and suffered the mob to carry him in bewildering procession to his capital and his prison. That great man who was watching French affairs with such consuming eagerness from distant Beaconsfield in our English Buckinghamshire, instantly divined that this procession from Versailles to the Tuileries marked the fall of the monarchy. ' A revolution in sentiment, manners, and moral opinions, the most important of all revolutions in a word,' was in Burke's judgment to be dated from the Sixth of October 1789.

The events of that day did, indeed, give its definite cast to the situation. The moral authority of the sovereign came to an end, along with the ancient and reverend mystery of the inviolability of his person. The Count d'Artois, the king's second brother, as incurably addicted to sinister and suicidal counsels in 1789 as he was when he overthrew his own throne forty years later, had run away from peril and from duty after the insurrection of July. On the insurrection of October, a troop of the nobles of the court followed him. The personal cowardice of the Emigrants was only matched by their political blindness. Many of the most unwise measures in the Assembly were only passed by small majorities, and the majorities would have been transformed into minorities, if in the early days of the Revolution these unworthy men had only stood firm at their posts. Selfish oligarchies have scarcely ever been wanting in courage. The emigrant noblesse of France are almost the only instance of a great privileged and territorial caste that had as little bravery as they had patriotism. The explanation is that they had been an oligarchy, not of power or duty, but of self-indulgence. They were crushed by Richelieu to secure the unity of the monarchy. They now effaced themselves at the Revolution, and this secured that far greater object, the unity of the nation.

The disappearance of so many of the nobles from France was not the only abdication on the part of conservative power. Cowed and terrified by the events of October, no less than three hundred members of the Assembly sought to resign. The average attendance even at the most important sittings was often incredibly small. Thus the Chamber came to have little more moral authority in face of the people of Paris than had the king himself. The people of Paris had themselves become, in a day, the masters of France.

This immense change led gradually to a decisive alteration in the position of Robespierre. He found the situation of affairs at last falling into perfect harmony with his doctrine. Rousseau had taught him that the people ought to be sovereign, and now the people were being recognised as sovereign *de facto* no less than *de jure*. Any limitations on the new divine right united the horror of blasphemy to the secular wickedness of political treason. After the Assembly had come to Paris, a famishing mob in a moment of mad fury murdered an unfortunate baker, suspected of keeping back bread. These paroxysms led to the enactment of a new martial law. Robespierre spoke vehemently against it; such a law implied a wrongful distrust of the people. Then discussions followed as to the property qualification of an elector. Citizens were classed as active and passive. Only those were to have votes who paid direct taxes to the amount of three days' wages in the year. Robespierre flung himself upon this too famous distinction with bitter tenacity. If all men are equal, he cried, then all men ought to have votes ; if he who only pays the amount of one day's work has fewer rights than another who pays the amount of three days, why should not the man who pays ten days have more rights than the other who only pays the earnings of three days ? This kind of reasoning had little weight with the Chamber, but it made the reasoner very popular with the throng in the galleries. Even within the Assembly, influence gradually came to the man who had a parcel of immutable axioms and postulates, and who was ready with a deduction and a phrase for each case as it arose. He began to stand out like a needle of sharp rock, amid the flitting shadows of uncertain purpose and vapoury drift.

Robespierre had no social conception, and he had nothing that can be described as a policy. He was the prophet of a sect, and had at this period none of the aims of the chief of a political party. What he had was democratic doctrine, and an intrepid logic. And Robespierre's intrepid logic was the nearest approach to calm force and coherent character the first three years of the Revolution brought into prominence. When the Assembly met, Necker was the popular idol. Almost within a few weeks, this well-meaning but incompetent divinity had slipped from his woolsack, and Lafayette had taken his place. Mirabeau came next. The ardent and animated genius of his eloquence fitted him above all

men to ride the whirlwind and direct the storm.
And on the memorable Twenty-third of June 1789,
he had shown the genuine audacity and resource of
a revolutionary statesman, when he stirred the
Chamber to defy the king's demand, and hailed the
royal usher with the resounding words : ' You, sir,
have neither place nor right of speech. Go tell those
who sent you that we are here by the will of the
people, and only bayonets shall drive us hence ! '
But Mirabeau bore a tainted character, and was
distrusted. ' Ah, how the immorality of my youth,'
he used to say, in words that sum up the tragedy
of many a puissant life, ' how the immorality of
my youth hinders the public good ! ' The event
proved that the popular suspicion was just : the
patriot is now no longer merely suspected, but known
to have sullied his hands with the money of the court.
He did not sell himself, it has been said ; he allowed
himself to be paid. The distinction was too subtle
for men doing battle for their lives and for freedom,
and Mirabeau's popularity waned towards the middle
of 1790. The next favourite was Barnave, the
generous and high-minded spokesman of those
sanguine spirits who to the very end hoped against
hope to save both the throne and its occupant. By
the spring of 1791 Barnave followed his predecessors
into disfavour. The Assembly was engaged on the
burning question of the government of the colonies.
Were the negro slaves to be admitted to citizenship,
or was a legislature of planters to be entrusted with

the task of social reformation ? Our own generation
has seen in the Republic of the West what strife this
political difficulty is capable of raising. Barnave
pronounced against the negroes. Robespierre, on
the contrary, declaimed against any limitation of
the right of the negro, as a compromise with the
avarice, pride, and cruelty of a governing race, and
a guilty trafficking with the rights of man. Barnave
from that day saw that his laurel crown had gone
to Robespierre.

If the people ' called him noble that was now their
hate, him vile that was their garland,' they did not
transfer their affections without sound reason.
Barnave's sensibility was too easily touched. There
are many politicians in every epoch whose principles grow slack at the approach of the golden
sun of royalty. Barnave was one of those sent
to bring back the fugitive king and queen from
Varennes, and the coach journey by their side un-
strung his spirit. He became one of the court's
clandestine advisers. Men of this weak susceptibility
of imagination are not fit for times of revolution.
To be on the side of the court was to betray the
cause of the nation. We cannot take too much pains
to realise that the voluntary conversion of Louis the
Sixteenth to a popular constitution and the abolition
of feudalism, was practically as impossible as the
conversion of Pope Pius the Ninth to the doctrine
of a free church in a free state. Those who believe
in the miracle of free will may think of this as they

please. Sensible people who accept the sensible account of human character, know that the sudden transformation of a man or a woman brought up to middle age as the heir to centuries of absolutist tradition, into adherents of a government that agreed with the doctrines of Locke and Milton, was only possible on condition of supernatural interference. The king's good nature was no substitute for political capacity or insight. An instructive measure of the degree in which he possessed these two qualities may be found in that deplorable diary of his, where on such days as the Fourteenth of July, when the Bastille fell, and the Sixth of October, when he was carried in triumph from Versailles to the Tuileries, he made the simple entry, ' *Rien.*' And he had no firmness. It was as difficult to keep the king to a purpose, La Marck said to Mirabeau, as to keep together a number of well-oiled ivory balls. Louis, moreover, was guided by a more energetic and less compliant character than his own.

Marie Antoinette's high mien in adversity, and the contrast between the dazzling splendour of her first years and the scenes of outrage and bloody death that made the climax of her fate, could not but strike the imaginations of men. Such contrasts are the very stuff of which Tragedy, the gorgeous muse with scepter'd pall, loves to weave her most imposing raiment. But history must be just; and the character of the queen had far more concern in the disaster of the first five years of the Revolution

than had the character of Robespierre. The popular
hatred for Marie Antoinette sprang from a sound
instinct. We shall never know how much or how
little truth was in those frightful charges against
her, that may still be read in a thousand pamphlets.
These imputed depravities far surpass anything that
John Knox ever said against Mary Stuart, or that
Juvenal has recorded against Messalina ; and, perhaps, for the only parallel, we must look to the
stories of the Byzantine secretary against Theodora,
the too famous empress of Justinian and the per-
secutor of Belisarius. We have to remember that
all the revolutionary portraits are distorted by
furious passion, and that Marie Antoinette may no
more deserve to be compared to Mary Stuart than
Robespierre deserves to be compared to Ezzelino or
to Alva. The aristocrats were the libellers, if libels
they were. It is at least certain that, from the
unlucky hour when the Austrian archduchess crossed
the French frontier, a childish bride of fourteen,
down to the hour when the Queen of France made
the attempt to recross it in resentful flight one-
and-twenty years afterwards, Marie Antoinette was
ignorant, unteachable, blind to events and deaf to
good counsels, a bitter grief to her heroic mother, the
evil genius of her husband, the despair of her truest
advisers, and an exceedingly bad friend to the people
of France. When Burke had that immortal vision
of her at Versailles—' just above the horizon, decorat-
ing and cheering the elevated sphere she just began

to move in, glittering like the morning star, full of life and splendour and joy'—we know from the correspondence between Maria Theresa and her minister at Versailles, that what Burke really saw was no divinity, but a troublesome schoolgirl, an accomplice in all the ignoble intrigues, and a sharer of all the small busy passions, that convulse an unordered court. The levity that came with her Lorraine blood, broke out in incredible dissipations; in indiscreet visits to the masked balls at the opera; in midnight parades and mystifications on the terrace at Versailles; in insensate gambling. 'The court of France is turned into a gaming-hell,' said the Emperor Joseph, the queen's own brother: 'if they do not amend, the revolution will be cruel.' These vices or follies were less mischievous than her intervention in affairs of state. Here her levity was as marked as in the affairs of the boudoir and the ante-chamber, and here to levity she added both dissimulation and vindictiveness. It was the Queen's influence that procured the dismissal of the two virtuous ministers by whose aid the king was striving to arrest the decay of the government of his kingdom. Malesherbes was distasteful to her for no better reason than that she wanted his post for some favourite's favourite. Against Turgot she conspired with tenacious animosity, because he had suppressed a sinecure she designed for a court parasite, and because he would not support her caprice on behalf of a worthless creature of her faction. These two admirable men

were disgraced on the same day. The queen wrote
to her mother that she had not meddled in the affair.
This was false, for she had even sought to have
Turgot thrown into the Bastille. 'I am as one
dashed to the ground,' cried Voltaire, now nearing
his end. 'Never can we console ourselves for having
seen the golden age dawn and vanish. My eyes see
only death in front of me, now that Turgot is gone.
The rest of my days must be all bitterness.'

When people write hymns of pity for the queen,
we may recall the poor woman whom Arthur Young
met, as he was walking up a hill to ease his horse
near Mars-le-Tour. Though the unfortunate creature
was only twenty-eight, she might have been taken for
sixty or seventy, her figure was so bent, her face so
furrowed and hardened by toil. Her husband, she
said, had a morsel of land, one cow, and a poor little
horse, yet he had to pay forty-two pounds of wheat
and three chickens to one Seigneur, and one hundred
and sixty pounds of oats, one chicken, and one franc
to another, besides very heavy *tailles* and other taxes ;
and they had seven children. She had heard that
'something was to be done by some great folks for
such poor ones, but she did not know who nor how,
but God send us better, for the *tailles* and the dues
grind us to the earth.' It was such hapless drudges
as this who replenished the queen's gaming tables
at Versailles. Thousands of them dragged on the
burden of their harassed and desperate days, less like
men and women than beasts of the field wrung and

tortured and mercilessly overladen, in order that the
queen might gratify her childish passion for diamonds,
or lavish money and estates on worthless female
Polignacs and Lamballes, or kill time at a cost of
five hundred louis a night at lansquenet and the faro
bank. The queen, it is true, was in all this no worse
than other dissipated women. She did not realise
that it was the system to which she had stubbornly
committed herself, that drove the people of the fields
to cut their crops green, to be baked in the oven,
because their hunger could not wait ; or made them
cower whole days in their beds, because misery
seemed to gnaw them there with a duller fang. That
she was unconscious of its effect, makes no difference
in the real drift of her policy ; makes no difference
in the judgment we ought to pass upon it, nor
in the gratitude that is owed to the stern men who
rose up to consume her and her court with flame.
The queen and the courtiers, and the hard-faring
woman of Mars-le-Tour, and that whole generation,
have long been dust and shadow ; they have vanished
from the earth, as if they were no more than the fire-
flies that the peasant of the Italian poet saw dancing
in the vineyard as he took his evening rest on the
hillside. They have all fled back into the impenetrable shade whence they came ; and if social equity
is not a chimera, Marie Antoinette was the protagonist
of the worst of causes.

Let us return to the shaping of the Constitution,

T

not forgetting that its stability was to depend upon the queen. Robespierre left some characteristic marks on the final arrangements. He imposed upon the Assembly a motion prohibiting any member of it from accepting office under the Crown for a period of four years after the dissolution. Robespierre from this time forth constantly illustrated a very singular and unfortunate truth; namely, that the most ostentatious faith in humanity in general seems always to beget the sharpest distrust of all human beings in particular. He proceeded further in the same direction. It was Robespierre who persuaded the Chamber to pass a self-denying ordinance. All its members were declared ineligible for a seat in the legislature that was to replace them. The members of the Right on this occasion went with their bitter foes of the Extreme Left, and to both parties have been imputed sinister and Machiavellian motives. The Right, aware that their own return to the new Assembly was impossible, were delighted to reduce the men with whom they had been carrying on incensed battle for two long years, to their own obscurity and impotence. Robespierre, on the other hand, is accused of a jealous desire to exclude Barnave from power. He is accused also of a deliberate intention to weaken the new legislature, in order to secure the preponderance of the Parisian clubs. There is no evidence that these malignant feelings were in Robespierre's mind. The reasons he gave were exactly of the kind that we should have expected to weigh with a man of his calibre. There is even a certain truth in them, not inconsistent with the experience of a parliamentary country like our own. To talk, he said, of the transmission of light and experience from one Assembly to another, was to distrust the public spirit. The influence of opinion and the general good grows less, as the influence of parliamentary orators grows greater. He had no taste, he proceeded with one of his chilly sneers, for the new science that was styled the tactics of great assemblies; it was too like intrigue. Nothing but truth and reason ought to reign in a legislature. He did not like the idea of clever men becoming dominant by skilful tactics, and then perpetuating their empire from one Assembly to another. He wound up his discourse with some theatrical talk about disinterestedness. When he sat down, he was greeted with enthusiastic acclamations, such as a few months before used to greet the stormful Mirabeau, now wrapped in eternal sleep amid the stillness of the new Pantheon. The folly of Robespierre's inferences is obvious enough. If only truth and reason ought to weigh in a legislature, then it is all the more important not to exclude any body of men with whom truth and reason may possibly enter. Robespierre had striven hard to remove all restrictions from admission to the electoral franchise. He did not see that to limit the choice of candidates was in itself the most grievous of all restrictions.

The common view has been that the Constitution of 1791 perished because its creators were thus disabled from defending the work of their hands. This view led to a grave mistake four years later, after Robespierre had gone to his grave. The Convention, framing the Constitution of the Year III., decided that two-thirds of the existing assembly should keep their places, and only one-third should be popularly elected. This led to the revolt of the Thirteenth Vendémiaire, and afterwards to the *coup d'État* of the Eighteenth Fructidor. In that sense, no doubt, Robespierre's proposal was the indirect root of much mischief. But it is childish to believe that if a hundred of the most prominent members of the Constituent had found seats in the new Assembly, they would have saved the Constitution. Their experience, the loss of which it is the fashion to deplore, could have had no application to the strange combinations of untoward circumstance now rising up with such deadly rapidity in every quarter of the horizon, like vast sombre banks of impenetrable cloud. Prudence in new cases can do nothing on grounds of retrospect. The work of the Constituent was doomed by the very nature of things. Their assumption that the Revolution was made, while all France was still torn by fierce and unappeasable disputes as to seignorial rights, was one of the most striking pieces of self-deception in history. It is told how in the eleventh century, when the fervent hosts of the Crusaders tramped across Europe on

their way to deliver the Holy City from the hands
of the unbelievers, the wearied children, as they
espied each new town that lay in their interminable
march, cried out with joyful expectation, ' Is not
this, then, Jerusalem ? ' So France had set out on
a portentous journey, little knowing how far off was
the end ; lightly taking each poor halting-place for
the deeply - longed - for goal ; and waxing more
fiercely disappointed, as each new height they gained
only disclosed yet farther and more unattainable
horizons. ' Alas,' said Burke, ' they little know how
many a weary step is to be taken, before they can
form themselves into a mass which has a true political
personality.'

An immense revolution had been effected, but by
what force were its fruits to be guarded ? Each step
in the Revolution had raised a host of irreconcilable
enemies. The rights of property, the old and jealous
associations of local independence, the traditions of
personal dignity, the relations of the civil to the
spiritual power—these were the momentous matters
about which the lawmakers of the Constituent had
exercised themselves. The parties of the Chamber
had for these two years past been laying mine and
counter-mine among the very deepest foundations of
society. One by one each great corporation of the
old order had been alienated from the new. It was
inevitable. Let us look at one or two examples.
The monarchy had imposed administrative centralisa-
tion upon France without securing national unity.

The great provinces that had been slowly added one after the other to the monarchy, while becoming members of the same kingdom, still retained different institutions and isolated usages. The time was now come when France should be France, and its inhabitants Frenchmen, and no longer Bretons, Normans, Gascons, Provençals. The Assembly by a single decree (1790) redivided the country into eighty-three departments. It wiped out at a stroke the separate administrations, the separate parliaments, the peculiar privileges, and even the historic names of the old provinces. We need not dwell on the significance of this change here, but will only remark in passing that the stubborn disputes from the time of the Regency downwards between the Crown and the provincial parliaments turned, under other names and in other forms, upon this very issue of the unification of the law. The Crown was with the progressive party, but it lacked the strength and courage to set aside retrograde local sentiment as the Constituent Assembly was able to set it aside.

Then this prodigious change in the distribution of government was accompanied by no less prodigious a change in the source of power. Popular election replaced the old system of territorial privilege and aristocratic prerogative. The effect of this vital innovation, followed as it was a few months later by a decree abolishing titles and armorial bearings, was to complete the estrangement of the old privileged classes from the revolutionary movement. All that they had meant to concede was the payment of an equal land tax. What was life worth to the noble, if common people were to be allowed to wear arms and to command a company of foot or a troop of horse ; if he was no longer to have thousands of acres left waste for the chase ; if he was compelled to sue for a vote where he had only yesterday reigned as manorial lord ; if, in short, he was at a stroke to lose all those delights of insolence and vanity that had made, not the decoration, but the very substance, of his days ?

Nor were the nobles of the sword and the red-heeled slipper the only outraged class. The magistracy of the provincial parliaments were inflamed with resentment against changes that stripped them of the power of exciting against the new government the same factious and impracticable spirit with which they had on so many occasions embarrassed the old. The clergy were thrown even still more violently into opposition. The Assembly, sorely pressed for resources, declared the property held by ecclesiastics, amounting to a revenue of not less than eight million pounds sterling a year, or double that amount in modern values, to be the property of the nation. Talleyrand carried a measure decreeing the sale of the ecclesiastical domain. The clergy were as intensely irritated as laymen would have been by a similar assertion of sovereign right. And their irritation was made still more dangerous by the next set of measures against them.

The Assembly withdrew all recognition of Catholicism as the religion of the State ; monastic vows were abolished, and orders and congregations suppressed ; the ecclesiastical divisions were made to coincide with the civil divisions, a bishop being allotted to each department. What was a more important revolution than all, bishops and incumbents were henceforth to be appointed by popular election. The Assembly, who had always the institutions of our own country before them, meant to introduce into France the system of the Church of England, that was even then an anachronism in the land of its birth ; much more was such a system an anachronism, after belief had been sapped by a Voltaire and an Encyclopædia. The clergy both showed and excited a mutinous spirit. The Assembly, by way of retort, decreed that all ecclesiastics should take the oath of allegiance to the civil constitution of the clergy, on pain of forfeiture of their benefices. Five-sixths of the clergy refused, and the result was an outbreak of religious fury in the great towns of the south and elsewhere, that recalled the violence of the sixteenth century and the Reformation.

Thus when the Constituent Assembly ceased from its labours, the popular party had to face the mocking and defiant privileged classes ; the magistracy, whose craft and calling were gone ; and the clergy and as many of the flocks as shared the vindictiveness of their pastors. Immense material improvements had been made, but who was to guard them against all these powerful and exasperated bands? No chamber could execute so portentous an office, least of all a chamber that was bound to work in accord with a king, who at the very moment when he was swearing fidelity to the new order of things, was sending entreaties to the King of Prussia and to the Emperor, his brother-in-law, to overthrow the new order and bring back the old. If the Revolution had achieved priceless gains for France, they could only be preserved on condition that public action was directed by those who valued these gains for themselves and for their children above all things else—above the monarchy, above the constitution, above peace, above their own sorry lives. There was only one party who showed this passionate devotion, this fanatical resolution not to suffer to be undone the work that had been done, and never to allow France to sink back from exalted national life into the lethargy of national death. That party was the Jacobins, and, above all, the austere and rigorous Jacobins of Paris. On their ascendancy depended the triumph of the Revolution, and on the triumph of the Revolution depended the salvation of France. Their ascendancy meant a Jacobin dictatorship, and against this, as against dictatorship in all its forms, many things have been said, and truly said. But the one most important thing that can be said about Jacobin dictatorship is that, in spite of all the dolorous mishaps and hateful misdeeds that marked its course, it was still the only instrument capable of concentrating and utilising the dispersed social energy of the French people.

The great popular club of Paris was the centre of all those who looked at events in this spirit. The Legislative Assembly, the successor of the Constituent, met in the month of October 1791. Like its predecessor, the Legislative contained a host of excellent and patriotic men, and they at once applied themselves to the all-important task, which the Constituent had left so incomplete, of finally breaking down the old feudal rights. The most important group in the new chamber were the deputies from the Gironde. Events soon revealed violent dissents between Girondins and Jacobins, but, for some months after the meeting of the Legislative, Girondins and Jacobins represented together in unbroken unity the great popular party. From this time until the fall of the monarchy, the whole of this popular party in all its branches found their rallying-place, not in the Assembly, but in the Jacobin Club; and the ascendancy of the Jacobin Club embodied the dictatorship of Paris. It was only from Paris that the whole circle of events could be commanded. When the peasants had got what they wanted, that is to say the emancipation of the land, they were ready to think that the Revolution was in safety and at an end. They were in no position to see the enmity of the exiles, the dangerous selfishness of Austria and Prussia, the disloyal machinations of the court, the reactionary sentiment of La Vendée, the absolute unworkableness of the new constitution. Arthur Young, in the height of the agitations of the Constituent Assembly, found himself at Moulins, the capital of the Bourbonnais, and on the great post-road to Italy. He went to the best coffee-house in the town, and found as many as twenty tables spread for company, but as for a newspaper, he says he might as well have asked for an elephant. In the capital of a great province, the seat of an Intendant, at a moment like that, with a National Assembly voting a revolution, and not a newspaper to tell the people whether Lafayette, Mirabeau, or Louis XVI. were on the throne! Could such a people as this, he cries, ever have made a revolution or become free? 'Never in a thousand centuries: the enlightened mob of Paris have done the whole.' And that was the plain truth. What was involved in such a truth, we shall see presently.

Robespierre had now risen to be one of the foremost men in France. To borrow the figure of an older chief of French faction, from trifling among the violins in the orchestra, he had ascended to the stage itself, and had a right to perform leading parts. Disqualified for sitting in the Assembly, he wielded greater power than ever in the Club. The Constituent had been full of his enemies. 'Alone with my own soul,' he once cried to the Jacobins, 'how could I have borne struggles that were beyond any human strength, if I had not raised my spirit to God?' This isolation marked him with a kind of theocratic distinction. These communings with the unseen powers gave a certain indefinable prerogative to a man, even among the children of the century of Voltaire. Condorcet, the youngest of the intimates and disciples of Voltaire, of D'Alembert, of Turgot, was the first to sound bitter warning that Robespierre was at heart a priest. The suggestion was more than a gibe. By and by, from mere priest he developed into the deadlier carnivore, the Inquisitor.

The absence of advantages of bodily presence has never been fatal to the pretensions of the pontiff. Robespierre was only a couple of inches above five feet in height, but the Grand Monarch himself was hardly more. His eyes were small and weak, and he usually wore spectacles; his face was pitted by the marks of smallpox; his complexion was dull and sometimes livid; the tones of his voice were dry and shrill; and he spoke with the vulgar accent of his province. Such is the accepted tradition, and there is no reason to dissent from it. It is fair, however, to remember that Robespierre's enemies had command of his historic reputation at its source. So Robespierre's voice and person may have been maligned, just as Aristophanes may have been a calumniator when he accused Cleon of having an intolerably loud voice and smelling of the tan-yard. What is certain is that Robespierre was a master of effective oratory adapted for a violent popular audience, to impress, to persuade, and to command. The Convention would have yawned, if it had not

trembled under him, but the Jacobin Club never
found him tedious. Robespierre's style had no
richness either of feeling or of phrase; no fervid
originality, no happy violences. If we turn from a
page of Rousseau to a page of Robespierre, we feel
that the disciple has none of the sonorous thrill
of the master; the ardour has become metallic;
the long-drawn plangency is parodied by shrill
notes of splenetic complaint. Robespierre could
not rival the vivid and highly-coloured declamation of Vergniaud; his speeches were never heated
with the ardent passion that poured like a torrent of
fire through some of the orations of Isnard; nor,
above all, had he any mastery of that dialect of the
Titans, by which Danton convulsed an audience with
fear, with amazement, or with the spirit of defiant
endeavour. The absence of these intenser qualities
did not make Robespierre's speeches less effective
for their own purpose. On the contrary, when the
air has become torrid, and passionate utterance is
cheap, then severity in form is very likely to pass
for sense in substance. That Robespierre had decent
fluency, copiousness, and finish, need hardly be said.
He more than once showed himself ready with a
forcible reply on critical occasions : this only makes
him an illustration the more of the good oratorical
rule, that he is most likely to come well out of the
emergency of an improvisation, who is usually most
careful to prepare. Robespierre was as solicitous
about the correctness of his speech as he was about

the neatness of his clothes ; he no more grudged the pains given to the polishing of his discourses than he grudged the time given every day to the powdering of his hair.

Nothing was more remarkable than his dexterity in presenting his case. James Mill used to point out to his son among other skilful arts of Demosthenes, these two : first, that he said everything important to his purpose at the exact moment when he had brought the minds of his hearers into the state most fitted to receive it ; second, that he insinuated gradually and indirectly into their minds ideas that would have roused opposition if they had been expressed more directly. Mill once called the attention of the present writer to exactly the same kind of rhetorical skill in the speeches of Robespierre. The reader may do well to turn, for excellent specimens of this, to the speech of January 11, 1792, against the war, or that of May 1794 against atheism. The logic is stringent, but the premisses are arbitrary. Robespierre is as one who should iterate indisputable propositions of abstract geometry and mechanics, while men are craving an architect who shall bridge the gulf of waters. Exuberance of high words no longer conceals the sterility of his ideas and the shallowness of his method. We should say of his speeches, as of so much of the speaking and writing of the time, that it is transparent and smooth, but there is none of that quality which the critics of painting call Texture.

His listeners, however, in the old refectory of the Convent of the Jacobins took little heed of these things; the matter was too absorbing, the issue too vital. A hundred years before, the hunted Covenanters of the Western Lowlands, with Claverhouse's dragoons a few miles off, exulted in the endless exhortations and expositions of their hill preachers : they relished nothing so keenly as three hours of Mucklewrath, followed by three hours more of Peter Poundtext. We now find the jargon of the Mucklewraths and the Poundtexts of the Solemn League and Covenant, dead as it is, still not devoid of the picturesque and the impressive. We cannot say the same of the great preacher of the Declaration of the Rights of Man.

We have still to mark the trait that above everything else gave to Robespierre the trust and confidence of Paris. As men listened to him, they had full faith in the integrity of the speaker. And Robespierre in one way deserved this confidence. He was possessor of a conscience. When the strain of circumstance in the last few months of his life pressed him towards wrong, at least before doing wrong he was forced to lie to his own conscience. This is a kind of honesty, as the world goes. In the Salon of 1791 an artist exhibited Robespierre's portrait, simply inscribing it, *The Incorruptible.* Throngs passed before it every day, and ratified the honourable designation by eager murmurs of approval. The democratic journals were loud in panegyric on the unsleeping sentinel of liberty. They loved to speak of him as the modern Fabricius, and delighted to recall the words of Pyrrhus, that it is easier to turn the sun from its course, than to turn Fabricius from the path of honour. Patriotic parents eagerly besought him to be sponsor for their children. Ladies of wealth, including at least one countrywoman of our own, vainly entreated him to accept their purses.

Robespierre's life was frugal and simple, as must always be seemly in the spokesman of the dumb multitude whose lives are hard. He had a single room in the house of Duplay, at the extreme west end of the long rue Saint Honoré, half a mile from the Jacobin Club, and less than that from the Riding School of the Tuileries, where the Constituent and Legislative Assemblies held session. His room, which served him for bed-chamber as well as for the uses of the day, was scantily furnished, and he shared the homely fare of his host. Duplay was a carpenter, a sworn follower of Robespierre, and the whole family cherished their guest as if he had been a son and a brother. Between him and the eldest daughter of the house a more tender sentiment grew up, and Robespierre looked forward to the joys of the hearth, so soon as his country should be delivered from the oppressors without and the traitors within.

Eagerly as Robespierre delighted in his popularity, he intended it to be a force and not a decoration. An occasion of testing his influence arose in the winter of 1791. The situation had become more and more difficult. The court was more disloyal and more perverse, as its hopes became fainter that the nightmare would come to an end. In the summer of 1791, the German Emperor, the King of Prussia, and minor champions of retrograde causes issued the famous Declaration of Pilnitz. The menace of intervention was the one element needed to make the position of the monarchy desperate. It roused France to fever heat. For along with the foreign kings were the French princes of the blood and the French nobles. In the spring of 1792, the Assembly forced the king to declare war against Austria. Robespierre, in spite of the strong tide of warlike feeling, led the Jacobin opposition to the war. This is one of the most sagacious acts of his career, for the hazards of the conflict were terrible. If the foreigners and the emigrant nobles were victorious, all that the Revolution had won would be instantly and irretrievably lost. If, on the other hand, the French armies were victorious, one of two disasters might follow. Either the troops might become a weapon in the hands of the court and the reactionary party, for the suppression of all the progressive parties alike ; or else their general might make himself supreme. Robespierre divined, what the Girondins did not, that Narbonne and the court, in accepting the cry for war, were secretly designing, first, to crush the faction of emigrant nobles, then to make the king popular at home, and thus finally to construct a strong royalist army. The Constitutional party in the Legislative

U

Assembly had the same ideas as Narbonne. The Girondins sought war; first, from a genuine, if not a profoundly wise, enthusiasm for liberty, which they would fain have spread all over the world; and next, because they thought that war would increase their popularity, and give them decisive control of the situation.

The first effect of the war declared in April 1792 was to shake down the throne. Operations had no sooner begun than the king became an object of bitter and amply warranted suspicion. Neither the leaders nor the people had forgotten his flight a year before, to place himself at the head of the foreign invaders, nor the letter that he had left behind him for the National Assembly, protesting against all that had been done. They were again reminded of what short shrift they might expect if the king's friends should come back. The Duke of Brunswick at the head of the foreign army set out on his march, and issued his famous proclamation to the inhabitants of France. He demanded immediate and unconditional sub-mission; he threatened with fire and sword every town, village, or hamlet, that should dare to defend itself; and finally, he swore that if the smallest violence or insult were done to the king or his family, the city of Paris should be handed over to military execution and absolute destruction. This insensate document bears marks in every line of the implacable hate and burning thirst for revenge that consumed the aristocratic refugees. Only civil war can awaken

such rage as Brunswick's manifesto betrayed. It
was drawn up by the French nobles at Coblenz. He
merely signed it. The reply to it was the memorable
insurrection of the Tenth of August 1792. The king
was thrown into prison, and the Legislative Assembly
made way for the National Convention.

Robespierre's part in the great rising of August
was only secondary. A few weeks before he had
started a journal and written articles in a constitutional sense. M. d'Héricault believes a story
that Robespierre's aim in this had been to have himself accepted as tutor for the young dauphin. It is
impossible to prove a negative, but we find great
difficulty in believing that such a post could ever
have been an object of Robespierre's ambition. Now
and always he showed a rather singular preference
for the substance of power over its glitter. He was
vain and an egoist, but in spite of this, and in spite
of his passion for empty phrases, he was not without
a sense of reality.

The insurrection of the Tenth of August, however,
was the idea, not of Robespierre, but of a more commanding personage, who now became one of the
foremost of the Jacobin chiefs. De Maistre, that
ardent champion of reaction, found a striking argument for the presence of the divine hand in the
Revolution, in the intense mediocrity of the revolutionary leaders. How could such men, he asked,
have achieved such results, if they had not been
instruments of the directing will of heaven? Danton

at any rate is above this caustic criticism. Danton was of the Herculean type of a Luther, though without Luther's deep vision of spiritual things; or a Chatham, though without Chatham's august majesty of life; or a Cromwell, though without Cromwell's unshaken steadfastness of patriotic purpose. His visage and port seemed to declare his character: dark overhanging brows; eyes that had the gleam of lightning; a savage mouth; an immense head; the voice of a Stentor. Madame Roland pictured him as a fiercer Sardanapalus. Artists called him Jove the Thunderer. His enemies saw in him the Satan of the *Paradise Lost.* He was no moral regenerator; the difference between him and Robespierre is typified in Danton's version of an old saying, that he who hates vices hates men. He was not free from the careless life-contemning desperation that sometimes belongs to forcible natures. He was too heedless of his good name, and too blind to the truth that, though right and wrong may be near neighbours, yet the line that separates them is of an awful sacredness. If Robespierre passed for a hypocrite by reason of his scruple, Danton seemed a desperado by his airs of ' immoral thoughtlessness.' But the world forgives much to a royal size, and Danton was one of the men who strike deep notes. He had the largeness of motive, fullness of nature, and capaciousness of mind that will always redeem a multitude of infirmities.

Though the author of some of the most tremendous

and far-sounding phrases of an epoch that was only too rich in them, yet phrases had no empire over him ; he was their master, not their dupe. Of all the men who succeeded Mirabeau as directors of the unchained forces, we feel that Danton alone was in his true element. Action, which poisoned the blood of such men as Robespierre, and drove such men as Vergniaud out of their senses with exaltation, was to Danton his native sphere. When France was for a moment discouraged, it was he who nerved her to new effort by the electrifying cry, ' *We must dare, and again dare, and without end dare !* ' If his rivals or his friends seemed too intent on trifles, too apt to confound side-issues with the central aim of the battle, Danton was ever ready to urge them to take a juster measure : ' *When the edifice is all ablaze, I take little heed of the knaves who are pilfering the household goods ; I rush to put out the flames.*' When base egoism was compromising a cause more priceless than the personality of any man, it was Danton who made them ashamed by the inspiring exclamation, ' *Let my name be blotted out and my memory perish, if only France may be free.*' The Girondins denounced the popular clubs of Paris as hives of lawlessness and outrage. Danton warned them that it were wiser to go to these seething societies and to guide them, than to waste breath in futile denunciation. ' A nation in revolution,' he cried to them, in a superb figure, ' is like the bronze boiling and foaming and purifying itself in the cauldron. Not yet is the

statue of Liberty cast. Fiercely boils the metal;
have an eye on the furnace, or the flame will surely
scorch you.' If there was murderous work below
the hatches, that was all the more reason why the
steersman should keep his hand strong and ready
on the wheel, with an eye quick for each new drift in
the hurricane, and each new set in the raging currents.
This is ever the figure under which one conceives
Danton—a Titanic shape doing battle with the fury
of the seas, yielding while flood upon flood sweeps
wildly over him, and then with undaunted front
once more surveying the waste of waters, and striving
with dexterous energy to force the straining vessel
over the waters of the bar.

Lafayette had called the huge giant of popular
force from its squalid lurking-places, and now he
trembled before its presence, and fled from it shrieking, with averted hands. Marat thrust swords into
the giant's half-unwilling grasp, and plied him with
bloody incitement to slay hip and thigh, and so filled
the land with a horror that has not faded from out
of men's minds to this day. Danton instantly discerned that the problem was to preserve revolutionary
energy, and still to persuade the insurgent forces to
retire once more within their boundaries. Robespierre discerned this too, but he was paralysed and
bewildered by his own principles, as the convinced
doctrinaire is so apt to be amid the perplexities of
practice. The teaching of Rousseau was ever pour-
ing like thin smoke among his ideas, and clouding

his view of actual conditions. The Tenth of August produced a considerable change in Robespierre's point of view. It awoke him to the steepness of the slope down which the revolutionary car was rushing headlong. His faith in the infallibility of the people suffered no shock, but he was in a moment alive to the need of walking warily, and his whole march from now until the end, twenty-three months later, became timorous, cunning, and oblique.

The enthusiastic pedant, with his narrow understanding, his thin purism, and his idyllic sentimentalism, found that the summoning archangel of his paradise proved to be a ruffian with a pike. The shock must have been tremendous. Robespierre did not quail nor retreat; he only revised his notion of the situation. A curious interview once took place between him and Marat. Robespierre began by assuring the Friend of the People that he quite understood the atrocious demands for blood with which the columns of Marat's newspaper were filled, to be merely useful exaggerations of his real designs. Marat repelled the disparaging imputation of clemency and common sense, and talked in his familiar vein of poniarding brigands, burning despots alive in their palaces, and impaling the traitors of the Assembly on their own benches. ' Robespierre,' says Marat, ' listened to me with affright; he turned pale and said nothing. The interview confirmed the opinion I had always had of him, that he united the integrity of a thoroughly honest man and the zeal of a good

patriot, with the enlightenment of a wise senator,
but that he was without either the views or the
audacity of a real statesman.' The picture is instructive, for it shows us Robespierre's invariable
habit of leaving violence and iniquity unrebuked ; of
conciliating the practitioners of violence and iniquity ;
and of contenting himself with an inward hope of
turning the world into a right course by fine words.
He had no audacity in Marat's sense, but he was no
coward. He knew, as all these men knew, that
almost from hour to hour he carried his life in his
hand, yet he declined to seek shelter in the obscurity
that saved such men as Sieyès. But if he had
courage, he had not the initiative of a man of action.
He invented none of the ideas or methods of the
Revolution, not even the Reign of Terror, but he
was very dexterous in accepting or appropriating what
more audacious spirits than himself had devised and
enforced. The pedant, cursed with the ambition to
be a ruler of men, is a curious study. He would be
glad not to go too far, and yet his chief dread is lest
he be left behind. His consciousness of pure aims
allows him to become an accomplice in the worst
crimes. Suspecting himself at bottom to be a
theorist, he hastens to clear his character as man
of practice by conniving at an enormity. Thus, in
September 1792, a band of miscreants committed the
atrocious massacres in the prisons of Paris. Robespierre, though the best evidence goes to show that
he not only did not abet the prison murders, but in

his heart deplored them, yet after the event did not scruple to justify what had been done. This was the beginning of a long course of compliance with sanguinary misdeeds, for which Robespierre has been as hotly execrated as if he prompted them. We are not measuring the relative degrees of guilt that attached to mere compliance on the one hand, and cruel origination on the other. But his position in the Revolution is not rightly understood, unless we recognise him as being in almost every case an accessory after the fact.

Between the fall of Louis in 1792 and the fall of Robespierre in 1794, France was the scene of two main series of events. One set comprises the repulse of the invaders, the suppression of an extensive civil war, and the attempted reconstruction of a social framework. The other comprises the rapid phases of an internecine struggle of violent and short-lived factions. By an unhappy fatality, due partly to anti-democratic prejudice, and partly to men's unfailing passion for melodrama, the Reign of Terror has been popularly taken for the central and most important part of the revolutionary epic. This is nearly as absurd as it would be to make Gustave Flourens' manifestation of the Fifth of October, or the rising of the Thirty-first of October, the most prominent features in a history of the war of French defence in a later day. In truth, the Terror was a mere episode ; and just as the rising of October 1870 was due to Marshal Bazaine's capitulation at Metz, it is easy to see that, with one exception, every violent movement in Paris, from 1792 to 1794, was due to menace or disaster on the frontier. Every one of the famous days of Paris was an answer to some enemy without. The storm of the Tuileries on the Tenth of August, as we have already said, was the response to Brunswick's proclamation. The bloody days of September were the reaction of panic at the capture of Longwy and Verdun by the Prussians. The surrender of Cambrai provoked the execution of Marie Antoinette. The defeat of Aix-la-Chapelle produced the abortive insurrection of the Tenth of March; and the treason of Dumouriez, the reverses of Custine, and the rebellion in La Vendée, produced the effectual insurrection of the Thirty-first of May 1793. The last of these two risings of Paris, headed by the Commune, against the Convention that was until then controlled by the Girondins, at length gave the government of France and the defence of the Revolution definitely over to the Jacobins. Their patriotic dictatorship lasted unbroken for a short period of ten months, and then the great party broke up into factions. The splendid triumphs of the dictatorship have been, in England at any rate, too usually forgotten, and only the crimes of the factions remembered. Robespierre's history belongs to the less important battle.

II.

The Girondins were driven out of the Convention by the insurgent Parisians at the beginning of June 1793. The movement may be roughly compared to that of the Independents in our own Rebellion, when the army compelled the withdrawal of eleven of the Presbyterian leaders from the parliament; or it may recall Pride's memorable Purge of the same famous assembly. Both cases illustrate the common truth that large deliberative bodies, be they never so excellent for purposes of legislation, and even for a general control of the executive government in ordinary times, are found to be essentially unfit for directing a military crisis. If there are any historic examples that at first seem to contradict such a proposition, it will be found that the bodies in question were close aristocracies, like the Great Council of Venice, or the Senate of Rome in the strong days of the Commonwealth; they were never the creatures of popular election, with varying aims and a diversified political spirit. Modern publicists have substituted the divine right of assemblies for the old divine right of monarchies. Those who condone the violence done to the king on the Tenth of August, and even acquiesce in his execution five months afterwards, are relentless against the violence done to the Convention on the Thirty-first of May. It is hard to follow this transfer of the superstition of sacrosanctity from a king to a chamber. No doubt, the sooner a nation acquires a settled government, the better for it, provided the government be efficient. But if it be not efficient, the mischief of actively suppressing it may well be fully outweighed by the mischief of retaining it. We have no wish to smooth over the perversities of a revolutionary time; they cost a nation very dear; but if all the elements of the state are in furious convulsion and uncontrollable effervescence, then it is childish to measure the march of events by the standard of happier days of social peace and political order. The prospect before France at the violent close of Girondin supremacy was as formidable as any nation has ever yet had to confront in the history of the world. Rome was not more critically placed when the defeat of Varro on the plain of Cannæ had broken up her alliances and ruined her army. The brave patriots of the Netherlands had no gloomier outlook at that moment when the Prince of Orange had left them, and Alva had been appointed to bring them back by rapine, conflagration, and murder, under the loathed yoke of the Spanish tyrant.

Let us realise the conditions Robespierre and Danton and the other Jacobin leaders had now to face. In the north-west one division of the fugitive Girondins was forming an army at Caen; in the south-west another division was doing the same at Bordeaux. Marseilles and Lyons were rallying all the disaffected and reactionary elements in the south-east. La Vendée had flamed out in wild rebellion for Church and King. The strong places on the north frontier, and the strong places on the east, were in the hands of the foreign enemy. The fate of the Revolution lay in the issue of a struggle between Paris, with less than a score of departments on her side, and all the rest of France and the whole European coalition marshalled against her. And even this was not the worst. In Paris itself a very considerable proportion of its half-million of inhabitants were disaffected to the revolutionary cause. Reactionary historians dwell on the fact that such risings as that of the Tenth of August were devised by no more than half of the sections into which Paris was divided. It was common, they say, for half a dozen individuals to take upon themselves to represent the fourteen or fifteen hundred other members of a section. But what better proof can we have that if France was to be delivered from restored feudalism and foreign spoliation, the momentous task must be performed by those who had sense to discern the awful peril, and energy to encounter it?

The Girondins had made their incapacity plain. The execution of the king had filled them with alarm, and with hatred against the ruder and more robust party who had forced that startling act of vengeance upon them. Puny social disgusts prevented them from co-operating with Danton or with Robespierre. Prussia and Austria were not more redoubtable or more hateful to them than was Paris, and they wasted, in futile recriminations about the September massacres or the alleged peculations of municipal officers, the time and the energy that should have been devoted without let or interruption to the settlement of the administration and the repulse of the foe. It is impossible to think of such fine characters as Vergniaud or Madame Roland without admiration, or of their untimely fate without pity. But the deliverance of a people beset by strong and implacable enemies could not wait on good manners and fastidious sentiments, when these comely things were in company with the most stupendous want of foresight ever shown by a political party. How can we measure the folly of men who so missed the conditions of the problem as to cry out in the Convention itself, almost within earshot of the Jacobin Club, that if any insult were offered to the national representation, the departments would rise, ' Paris would be annihilated ; and men would come to search on the banks of the Seine whether such a city had ever existed ! ' ?   It was to no purpose that Danton urgently rebuked the senseless animosity with which the Right poured incessant malediction on the Left, and the wild shrieking hate with which the Left retaliated on the Right.   The battle was to the death, and it was the Girondins who first menaced their political foes with vengeance and the guillotine.   As it happened, the treason of Dumouriez and their own ineptitude destroyed them before revenge was within reach. Such a consummation was fortunate for their country. It was the Girondins whose want of union and energy

had by the middle of 1793 brought France to dis-
traction and imminent ruin. It was a short year of
Jacobin government that by the summer of 1794
had welded the nation together again, and finally
conquered the invasion. The city of the Seine had
once more shown itself what it had been for nine
centuries, ever since the days of Odo, Count of Paris
and first King of the French, not merely a capital,
but France itself, ' its living heart and surest bulwark.'

The immediate instrument of so rapid and extraordinary an achievement was the Committee of
Public Safety. The French have never shown their
quick genius for organisation with more triumphant
vigour. While the Girondins were still powerful,
nine members of the Convention had been constituted
an executive committee, April 6, 1793. They were
in fact a kind of permanent cabinet, with practical
irresponsibility. In the summer of 1793 the number
was increased from nine to twelve, and these twelve
were the centre of the revolutionary government.
They fell into three groups. First, there were the
scientific or practical administrators, of whom the
most eminent was Carnot. Next came the directors
of internal policy, the pure revolutionists, headed by
Billaud-Varennes. Finally, there was a trio whose
business it was to translate action into the phrases of
revolutionary policy. This famous group was Robespierre, Couthon, and Saint-Just.

Besides the Committee of Public Safety there was
another chief governmental committee, that of

General Security. Its functions were mainly connected with the police, the arrests, and the prisons, but in all serious affairs the two Committees deliberated in common. There were also fourteen other groups of various size, taken from the Convention; they applied themselves with admirable zeal, and usually not with more zeal than skill, to schemes of public instruction, of finance, of legislation, of the administration of justice, and a host of other civil reforms, of all of which Napoleon was by and by to reap the credit. These bodies completed the civil revolution, which the Constituent and the Legislative Assemblies had left so mischievously incomplete that, as soon as ever the Convention had assembled, it was besieged by a host of petitioners praying them to explain and to pursue the abolition of the old feudal rights. Everything had still been left uncertain in men's minds, even upon that greatest of all the revolutionary questions. The feudal division of the committee of general legislation had in this eleventh hour to decide innumerable issues, from those of the widest practical importance, down to the prayer of a remote commune to be relieved from the charge of maintaining a certain mortuary lamp that had been a matter of seignorial obligation. The work done by the radical jurisconsults was never undone. It was the great and durable reward of the struggle. And we have to remember that these industrious and efficient bodies, as well as all other public bodies and functionaries whatever, were placed

by the definite revolutionary constitution of 1793
under the direct orders of the Committee of Public
Safety.

It is hardly possible even now for any one who
exults in the memory of the great deliverance of a
brilliant and sociable people, to stand unmoved before
the walls of the palace which Philibert Delorme
reared for Catherine de' Medici, and which was thrown
into ruin by the madness of a band of desperate men
in 1871. Louis had walked forth from the Tuileries
on the fatal morning of the Tenth of August, holding
his children by the hand, and lightly noticing, as he
traversed the gardens, how early that year the leaves
were falling. He had by this time followed the fallen
leaves into nothingness. The palace of the kings
was now styled the Palace of the Nation, and the
new Republic carried on its work surrounded by the
outward associations of the old monarchy. The
Convention after the spring of 1793 held its sittings
in what had formerly been the palace theatre. Fierce
men from the Faubourgs of St. Antoine and St.
Marceau, and fiercer women from the markets, shouted
savage applause or menace from galleries where not
so long ago the Italian buffoons had amused the
perpetual leisure of the finest ladies and proudest
grandees of France. The Committee of General
Security occupied the Pavillon de Marsan, looking
over a dingy space that the conqueror at Rivoli afterwards made the most dazzling street in Europe. The

Committee of Public Safety sat in the Pavillon de
Flore, at the opposite end of the Tuileries on the river
bank. The approaches were protected by guns and
by a bodyguard, while inside there flitted to and fro
a cloud of familiars, who have been compared by the
enemies of the Great Committee to the mutes of the
court of the Grand Turk. Any one who had business
with this awful body had to grope his way along
gloomy corridors, that were dimly lighted by a single
lamp at either end. The room in which the Committee sat round a table of green cloth, was incon-
gruously gay with the clocks, the bronzes, the mirrors,
the tapestries, of the ruined court. The members
met at eight in the morning and worked until one;
from one to four they attended the sitting of the
Convention. In the evening they met again, and
usually sat until night was far advanced. It was
no wonder if their hue became cadaverous, their
eyes hollow and bloodshot, their brows stern, their
glance preoccupied and sinister. Between ten and
eleven every evening a sombre piece of business was
transacted, that has half effaced in the memory
of posterity all the heroic industry of the rest of the
twenty-four hours. It was then that Fouquier-
Tinville, the public prosecutor, brought an account
of his day's labour; how the Revolutionary Tribunal
was working, how many had been convicted and how
many acquitted, how large or how small had been the
batch of the guillotine since the previous night.
Across the breadth of the gardens, beyond their

trees and fountains, stood the Monster itself, with
its cruel symmetry, its colour as of the blood of the
dead, its unheeding knife, neutral as the Fates.

Robespierre has been held responsible for all the
violences of the revolutionary government, and his
position on the Committee appeared to be exceedingly
strong. It was, however, for a long time much less
strong in reality than it seemed : all depended upon
successfully playing off one force against another, and
at the same time maintaining himself at the centre
of the see-saw. Robespierre was the literary and
rhetorical member of the band ; he was the author
of the strident manifestoes in which Europe listened
with exasperation to the audacious hopes and un-
faltering purpose of the new France. This had the
effect of investing him in the eyes of foreign nations
with supreme and undisputed authority over the
government. The truth is, that Robespierre was
both disliked and despised by his colleagues. They
thought of him as a mere maker of useful phrases ;
he in turn secretly looked down upon them, as the
man who has a doctrine and a system in his head
always looks down upon the man who lives from hand
to mouth. If the Committee had been in the place
of a government that has no opposition to fear,
Robespierre would have been one of its least powerful
members. But although the government was strong,
there were at least three potent elements of opposition
even within the ranks of the dominant revolutionary
party itself.

Three bodies in Paris were, each of them, the centre of an influence that might at any moment become the triumphant rival of the Committee of Public Safety. These bodies were the Convention, the Commune of Paris, and the Jacobin Club. The jealousy thus existing outside the Committee would have made any failure instantly destructive. At one moment, at the end of 1793, it was only the surrender of Toulon that saved the Committee from a hostile motion in the Convention, and such a motion would have sent half of them to the guillotine. They were reviled by the extreme party who ruled at the Town Hall for not carrying the policy of extermination far enough. They were reproached by Danton and his powerful section for carrying that policy too far. They were discredited by the small band of intriguers, like Bazire, who identified government with peculation. Finally, they were haunted by the shadow of a fear, which events were by and by to prove only too substantial, lest one of their military agents on the frontier should make himself their master. The key to the struggle of the factions between the winter of 1793 and the revolution of the summer of 1794 is the vigorous resolve of the governing Committees not to part with power. The drama is one of the most exciting in the history of faction; it abounds in rapid turns and unexpected shifts upon which the student may spend many a day and many a night, and after all he is forced to leave off in despair of threading an accurate way through the labyrinth of passion and intrigue. The broad traits of the situation, however, are tolerably simple. The difficulty was to find a principle of government that the people could be induced to accept. ' The rights of men and the new principles of liberty and equality,' Burke said, ' were very unhandy instruments for those who wished to establish a system of tranquillity and order. The factions,' he added with fierce sarcasm, ' were to accomplish the purposes of order, morality, and submission to the laws, from the principles of atheism, profligacy, and sedition. They endeavoured to establish distinctions, by the belief of which they hoped to keep the spirit of murder safely bottled up and sealed for their own purposes, without endangering themselves by the fumes of the poison which they prepared for their enemies.' This ferocious and passionate version is substantially no unreal account of the position.

Upon one point all parties agreed, and that was the necessity of founding the government upon force, and force naturally meant Terror. Their plea was that of Dido to Ilioneus and the storm-beaten sons of Dardanus, when they complained that her people had drawn the sword upon them, and barbarously denied the hospitality of the sandy shore :—

> Res dura et regni novitas me talia cogunt
> Moliri.

And the pithy chapter in Machiavelli's *Prince* that treats of cruelty and clemency, and whether it be better to be loved or feared, anticipates the defence of the Terrorists, in the maxim that for a new prince it is impossible to avoid the name of cruel, because all new states abound in many perils. The difference arose on the question when Terror should be considered to have done as much of its work as it could be expected to do. This difference again was connected with difference of conception as to the type of the society that was ultimately to emerge from the existing chaos. Billaud-Varennes, the guiding spirit of the Committees, was without any conception of this kind. He was a man of force pure and simple. Danton was equally untouched by dreams of social transformation; his philosophy, so far as he had one, was, in spite of one or two inconsistent utterances, materialistic: and materialism, when it takes root in a sane, perspicacious, and indulgent character, as in the case of Danton, and, to take a better-known example, in the case of Jefferson, usually leads to a sound and positive theory of politics; chimeras have no place in it, though a rational social hope has the first place of all. Neither Danton nor Billaud expected a millennium; their only aim was to shape France into a coherent political personality, and the war between them turned upon the policy of prolonging the Terror after the frontiers had been saved and the risings in the provinces put down. There were, however, two parties who took the literature of the century in earnest; they thought that the hour had struck for translating, one of them, the sentimentalism of Rousseau, the other of them, the rationalism of Voltaire and Diderot, into terms of politics that should form the basis of a new social life. The strife between the faction of Robespierre and the faction of Chaumette was the reproduction, under the shadow of the guillotine, of the deep literary strife of a quarter of a century before, between Jean Jacques and the writers whom he contemptuously styled Holbachians. The battle of the books had become a battle between bands of infuriated men. The struggle between Hébert and Chaumette and the Common Council of Paris on the one part, and the Committee and Robespierre on the other, was the concrete form of the deepest controversy that lies before modern society. Can the social union subsist without a belief in a Supreme Being ? Chaumette answered Yes, and Robespierre cried No. Robespierre followed Rousseau in thinking that any one who should refuse to recognise the existence of a God, should be exiled as a monster devoid of the faculties of virtue and sociability. Chaumette followed Diderot, and Diderot told Samuel Romilly in 1783 that belief in God, as well as submission to kings, would be at an end all over the world in a very few years. The theists and the atheists, Chaumette and Robespierre, each of them accepted the doctrine that it was in the power of the armed legislator to impose any belief and any rites he pleased upon the country at his feet. Theism or atheism depended, as they thought, on the issue of the war for authority between the Hébertists in the Common Council of Paris, and the Committee of

Public Safety. That was the religious side of the
attitude of the government to the opposition, and
it is the side that possesses most historic interest.
Billaud cared very little for religion in any way ; his
quarrel with the Commune and with Hébert was
political. What Robespierre's drift appears to have
been, was to use the political animosity of the
Committee as a means of striking foes against
whom his own animosity was both political and
religious.

It would doubtless show a very dull apprehension
of the violence and confusion of the time to suppose
that even Robespierre, with all his love for concise
theories, was accustomed to state his aim to himself
with the definite neatness in which it appears when
reduced to literary statement. Pedant as he was, he
was yet enough of a politician to see the practical
urgency of restoring material order, whatever spiritual
belief or disbelief might accompany it. The prospect
of a rallying point for material order was incessantly
changing, and Robespierre turned to different quarters
in search of it almost from week to week. He was
only able to exert a certain limited authority over his
colleagues in the government, by virtue of his influence
over the various sections of possible opposition, and
this was a moral, and not an official, influence. It
was acquired not by marked practical gifts, for in
truth Robespierre did not possess them, but by his
good character, by his rhetoric, and by the skill with
which he kept himself prominently before the public

eye. The effective seat of his power, notwithstanding many limits and incessant variations, was the Jacobin Club. There a speech from him threw his listeners into ecstasies that have been disrespectfully compared to the paroxysms of Jansenist convulsionaries, or the hysterics of Methodist negroes on a cotton plantation. We naturally think of those grave men who a few years before had founded the Republic in America. Jefferson served with Washington in the Virginian legislature and with Franklin in Congress, and he afterwards said that he never heard either of them speak ten minutes at a time; while John Adams declared that he never heard Jefferson utter three sentences together. Of Robespierre it is stated on good authority that for eighteen months there was not a single evening on which he did not make to the assembled Jacobins at least one speech, and that never a short one.

Strange as it may seem, Robespierre's credit with this grim assemblage was due to his truly Philistine respectability and his literary faculty. He figured as the philosopher and bookman of the party : the most iconoclastic politicians are usually willing to respect the scholar, provided they are sure of his being on their side. Robespierre had from the first discountenanced the fantastic caprices of some too excitable allies. He distrusted the noisy patriots of the middle class, who curried favour with the crowd by clothing themselves in coarse garments, clutching a pike, and donning the famous cap of red woollen

that had been the emblem of the emancipation of a
slave in ancient Rome. One night at the Jacobin
Club, Robespierre mounted the tribune, dressed with
his usual elaborate neatness, and still wearing powder
in his hair. An onlooker unceremoniously planted
on the orator's head the red cap demanded by revolutionary etiquette. Robespierre threw the sacred
symbol on the ground with a severe air, and then
proceeded with a discourse of much austerity. Not
that he was averse to a certain seemly decoration, or
to the embodiment of revolutionary sentiment by
means of a symbolism that strikes our cooler imagination as puerile. He was as ready as others to use
the arts of the theatre for the liturgy of patriots.
One of the most touching of all the minor dramatic
incidents of the Revolution was the death of Barra.
This was a child of thirteen who enrolled himself as
a drummer, and marched with the Blues to suppress
the rebel Whites in La Vendée. One day he advanced
too close to the enemy's post, intrepidly beating the
charge. He was surrounded, but the peasant soldiers
were loth to strike. ' Cry *Long live the King !* ' they
shouted, ' or else death ! ' ' Long live the Republic ! '
was the poor little hero's answer, as a ball pierced his
heart. Robespierre described the incident to the
Convention, and amid prodigious enthusiasm demanded that the body of the young martyr of liberty
should be transported to the Pantheon with special
pomp, and that David, the artist of the Revolution,
should be charged with the duty of devising and

embellishing the festival. As it came to pass, the arrangements were made for the ceremony to take place on the Tenth of Thermidor—a day on which Robespierre and all Paris were concerned about a celebration of bloodier import. Thermidor, however, was still far off; and the red sun of Jacobin enthusiasm seemed as if it would shine unclouded for ever.

Even at the Jacobins, however, popular as he was, Robespierre felt every instant the necessity of walking cautiously. He was as far removed as possible from the position of Dictator that some historians persist in ascribing to him, even at the moment when they are enumerating the defeats which the party of Hébert was able to inflict upon him in the very bosom of the Mother Club itself. They make him the sanguinary dictator in one sentence, and the humiliated intriguer in the next. The latter is much the more correct account of the two, if we choose to call a man an intriguer who was honestly anxious to suppress what he considered a wicked faction, and yet had need of some dexterity to keep his own head upon his shoulders.

In the winter of 1793 the Municipal party, guided by Hébert and Chaumette, made their memorable attempt to extirpate Christianity in France. The doctrine of D'Holbach's supper-table had for a short space the arm of flesh and the sword of the temporal power on its side. It was the first appearance of dogmatic atheism in Europe as a militant political force. This makes it one of the most remarkable moments in the Revolution, just as it makes the Revolution itself the most remarkable moment in modern history. On the whole it is a very mild story compared with the atrocities of the Jewish records or the crimes of Catholicism. The worst charge against the party of Chaumette is that they were intolerant, but this charge cannot lie in the mouth of persecuting churches.

Historical recriminations, however, are not very edifying. It is perfectly fair, when Catholics talk of the atheist Terror, to rejoin that the retainers of Anjou and Montpensier slew more men and women on the first day of the Saint Bartholomew than perished in Paris through the Years I. and II. But the retort does us no good beyond the region of dialectic; it rather brings us down to the level of the sectaries whom it crushes. Opinions are less important than the spirit and temper with which they possess us, and even good opinions are worth little unless we hold them in a broad, intelligent, and spacious way. Now some of the opinions of Chaumette were full of enlightenment and hope. He had a generous and vivid faith in humanity, and he showed the natural effect of abandoning belief in another life by his energetic interest in arrangements for improving the lot of man in this life. But it would be far better to share the opinions of a virtuous and benignant priest like the Bishop in Victor Hugo's *Misérables*, than to hold those opinions of Chaumette as he held them, with a rancorous intolerance, a reckless disregard of the rights and feelings of others, and a shallow forgetfulness of all that great and precious part of our natures that lies out of the immediate domain of the logical understanding. One can understand how an honest man would abhor the darkness and tyranny of the church. But then to borrow the same absolutism in the interests of new light, was inevitably to bring the new light into the same abhorrence as had befallen the old system of darkness. And this is exactly what happened. In every family where a mother sought to have her child baptized, or where sons and daughters sought to have the dying spirit of the old consoled by the last sacrament, there sprang up a bitter enemy to the government that had closed the churches and proscribed the priests.

How could a society whose spiritual life had been nourished in the solemn mysticism of the Middle Ages, suddenly turn to embrace a gaudy paganism ? The common self-respect of humanity was outraged by apostate priests who, whether under the pressure of fear of Chaumette, or in a very superfluity of folly, hastened to proclaim the charlatanry of their past lives, as they filed before the Convention, led by the Archbishop of Paris, and accompanied by rude acolytes bearing piles of the robes and the vessels of silver and gold with which they had once served their holy offices. ' Our enemies,' Voltaire had said, 'have always on their side the fat of the land, the sword, the strong-box, and the *canaille*.' For a moment all these forces were on the other side.

Instead of defying the church by the theatrical march of the Goddess of Reason under the great sombre arches of Notre Dame, Chaumette should have found comfort in a firm calculation of the conditions. 'You,' he might have said to the priests,— 'you have so debilitated the minds of men and women by your promises and your dreams, that many a generation must come and go before Europe can throw off the yoke. We give you all the advantages that you can get from the sincerity and worth of the good and simple among you. We give you all that the bad among you may get by resort to your system,—its bribes to mental indolence, its hypocritical affectations in the pulpit, its tyranny in the closet, its false speciousness in the world, its menace at the deathbed. We will not attack you as Voltaire did; we shall explain you. History will place your dogma in its class; from being the guide to millions of human lives, it will become a chapter in a book. As History explains your dogma, so Science will dry it up; the conception of law will silently make the conception of the daily miracle seem impossible; the mental climate will gradually deprive your symbols of their nourishment, and men will turn their backs on you, not because they have confuted you, but because, like witchcraft or astrology, you have ceased to interest them.'

Alas, the speculation of the century had not rightly attuned men's minds to this firm confidence in the virtue of liberty, sounding like a bell through all distractions. None of these high things were said. The temples were closed, the sacred symbols defiled, the priests maltreated, the worshippers dispersed. The Commune of Paris imitated the policy of the King of France who revoked the Edict of Nantes, and democratic atheism parodied the dragonnades of absolutist Catholicism.

Robespierre was unutterably outraged by the proceedings of the atheists. They perplexed him as a politician intent upon order, and they afflicted him sorely as an ardent disciple of the Savoyard Vicar. Hébert, however, was so strong that it needed some courage to attack him, nor did Robespierre dare to withstand him to the face. But he did not flinch from making an energetic assault upon atheism and the excesses of its partisans. His admirers usually count his speech of the Twenty-first of November one of the most admirable of his oratorical successes. The Sphinx still sits inexorable at our gates, and his words have lost none of their interest. ' Every philosopher and every individual,' he said, ' may adopt whatever opinion he pleases about atheism. Any one who wishes to make such an opinion into a crime is an insensate ; but the public man or the legislator who should adopt such a system, would be a hundred times more insensate still. The National

Convention abhors it. The Convention is not the author of a scheme of metaphysics. It was not to no purpose that it published the Declaration of the Rights of Man in presence of the Supreme Being. I shall be told perhaps that I have a narrow intelligence, that I am a man of prejudice, and a fanatic. I have already said that I spoke neither as an individual nor as a philosopher with a system, but as a representative of the people. *Atheism is aristocratic. The idea of a great Being who watches over oppressed innocence and punishes triumphant crime is essentially the idea of the people.* This is the sentiment of Europe and the Universe; it is the sentiment of the French nation. That nation is attached neither to priests, nor to superstition, nor to ceremonies; it is attached only to worship in itself, or in other words to the idea of an incomprehensible Power, the terror of wrong-doers, the stay and comfort of virtue, to which it delights to render words of homage that are all so many anathemas against injustice and triumphant crime.'

This is Robespierre's favourite attitude, the priest posing as statesman. Like others, he declares the Supreme Power incomprehensible, and then describes him in terms of familiar comprehension. He first declares atheism an open choice, and then he brands it with the most odious epithet in the accepted vocabulary of the hour. Danton followed practically the same line, though saying much less about it. ' If Greece,' he said in the Convention, ' had its Olympian

games, France too shall solemnise her sans-culottid
days. The people will have high festivals; they
will offer incense to the Supreme Being, to the master
of nature; for we never intended to annihilate the
reign of superstition in order to set up the reign of
atheism. . . . If we have not honoured the priest of
error and fanaticism, neither do we wish to honour
the priest of incredulity: we wish to serve the people.
I demand that there shall be an end of these anti-
religious masquerades in the Convention.'

There was an end of the masquerading, but the
Hébertists still kept their ground. Danton, Robespierre, and the Committee were all equally impotent
against them for some months longer. The revolutionary force had been too strong to be resisted by
any government since the Paris insurgents had carried
both king and Assembly in triumph from Versailles
in the October of 1789. It was now too strong for
those who had begun to strive with all their might to
build a new government out of the agencies that had
shattered the old. For some months the battle that
had been opened by Robespierre's remonstrance
against atheistic intolerance, degenerated into a series
of masked skirmishes. The battle-ground of rival
principles was overshadowed by the baleful wings of
the genius of demonic Hate. *Vexilla regis prodeunt
inferni*; the banners of the King of the Pit came
forth. The scene at the Cordeliers for a time became
as frantic as a Council of the Early Church settling
the true composition of the Holy Trinity. Or it

Y

recalls the fierce and bloody contentions between
Demos and Oligarchy in an old Greek town. We
think of the day in the harbour of Corcyra when the
Athenian admiral who had come to deliver the people,
sailed out to meet the Spartan enemy, and on turning
round to see if his Corcyrean allies were following,
saw them following indeed, but the crew of every
ship striving in enraged conflict with one another.
Collot d'Herbois had come back in hot haste from
Lyons, where, along with Fouché, he had done his
best to carry out the decree of the Convention, that
not one stone of the city should be left on the top of
another, and that even its very name should cease
from the lips of men. Carrier was recalled from
Nantes, where his feats of ingenious massacre had
rivalled the exploits of the cruellest and maddest of
the Roman Emperors. The presence of these men
of blood gave new courage and resolution to the
Hébertists. Though the alliance was informal, yet
as against Danton, Camille Desmoulins, and the rest
of the Indulgents, as well as against Robespierre,
they made common cause.

Camille Desmoulins attacked Hébert in successive
numbers of a journal that is perhaps the one truly
literary monument of this stage of the Revolution.
Hébert retaliated by impugning the patriotism of
Desmoulins in the Club, and the unfortunate wit,
notwithstanding the efforts of Robespierre on his
behalf, was for a while turned out of the sacred
precincts. The power of the extreme faction was

shown in relation to other prominent members of the party whom they loved to stigmatise by the deadly names of Indulgent and Moderantist. Even Danton himself was attacked (December 1793), and the integrity of his patriotism brought into question. Robespierre made an energetic defence of his great rival in the hierarchy of revolution, and the defence saved Danton from the mortal ignominy of expulsion from the communion of the orthodox. On the other hand, Anacharsis Clootz, that guileless ally of the party of delirium, was less fortunate. Robespierre assailed the cosmopolitan for being a German baron, for having four thousand pounds a year, and for striking his sans-culottism some notes higher than the regular pitch. Even M. Louis Blanc calls this an iniquity, and sets it down as the worst page in Robespierre's life. Others have described Robespierre as struck at this time by the dire malady of kings—hatred of the Idea. It seems, however, a hard saying that devotion to the Idea is to extinguish common sense. Clootz, notwithstanding his simple and disinterested character, and his possession of some rays of the modern illumination, was one of the least sane of all the men who in the exultation of their foolish gladness were suddenly caught up by that great wheel of fire. All we can say is that Robespierre's bitter demeanour towards Clootz was ungenerous ; but then this is only natural in him. Robespierre often clothed cool policy in the semblance of clemency, but I cannot hear in any phrase he ever used, or see in any measure he ever proposed, the mark of true generosity ; of kingliness of spirit, not a trace. He had no element of ready and cordial propitiation, an element that can never be wanting in the greatest leaders in time of storm. If he resisted the atrocious proposals to put Madame Elizabeth to death, he was thinking not of mercy or justice, but of the mischievous effect that her execution would have upon the public opinion of Europe.

This did not prevent him from seeing and denouncing the bloody extravagances of the Proconsuls, the representatives of Parisian authority in the provinces ; nor from standing firm against the execution of the Seventy-Three, who had been bold enough to question the purgation of the National Convention on the Thirty-first of May. But the return of Collot d'Herbois made the situation more intricate. Collot was by his position the ally of Billaud, and to attack him, therefore, was to attack the most powerful member of the Committee of Public Safety. Billaud was too formidable. He was always the impersonation of the ruder genius of the Revolution, and the incarnation of the philosophy of the Terror, not as a delirium, but as a piece of deliberate policy. His pale, sober, and concentrated physiognomy seemed a perpetual menace. He had no gifts of speech, but his silence made people shudder.

Robespierre began to suspect that he had been premature ; and a convenient illness, which some suppose to have been feigned, excused his withdrawal for some weeks from a scene where he felt that he could no longer see clear. We cannot doubt that both he and Danton were perfectly assured that the anarchic party must unavoidably roll headlong into the abyss. But the hour of doom was uncertain. To make a mistake as to the right moment, to hurry the crisis, was instant death. Robespierre was a more adroit calculator than Danton. But his habit of waiting on force, instead of, like the other, taking the initiative with force, had trained his sight. The mixture of astuteness with his scruple, of egoistic policy with his stiffness for doctrine, gave him an advantage over Danton, that made his life worth exactly three months' more purchase than Danton's. It has been said that Spinozism or Transcendentalism in poetic production becomes Machiavellism in reflection : for the same reasons we may always expect sentimentalism in theory to become under the pressure of action a very self-protecting guile. Robespierre's mind was not rich nor flexible enough for true statesmanship, and it is a grave mistake to suppose that the various cunning tacks in which his career abounds, were any sign of genuine versatility or resource or political growth and expansion. They were, in fact, the resort of a man whose nerves were weaker than his volition. Force of head did not match Robespierre's spiritual ambition. He was not, we repeat, a coward in any common sense ; in that case he would have remained quiet among the croaking frogs of the Marsh, and by and by have

come to hold a portfolio under the first Consul. He
did not fear death, and he envied with consuming
envy those to whom nature had given the qualities
of initiative. But his nerves played him false.
The consciousness of having to resolve to take
a decided step alone, was the precursor of a fit of
trembling. His heart did not fail, but he could not
control the parched voice, nor the twitching features,
nor the palsy of inner misgiving. In this respect
Robespierre recalls a more illustrious man ; we think
of Cicero calling upon the Senate to decide for him
whether he should order the execution of the Cati-
linarian conspirators. It is to be said, however, in
his favour that he had the art, which Cicero lacked,
to hide his pusillanimity. Robespierre knew himself,
and did his best to keep his own secret

His absence during the final crisis ot the anarchic
party allowed events to ripen, without committing
him to the initiative in dangerous action that he
had dreaded on the Tenth of August, as he dreaded
it on every other decisive day of this burning time.
The party of the Commune became more and more
daring in their invectives against the Convention and
the Committees. At length they proclaimed open
insurrection. But Paris was cold, and opinion was
divided. In the night of the Thirteenth of March,
Hébert, Chaumette, Clootz were arrested. The next
day Robespierre recovered sufficiently to appear at
the Jacobin Club. He joined his colleagues of the
Committee of Public Safety in striking the blow.

On the Twenty-fourth of March the Ultra-Revolutionist leaders were beheaded.

This first bloody breach in the Jacobin ranks was speedily followed by the second. The Right wing of the opposition to the Committee soon followed the Left down the ways to dusty death, and the execution of the Anarchists only preceded by a week the arrest of the Moderates. When the seizure of Danton had once before been discussed in the Committee, Robespierre resisted the proposal violently. We have already seen how he defended Danton at the Jacobin Club, when the Club underwent the process of purification in the winter. What produced this sudden tack? How came Robespierre to assent in March to a violence he had angrily discountenanced in February? There had been no change in the policy or attitude of Danton himself. The military operations against the domestic and foreign enemies were no sooner fairly in the way of success, than Danton began to meditate in serious earnest the consolidation of a republican system of law and justice. He would fain have stayed the Terror. ' Let us leave something,' he said, ' to the guillotine of opinion.' He aided, no doubt, in the formation of the Revolutionary Tribunal, but this was exactly in harmony with his usual policy of controlling popular violence without alienating the strength of popular sympathy. The process of the tribunal was rough and summary, but it was fairer—until Robespierre's Law of Prairial—than people usually suppose, and it was the very temple of the goddess of Justice herself compared with the September massacres. ' Let us prove ourselves terrible,' Danton said, ' to relieve the people from the necessity of being so.' His activity had been incessant in urging and superintending the great levies against the foreigner; he had gone repeatedly on distant and harassing expeditions, as the representative of the Convention at the camps on the frontier. In the midst of all this he found time to press forward measures for the instruction of the young, and for the due appointment of judges, and his head was full of ideas for the construction of a permanent executive council. It was this that made him eager for a cessation of the method of Terror, and it was this that made the Committee of Public Safety his implacable enemy.

Why, then, did Robespierre, who also passed as a man of order and humanity, not continue to support Danton after the suppression of the Hébertists, as he had supported him before ? The common and facile answer is that he was moved by a malignant desire to put a rival out of the way. On the whole, the evidence seems to support Napoleon's opinion that Robespierre was incapable of voting for the death of anybody in the world on grounds of personal enmity. And his acquiescence in the ruin of Danton is intelligible enough on the grounds of policy. The Committee hated Danton for the good reason that he had openly attacked them, and his cry for clemency was an inflammatory and dangerous protest against their system. Now Robespierre, rightly or wrongly, had made up his mind that the Committee was the instrument by which, and which only, he could work out his own vague schemes of power and reconstruction. And, in any case, how could he resist the Committee ? The famous insurrectionary force of Paris, which Danton had been the first to organise against a government, had just been chilled by the fall of the Hébertists. Least of all could this force be relied upon to rise in defence of the very chief whose every word for many weeks past had been a protest against the Communal leaders. In separating himself from the Ultras, Danton had cut off the great reservoir of his peculiar strength.

It may be said that the Convention was the proper centre of resistance to the designs of the Committee, and that if Danton and Robespierre had united their forces in the Convention they would have defeated Billaud and his allies. This seems more than doubtful. The Committee had acquired an immense preponderance over the Convention. They had been eminently successful in the immense tasks imposed upon them. They had the prestige not only of being the government—so great a thing in a country that had just emerged from the condition of a centralised monarchy ; they had also the prestige of being a government that had done its work triumphantly. We are now in March. In July we shall find that Robespierre adopted the very policy we are now discussing, of playing off the Convention against the

Committee. In July that policy ended in his headlong fall. Why should it have been any more
successful four months earlier ?

What we may say is, that Robespierre was bound
in all morality to defend Danton in the Convention
at every hazard. Possibly ; but then to run risks
for chivalry's sake was not in Robespierre's nature,
and a man cannot climb out beyond the limitations of
his own character. His narrow head and thin blood
and unstable nerve, his calculating humour and his
frigid egoism, disinclined him to all games of chance.
His apologists have sought to put a more respectable
colour on his abandonment of Danton. The precisian,
they say, disapproved of Danton's lax and heedless
courses. Danton said to him one day : ' What do I
care ? Public opinion is a strumpet, and posterity
a piece of nonsense.' How should the puritanical
lawyer endure such cynicism as this ? And Danton
delighted in inflicting these coarse shocks. Again,
Danton had given various gross names of contempt
to Saint-Just. Was Robespierre not to feel insults
offered to the ablest and most devoted of his
lieutenants ? What was more important than
all, the acclamations with which the partisans of
reaction greeted the fall of the Ultras, made it
necessary to give instant and unmistakable notice
to the foes of the Revolution that the goddess of the
scorching eye and fiery hand still grasped the axe of
vengeance.

These are pleas invented after the fact. All goes

to show that Robespierre was really moved by nothing
more than his invariable dread of being left behind,
of finding himself on the weaker side, of not seeming
practical and political enough. And having made up
his mind that the stronger party was bent on the
destruction of the Dantonists, he became fiercer than
Billaud himself. It is constantly seen that the
waverer, of nervous atrabiliar constitution, no sooner
overcomes the agony of irresolution, than he flings
himself on his object with a vindictive tenacity that
seems to repay him for all the moral humiliation
inflicted on him by his stifled doubts. He redeems
the slowness of his approach by the fury of his spring.
' Robespierre,' says M. d'Héricault, ' precipitated
himself to the front of the opinion that was yelling
against his friends of yesterday. In order to keep
his usual post in the van of the Revolution, in order
to secure the advantage to his own popularity of an
execution which the public voice seemed to demand,
he came forward as the author of that execution,
though only the day before he had hesitated about
its utility, and though it was, in truth, far less useful to him than it proved to be to his future antagonists.'

Robespierre first alarmed Danton's friends by
assuming a certain icy coldness of manner, and by
some menacing phrases about the faction of the so-
called Moderates. Danton had gone, as he often did,
to his native village of Arcis-sur-Aube, to seek repose
and a little clearness of sight in the night that wrapped

him about. He was devoid of personal ambition ; he never had any humour for mere factious struggles. His, again, was the temperament of violent force, and in such types the reaction is tremendous. The indomitable activity of the last twenty months had bred weariness of spirit. The nemesis of a career of strenuous Will in large natures is apt to be a sudden sense of the irony of things. In Danton, as with Byron, it happened afterwards, the vehemence of the revolutionary spirit was touched by this desolating irony. His friends tried to rouse him. It is not clear that he could have done anything. The balance of force, after the suppression of the Hébertists, was irretrievably against him, as calculation had already revealed to Robespierre.

There are various stories of the pair having met at dinner almost on the eve of Danton's arrest, and parting with sombre disquietude on both sides. The interview, with its champagne, its interlocutors, its play of sinister repartee, may possibly have taken place, but the alleged details are plainly apocryphal. After all, *Religion ist in der Thiere Trieb*, says Wallenstein ; ' the very savage drinks not with the victim, into whose breast he means to plunge a sword.' Danton was warned that Robespierre was plotting his arrest. ' If I thought he had the bare idea,' said Danton with something of Gargantuan hyperbole, ' I would eat his bowels out.' Such was the disdain with which the ' giant of the mighty bone and bold emprise ' thought of our meagre-hearted pedant. With singular baseness, Robespierre handed over to Saint-Just a collection of notes, to serve as material for the indictment which Saint-Just was to present to the Convention. They comprised everything that suspicion could interpret malignantly, from the most conspicuous acts of Danton's public life, down to the casual freedom of private discourse.

Worse was to follow. After the arrest, and on the proceedings to obtain the assent of the Convention to the trial of Danton and others of its members, one only of their friends had the courage to rise and demand that they should be heard at the bar. Robespierre burst out in cold rage; he asked whether they had undergone so many heroic sacrifices, counting among them these acts of ' painful severity,' only to fall under the yoke of a band of domineering intriguers; and he cried out impatiently that they would brook no claim of privilege, and suffer no rotten idol. The word was felicitously chosen, for the Convention dreaded to have its independence suspected, and it dreaded this all the more because at this time its independence did not really exist. The vote against Danton was unanimous. On the afternoon of the Sixteenth Germinal (April 5, 1794) Paris in amazement and some stupefaction saw the once-dreaded Titan of the Mountain fast bound in the tumbril. ' I leave it all in a frightful welter,' Danton is reported to have said. ' Not a man of them has an idea of government. Robespierre will follow me;

he is dragged down by me. Ah, better be a poor
fisherman than meddle with the governing of men ! '

We may pause for a moment over a calmer
reminiscence. This was the very day on which the
virtuous and high-minded Condorcet quitted the
friendly roof that for nine months had concealed him
from the search of proscription. The same week he
was found dead in his prison. While Danton was
storming with impotent thunder before the tribunal,
Condorcet was writing the closing words of his *Sketch
of Human Progress.* ' How this picture of the human
race freed from all its fetters,—withdrawn from the
empire of chance, as from that of the enemies of
progress, and walking with firm and assured step
in the way of truth, of virtue, and happiness, presents
to the philosopher a sight that consoles him for the
errors, the crimes, the injustice, with which the earth
is yet stained, and of which he is not seldom the
victim ! It is in the contemplation of this picture
that he receives the reward of his efforts for the
progress of reason, for the defence of liberty. He
ventures to link them with the eternal chain of the
destinies of man : it is there he finds the true recompense of virtue, the pleasure of having done a lasting
good ; fate can no longer undo it, by any disastrous compensation that shall restore prejudice and
bondage. This contemplation is for him a refuge,
into which the recollection of his persecutors can never
follow him ; in which, living in thought with man

reinstated in the rights and the dignity of his nature, he forgets man tormented and corrupted by greed, by base fear, by envy ; it is here that he truly abides with his fellows, in an elysium that his reason has known how to create for itself, and that his love for humanity adorns with all purest delights.'

In following the turns of the drama that was to end in Thermidor, we perceive that after the fall of the anarchists and the death of Danton, the relations between Robespierre and the Committees underwent a change. He, who had hitherto been on the side of government, became in turn an agency of opposition. He did this in the interest of ultimate stability, but the difference between the new position and the old is that he now distinctly associated the idea of a stable Republic with the ascendancy of his own religious conceptions. How far the ascendancy of his own personality was involved, we have no means of judging. The vulgar accusation against him is that he now deliberately aimed at a dictatorship, and began to plot with that end in view. It is always difficult to draw a line between mere arrogant egoism on the one hand, and on the other the identi-fication of a man's personal elevation with the success of his public cause. The two ends probably become mixed in his mind, and if the cause be a good one, it is the height of pharisaical folly to quarrel with him, because he desires that his authority and renown shall receive some of the lustre of a far-shining

triumph. We need not discuss the charge that he
sought to make himself master. The important
thing is that his mastery could have served no great
end for France ; that it would have been like himself,
poor, barren, and hopelessly mediocre. And this
would have been seen on every side. France had
important military tasks to perform before her
independence was assured. Robespierre hated war,
and was jealous of every victory. France was in
urgent need of stable government, of new laws, of
ordered institutions. Robespierre never said a word
to indicate that he had a single positive idea in his
head on any of these great departments. And, more
than this, he was incapable of making use of men
who were more happily endowed than himself. He
had never mastered that excellent observation of De
Retz, that of all the qualities of a good party chief,
none is so indispensable as being able to suppress on
many occasions, and to hide on all, even legitimate
suspicions. He was corroded by suspicion, and this
paralyses able servants. Finally, Robespierre had no
imperial quality, but only that bad imitation of it,
a lively irritability.

The base of Robespierre's schemes of social reconstruction now came clearly into view; an official
Supreme Being, and a regulated Terror. The one
was to fill up the spiritual void, and the other to
satisfy all the exigencies of temporal things. It is
to the credit of Robespierre's perspicacity that he
should have recognised the human craving for

religion, but this credit is little when we contemplate what passed for religion in his dim and narrow understanding. Rousseau had brought a new soul into the eighteenth century by the Savoyard Vicar's Profession of Faith, the most fervid expression of emotional deism that religious literature contains; vague, irrational, incoherent, cloudy; but the clouds all suffused with glowing gold. When we turn from that to the political version of it in Robespierre's discourse on the relations of religious and moral ideas with republican principles, we feel as one who revisits a landscape that had been made glorious to him by a summer sky and fresh liquid winds from the gates of the evening sun, only to find it dead under a grey heaven and harsh blasts from the north-east. Robespierre's words on the Supreme Being are never a stream of deep feeling; never the self-forgetting expansion of the religious soul, but only the composite of the rhetorician. Here, as in all else, his aspiration was far beyond his faculty; he yearned for great spiritual emotions, as he had yearned for great thoughts and great achievements, but his spiritual capacity was as meagre as his intelligence. And where Nature thus unequally yokes lofty objects in a man with a short mental reach, she stamps him with the very definition of mediocrity.

He seriously thought that he should conciliate the conservative and theological elements of the society at his feet, by such an opera-piece as the Feast of

z

the Supreme Being ?   This was designed as a triumphant ripost to the Feast of Reason that Chaumette
and his friends had celebrated in the winter. The
energumens of the Goddess of Reason had now been
some weeks in their bloody graves. Robespierre persuaded the Convention to decree an official recognition of the Supreme Being, and to attend a com-
memorative festival in honour of their mystic patron.
He contrived to be chosen president for the decade
in which the festival would fall. When the day
came (20th Prairial, June 8, 1794), he clothed himself with more than even his usual care. As he
looked out from the windows of the Tuileries upon
the jubilant crowd in the gardens, he was intoxicated
with enthusiasm. 'O Nature,' he cried, 'how sublime
thy power, how full of delight! How tyrants must
grow pale at the idea of such a festival as this!'
In pontifical pride he walked at the head of the
procession, with flowers and wheat-ears in his hand,
to the sound of chants and symphonies and choruses
of maidens. On the first of the great basins in the
gardens, David, the artist, had devised an allegorical
structure for which an inauspicious doom was prepared. Atheism, a statue of life size, was throned
in the midst of an amiable group of human Vices,
with Madness by her side, and Wisdom menacing
them with lofty wrath. Robespierre applied a torch
to Atheism, but the wind was hostile. Atheism and
Madness obstinately resisted the torch, and it was
hapless Wisdom who took fire. A great car was drawn

by milk-white oxen ; in the front were ranged sheaves
of golden grain ; at the back shepherds and shepherdesses posed with scenic graces. The whole mum-
mery was pagan, a bringing back of Cerealia and
Thesmophoria to earth.

The famous republican Calendar, with its Prairials
and Germinals, its Ventôses and Pluviôses, was an
anachronism of the same kind. The association of
worship and sacredness with the fruits of the earth,
with the forces of nature, with the power and variety
of the elements, could only be sincere so long as men
really thought of all these things as animated each
by a special will of its own. How could men go
back to adore an outer world, after they had found
out the secret that it is a mere huge group of phenomena, following fixed courses, and not obeying
spontaneous and unaccountable volitions of their
own ? And what could be more puerile than the
fanciful connection of the Supreme Being with a
pastoral simplicity of life ? This simplicity was gone,
irrecoverably gone, with the passage from nomad
times to the complexities of a modern society. To
typify, therefore, the Supreme Being as specially
interested in shocks of grain and in shepherds and
shepherdesses, was to make him a mere figure in an
idyll, the ornament of a rural mask, a god of the
garden, instead of the sovereign director of the
universal forces, and stern master of the destinies
of men. Chaumette's commemoration of the Divinity
of Reason was a sensible performance, compared with

Robespierre's farcical repartee. It was something, as Comte has said, to select for worship man's most individual attribute. If they could not contemplate society as a whole, it was at least a gain to pay homage to that faculty in the human rulers of the world, which had brought the forces of nature—its pluviosity, nivosity, germinality, and vendemiarity — under the yoke for the service of men.

On the day of the Feast of the Supreme Being, the guillotine was concealed in the folds of rich hangings. It was the Twentieth of Prairial. Two days later Couthon proposed to the Convention the memorable Law of the Twenty-second Prairial. Robespierre was the draftsman, and the text of it still remains in his own writing. Of all laws ever passed in the world it is the most nakedly iniquitous. Tyrants have often substituted their own will for the ordered procedure of a tribunal, but no tyrant before ever went through the atrocious farce of deliberately making a tribunal the organised negation of security for justice. Couthon laid its theoretic base in a fallacy that must always be full of seduction to shallow persons in authority : ' He who would subordinate the public safety to the inventions of jurisconsults, to the formulas of the court, is either an imbecile or a scoundrel.' As if public safety could mean anything but the safety of the public. The author of the Law of Prairial had forgotten the minatory word of the sage to whom he had gone on a pilgrimage in the days of his youth. ' All becomes legitimate and even virtuous,' Helvétius had written, ' on behalf of the public safety.' Rousseau inscribed on the margin, ' The public safety is nothing, unless individuals enjoy security.' What security was possible under the Law of Prairial ?

After the probity and good judgment of the tribunal, the two cardinal guarantees in state trials are accurate definition and proof. The offence must be capable of precise description, and the proof against an offender must conform to strict rule. The Law of Prairial violently infringed all three of these essential conditions of judicial equity. First, the number of the jury who had power to convict was reduced. Second, treason was made to consist in such vague and infinitely elastic kinds of action as inspiring discouragement, misleading opinion, depraving manners, corrupting patriots, abusing the principles of the Revolution by perfidious applications. Third, proof was to lie in the conscience of the jury ; there was an end of preliminary inquiry, of witnesses in defence, and of counsel for the accused. Any kind of testimony was evidence, whether material or moral, verbal or written, if it was of a kind ' likely to gain the assent of a man of reasonable mind.'

What was Robespierre's motive in devising this instrument ? The theory that he loved judicial murder for its own sake, can only be held by royalist or clerical partisans. It is like the theory

of the vulgar kind of Protestantism, that Mary Tudor
or Philip of Spain had a keen delight in shedding
blood. Robespierre, like Mary and like Philip, would
have been as well pleased if all the world would have
come round to his mind without the destruction of a
single life. The true inquisitor is a creature of policy,
not a man of blood by taste. What, then, was the
policy of Prairial ? We know what was the general
aim in Robespierre's mind at this point in the history
of the Revolution. His brother Augustin was then
the representative of the Convention with the army
of Italy, and General Bonaparte was on terms of
close intimacy with him. Bonaparte said long afterwards, when he was on his rock of St. Helena, that
he saw long letters from Maximilian to Augustin
Robespierre, all blaming the Conventional Commis-
sioners—Tallien, Fouché, Barras, Collot, and the rest
—for the horrors they perpetrated, and accusing
them of ruining the Revolution by their atrocities.
Again, there is abundant testimony that Robespierre
did his best to induce the Committee of Public Safety
to bring those malefactors to justice. The text of
the Law itself discloses the same object. The vague
phrases of depraving manners and applying revolutionary principles perfidiously, were exactly calculated to smite the band of men whose conduct was
to Robespierre the scandal of the Revolution. And
there was a curious clause in the law as originally
presented, that deprived the Convention of the right
of preventing measures against its own members.

Robespierre's general design in short was to effect a further purgation of the Convention. There is no reason to suppose that he deliberately aimed at any more general extermination. On the other hand, it is incredible that he should merely have had in view the equalisation of rich and poor before the tribunals, by withdrawing the aid of counsel and testimony to civic character from both rich and poor alike.

If Robespierre's design was what we believe it to have been, the result was ghastly failure. The Committee of Public Safety would not consent to apply his law against the men for whom he had specially designed it. The weapon that he had forged was seized by the Committee of General Security, and Paris was plunged into the fearful days of the Great Terror. The number of persons put to death by the Revolutionary Tribunal before the Law of Prairial had been comparatively moderate. From the creation of the Tribunal in April 1793, down to the execution of the Hébertists in March 1794, the number of persons condemned to death was 505. From the death of the Hébertists down to the death of Robespierre, the number of the condemned was 2158. One half of the entire number of victims, namely 1356, were guillotined after the Law of Prairial. Innocent women no less than innocent men, poor no less than rich, those in whom life was almost spent, no less than those in whom its pulse was strongest, virtuous no less than vicious, were sent off in woe-stricken batches all those summer days. A man was informed against; he was seized in his bed at five in the morning; at seven he was taken to the Conciergerie; at nine he received information of the charge against him; at ten he went into the dock; by two in the afternoon he was condemned; by four his head lay in the executioner's basket.

What stamps the system of the Terror at this date with a wickedness that cannot be effaced, is that at no moment was the danger from foreign or domestic foe less serious. We may forgive something to panic. The proscriptions of an earlier date in Paris were not excessively sanguinary, if we remember that the city abounded in royalists and other reactionists, who were dangerous in fomenting discouragement and spreading confusion. If there ever is an excuse for martial law, the French government were warranted in resorting to it in 1793. Paris in those days was like a city beleaguered, and the world does not use very harsh words about the commandant of a besieged town who puts to death traitors found within his walls. Opinion in England at this very epoch encouraged the Tory government to pass a Treason Bill, that introduced as vague a definition of treasonable offence as even the Law of Prairial itself. Windham did not shrink from declaring in parliament that he and his colleagues were determined to exact 'a rigour beyond the law.' And they were as good as their word. The Jacobins had no

monopoly of either cruel law or cruel breach of law
in the eighteenth century.   Only thirty years before,
opinion in Pennsylvania had prompted a hideous
massacre of harmless Indians as a deed acceptable
to God, and the grandson of William Penn proclaimed a bounty of fifty dollars for the scalp of
a female Indian, and three times as much for a
male. A man would have had quite as good a chance
of justice from the Revolutionary Tribunal, as at
the hands of Braxfield, the Scotch judge, who condemned Muir and Palmer for sedition in 1793, and
told the government, with a brazen front worthy of
Carrier or Collot d'Herbois themselves, that, if they
would only send him prisoners, he would find law
for them.

Robespierre was inflamed with resentment, not
because so many people were guillotined every day,
but because the objects of his own enmity were not
among them.   He was chagrined at the miscarriage
of his scheme ; but the chagrin had its root in his
desire for order, and not in his humanity.   A good
man—say, so imperfectly good a man as Danton—
could not have .endured life after enacting such a
law and seeing the ghastly work that it was doing.
He could hardly have contented himself with drawing
tears from the company in Madame Duplay's little
parlour, by his pathetic recitations from Corneille
and Racine, or with listening to melting notes from
the violin of Le Bas.   It is commonly said by Robespierre's defenders that he withdrew from the Com-

mittee of Public Safety as soon as he found out that
he was powerless to arrest the daily shedding of
blood. The older assumption used to be that he left
Paris, and ceased to be cognisant of the Committee's
deliberations. The minutes, however, prove that
this was not the case. Robespierre signed papers
nearly every day of Messidor—(June 19 to July 18)
the blood-stained month between Prairial and Thermidor—and was thoroughly aware of the doings of
the Committee.

In passing the Law of Prairial, Robespierre's
designs—and they were meritorious and creditable
designs enough in themselves—had been directed
against the corrupt chiefs, such as Tallien and Fouché,
and against the fierce and coarse spirits of the Committee of General Security, such as Vadier and
Voulland. Robespierre was above all a precisian.
He had a sentimental sympathy with the common
people in the abstract, but his spiritual pride, his
pedantry, his formalism, his personal fastidiousness,
were all wounded to the very quick by the kind
of men whom the Revolution had thrown to the
surface. Gouverneur Morris, then the American
minister, describes most of the members of the two
Committees as the very dregs of humanity, with
whom it is a stain to have any dealings ; as degraded
men only worthy of the profoundest contempt.
Danton had said : ' Robespierre is the least of a
scoundrel of any of the band.' The Committee of
General Security represented the very elements by

which Robespierre was most revolted. They offended his respectability; their evil manners seemed to tarnish the good name that his vanity hoped to make as revered all over Europe as it already was among his partisans in France. It was indispensable therefore to cut them off from the revolutionary government, just as Hébert and as Danton had been cut off. His colleagues of Public Safety refused to lend themselves to this. Henceforth, with characteristically narrow tenacity, he looked round for new combinations, with no broader design than to enable him to punish these particular objects of his very just detestation.

The position of sections and interests that ended in the Revolution of Thermidor, is one of the most entangled in the history of faction. It would take a volume to follow out all the peripeteias of the drama. Here we can only enumerate in a few sentences the parties to the contest and the conditions of the struggle. The reader will easily discern the difficulty in Robespierre's way of making an effective combination. First, there were the two Committees. Of these the one, the General Security, was thoroughly hostile to Robespierre; its members, as we have said, were wild and hardy spirits, with no political conception, and with a complete contempt for fine phrases and philosophical principles. They knew Robespierre's hatred for them, and they heartily returned it. They were the steadfast centre of the changing schemes that ended in his downfall. The

Committee of Public Safety was divided. Carnot
hated Saint - Just, and Collot d'Herbois hated
Robespierre, and Billaud had a sullen distrust of
Robespierre's counsels. The object of the Billaudists
was to retain their power, and their power was always
menaced from two quarters, the Convention and
Paris. If they let Robespierre have his own way
against his enemies, would they not be at his mercy
whenever he chose to devise a popular insurrection
against them ? Yet if they withstood Robespierre,
they could only do so through the agency of the
Convention, and to fall back upon the Convention
would be to give that body an express invitation to
resume the power that had, in the pressure of the
crisis a year before, been delegated to the Committee,
and periodically renewed afterwards. The dilemma
of Billaud seemed desperate, and events afterwards
proved that it was so.

If we turn to the Convention, we find the position
equally distracting. They, too, feared another insurrection and a second decimation. If the Right
helped Robespierre to destroy the Fouchés and
Vadiers, he would be stronger than ever ; and what
security had they against a repetition of the violence
of the Thirty-first of May ? If the Dantonists joined
in destroying Robespierre, they would be helping the
Right, and what security had they against a Girondin
reaction ? On the other hand, the Centre might
fairly hope, just what Billaud feared, that if the
Committee came to the Convention to crush Robes-

pierre this would end in a combination strong
enough to enable the Convention to crush the
Committees.

Much depended on military success. The victories
of the generals were the strength of the Committee.
For so long it would be difficult to turn opinion
against a triumphant administration. ' At the first
defeat,' Robespierre had said to Barère, ' I await
you.' But the defeat did not come. The plotting
went on with incessant activity; on one hand,
Robespierre, aided by Saint - Just and Couthon,
strengthening himself at the Jacobin Club, and
through that among the sections; on the other, the
Mountain and the Committee of General Security
trying to win over the Right, more contemptuously
christened the Marsh or the Belly, of the Convention.
The Committee of Public Safety was not yet fully
decided how to act.

At the end of the first week of Thermidor, Robespierre could endure the tension no longer. He had
tried to fortify his nerves for the struggle by riding,
but with so little success that he was lifted fainting
off his horse. He endeavoured to steady himself
by diligent pistol-practice. But nothing gave him
initiative and the sinews of action. Saint-Just urged
him to raise Paris. Some bold men proposed to
carry off the members of the Committee bodily from
their midnight deliberations. Robespierre declined,
and fell back on what he took to be his greatest
strength and most unfailing resource; he prepared

a speech. On the Eighth of Thermidor he delivered it to the Convention, amid intense excitement both within its walls and without. All Paris knew that they were now on the eve of one more of the famous Days; the Revolution of Thermidor had begun.

The speech of the Eighth Thermidor has seemed to men of all parties since a masterpiece of tactical ineptitude. If Robespierre had been a statesman instead of a phrasemonger, he had a clear course. He ought to have taken the line of argument that Danton would have taken. That is to say, he ought to have identified himself fully with the interests and security of the Convention; to have accepted the growing resolution to close the Terror; to have boldly pressed the abolition of the Committee of General Security, and the removal from the Committee of Public Safety of Billaud, Collot, Barère; to have proposed to send fifty persons to Cayenne for life; and to have urged a policy of peace with the foreign powers. This was the substantial wisdom and real interest of the position. The task was difficult, because his hearers had the best possible reasons for knowing that the author of the Law of Prairial was a Terrorist on principle. And in truth we know that Robespierre had no definite intention of erecting clemency into a rule. He had not mental strength enough to throw off the profound apprehension that the incessant alarms of the last five years had engendered in him; and the only device he could imagine for maintaining the Republic against traitors, was to stimulate the rigour of the Revolutionary Tribunal.

If, however, Robespierre lacked the grasp which might have made him the representative of a broad and stable policy, it was at least his interest to persuade the men of the Plain that he entertained no designs against them. And this is what in his own mind he intended. But to do it effectively, it was clearly best to tell his hearers, in so many words, whom he really wished them to strike. That would have relieved the majority, and banished the suspicion that had been busily fomented by his enemies, that he had in his pocket a long list of their names for proscription. But Robespierre, having for the first time in his life ventured on aggressive action without the support of a definite party, faltered. He dared not designate his enemies face to face by name. Instead of that, he talked vaguely of conspirators against the Republic, and calumniators of himself. There was not a single, definite, unmistakable sentence in the speech. The men of the Plain were insecure and doubtful; they had no certainty that among conspirators and calumniators he did not include too many of themselves. People are not so readily seized by grand phrases, when their heads are at stake. The sitting was long, and marked by changing currents and reverses. When they broke up, all was left uncertain. Robespierre had suffered a check. Billaud felt that he could no longer hesitate in joining the combination against his colleague.

Each party was aware that the next day must seal the fate of one or other of them. There is a legend that in the evening Robespierre walked in the Champs Elysées with his betrothed, accompanied as usual by his faithful dog, Brount. They admired the purple of the sunset, and talked of the prospect of a glorious to-morrow. But this is apocryphal. The evening was passed in no lover's saunterings, but amid the storm and uproar of the Club. He went to the Jacobins to read over again his speech of the day. 'It is my testament of death,' he said, amid the passionate protestations of his devoted followers. He had been talking for the last three years of his willingness to drink the hemlock, and to offer his breast to the poniards of tyrants. That was a fashion of the speech of the time, and in earlier days it had been more than a fashion of speech, for Brunswick would have given them short shrift. But now, when he talked of his last testament, Robespierre did not intend it to be such if he could prevent it. When he went to rest that night, he had a tolerably calm hope that he should win the next day's battle in the Convention, when he was aware that Saint-Just would attack the Committees openly and directly. If he would have allowed his band to invade the Pavillon de Flore, and carry off or slay the Committees who sat up through the night, the battle would have been won when he awoke. His friends are justified in saying that his strong respect for legality was the cause of his ruin.

Men in all ages have had a superstitious fondness for connecting awful events in their lives with portents among the outer elements. It was noticed that the heat during the terrible days of Thermidor was more intense than had been known within the memory of man. The thermometer never fell below sixty-five degrees in the coolest part of the night, and in the daytime men and women and beasts of burden fell down dead in the streets. By five o'clock in the morning of the Ninth Thermidor, the galleries of the Convention were filled by a boisterous and excited throng. At ten o'clock the proceedings began as usual with the reading of correspondence from the departments and from the armies. Robespierre, who had been escorted from his lodgings by the usual body of admirers, instead of taking his ordinary seat, remained standing by the side of the tribune. It is a familiar fact that moments of appalling suspense are precisely those in which we are most ready involuntarily to note a trifle; everybody observed that Robespierre wore the coat of violet-blue silk and the white nankeens in which a few weeks previously he had done honour to the Supreme Being.

The galleries seemed as enthusiastic as ever. The men of the Plain and the Marsh had lost the abject mien with which they usually cowered before Robespierre's glance; they wore a courageous air of judicial reserve. The leaders of the Mountain wandered restlessly to and fro among the corridors. At noon Tallien saw that Saint-Just had ascended the tribune.

2 A

Instantly he rushed down into the chamber, knowing
that the battle had now begun in fierce earnest.
Saint-Just had not got through two sentences before
Tallien interrupted him. He began to insist with
energy that there should be an end to the equivocal
phrases with which Paris had been too long alarmed
by the Triumvirate. Billaud, fearing to be outdone
in the attack, hastily forced his way to the tribune,
broke into what Tallien was saying, and proceeded
dexterously to discredit Robespierre's allies without
at once assailing Robespierre himself. Le Bas ran in
a fury to stop him; Collot d'Herbois, the president,
declared Le Bas out of order; the hall rang with
cries of ' To prison! To the Abbey! ' and Le Bas
was driven from the tribune. This was the beginning
of the tempest. Robespierre's enemies knew that
they were fighting for their lives, and this inspired
them with a strong and resolute power that is always
impressive in popular assemblies. He still thought
himself secure. Billaud pursued his accusations.
Robespierre, at last, unable to control himself, scaled
the tribune. There suddenly burst forth from Tallien
and his partisans vehement shouts of ' Down with
the tyrant! down with the tyrant! ' The galleries
were swept by a frenzy of vague agitation; the
president's bell poured loud incessant clanging into
the tumult; the men of the Plain held themselves
firm and silent; in the tribune raged ferocious groups,
Tallien menacing Robespierre with a dagger, Billaud
roaring out proposals to arrest this person and that,

Robespierre gesticulating, threatening, yelling, shrieking. His enemies knew that if he were once allowed
to get a hearing, his authority might even yet over-
awe the waverers. A penetrative word or a heroic
gesture might lose them the day. The majority of
the chamber still hesitated. They called for Barère,
in whose adroit faculty for discovering the winning
side they had the confidence of long experience.
Robespierre, recovering some of his calm, and perceiving now that he had really to deal with a serious
revolt, again asked to be heard before Barère. But
the cries for Barère were louder than ever. Barère
spoke, in a sense hostile to Robespierre, but warily
and without naming him.

Then there was a momentary lull. The Plain was
uncertain. The battle might even now turn either
way. Robespierre made another attempt to speak,
but Tallien with intrepid fury broke out into a torrent
of louder and more vehement invective. Robespierre's shrill voice was heard in disjected snatches,
amidst the violent tones of Tallien, the yells of the
president calling Robespierre to order, the murderous
clanging of the bell. Then came that supreme hour
of the struggle, whose tale has been so often told,
when Robespierre turned from his old allies of the
Mountain, and succeeded in shrieking out an appeal
to the probity and virtue of the Right and the Plain.
To his horror, even these despised men, after a slight
movement, remained mute. Then his cheeks blanched,
and the sweat ran down his face. But anger and

scornful impatience swiftly came back and restored him. *President of assassins*, he cried out to Thuriot, *for the last time I ask to be heard.* *Thou canst not speak*, called one, *the blood of Danton chokes thee.* He flung himself down the steps of the tribune, and rushed towards the benches of the Right. *Come no further*, cried another, *Vergniaud and Condorcet sat here.* He regained the tribune, but his speech was gone. He was reduced to the dregs of an impotent and gasping voiceless gesticulation, like the strife of one in a nightmare.

The day was lost. The Right, the Plain, even the galleries, despised the man who had succumbed. If Robespierre had possessed the physical strength of Mirabeau or Danton, the Ninth Thermidor would have been another of his victories. He was crushed by the relentless ferocity and endurance of his antagonists. A decree for his arrest was resolved upon by acclamation. He cast a glance at the galleries, as marvelling that they should remain passive in face of an outrage on his person. They were mute. The ushers advanced with hesitation to do their duty, and not without trembling carried him away, along with Couthon and Saint-Just. The brother, for whom he had made honourable sacrifices in days that seemed to be divided from the present by an abyss of centuries, insisted with fine heroism on sharing his fate, and Augustin Robespierre and Le Bas were led off to the prisons along with their leader and idol.

It was now a little after four o'clock. The Convention, with the self-possession that so often amazes us in its proceedings, went on with formal business for another hour. At five they broke up. For life, as the poets tell, is a daily stage-play ; men declaim their high heroic parts, then doff the buskin or the sock, wash away the paint from their cheeks, and gravely sit down to meat. The Conventionals, as they ate their dinners, were unconscious, apparently, that the crisis of the drama was still to come. The next twelve hours were to witness the climax. Robespierre had been crushed by the Convention ; it remained to be seen whether the Convention would not now be crushed by the Commune of Paris.

Robespierre was first conducted to the prisons of the Luxembourg. The gaoler, on some plea of informality, refused to receive him. The terrible prisoner was next taken to the Mairie, where he remained among joyful friends from eight in the evening until eleven. Meanwhile the old insurrectionary methods of the nights of June and of August in 1792, of May and of June in 1793, were again followed. The beating of the *rappel* and the *générale* was heard in all the sections ; the tocsin sounded its dreadful note, reminding all who should hear it that insurrection is the most sacred and indispensable of duties. Hanriot, the commandant of the forces, had been arrested in the evening, but he was speedily released by the agents of the Commune. The Council issued manifestoes and decrees from the

Common Hall every moment. The barriers were closed. Cannon were posted opposite the doors of the hall of the Convention. The quays were thronged. Emissaries sped to and fro between the Jacobin Club and the Common Hall, and between these two centres and each of the forty-eight sections. It is one of the inscrutable mysteries of this delirious night, that Hanriot did not at once use the force at his command to break up the Convention. The members of the Convention had reassembled after their dinner, towards seven o'clock. The hall that had resounded with the shrieks and yells of the furious gladiators of the factions all day, now lent a lugubrious echo to gloomy reports which one member after another delivered from the shadow of the tribune. Towards nine o'clock the members of the two dread Committees came in panic to seek shelter among their colleagues, ' as dejected in their peril,' says an eye-witness, ' as they had been cruel and insolent in the hour of their supremacy.' When they heard that Hanriot had been released, and that guns were at their door, all gave themselves up for lost and made ready for death. News came that Robespierre had broken his arrest, and gone to the Common Hall. Robespierre, after urgent and repeated solicitations, had been at length persuaded about an hour before midnight to leave the Mairie and join his partisans of the Commune. This was an act of revolt against the Convention, for the Mairie was a legal place of detention, and so long as he was there, he was within the law. The Convention with heroic intrepidity declared both Hanriot and Robespierre beyond the pale of the law. This prompt measure was its salvation. Twelve members were instantly named to carry the decree to all the sections. With the scarf of office round their waists, and a sabre in hand, they sallied forth. Mounting horses, and escorted by attendants with flaring torches, they scoured Paris, calling all good citizens to the succour of the Convention, haranguing crowds at the street corners with power and authority, and striking the imagination of men. At midnight heavy rain began to fall.

The leaders of the Commune meanwhile, in full confidence that victory was sure, contented themselves with incessant issue of paper decrees, to each of which the Convention replied by a counter-decree. Those who have studied the situation most minutely are of opinion that even so late as one o'clock in the morning, the Commune might have made a successful defence, although it had lost the opportunity, that it had certainly possessed up to ten o'clock, of destroying the Convention. But on this occasion the genius of insurrection slumbered. And there was a genuine division of opinion in the eastern quarters of Paris, the result of a grim distrust of the man who had helped to slay Hébert and Chaumette. At a word this distrust began to declare itself. The opinion of the sections became more and more distracted. One armed group cried, *Down with the Convention!* Another armed group cried, *The Con-*

vention for ever, and down with the Commune ! The
two great faubourgs were all astir, and three battalions
were ready to march. Emissaries from the Convention actually succeeded in persuading them—such
the dementia of the night—that Robespierre was a
royalist agent, and that the Commune were about to
deliver the little Louis from his prison in the Temple.
One body of communist partisans after another was
detached from its allegiance. The deluge of rain
emptied the Place de Grève, and when companies
came up from the sections in obedience to orders
from Hanriot and the Commune, the silence made
them suspect a trap, and they withdrew towards the
great metropolitan church or elsewhere.

Barras, whom the Convention had charged with
its military defence, gathered together some six
thousand men. With the right instinct of a man who
had studied the history of Paris since the July of
1789, he foresaw the advantage of being the first to
make the attack. He arranged his forces into two
divisions. One of them marched along the quays to
take the Common Hall in front ; the other along the
rue Saint Honoré to take it in flank. Inside the
Common Hall the staircases and corridors were alive
with bustling messengers, and those mysterious busy-
bodies who are always found lingering without a
purpose on the skirts of great historic scenes.
Robespierre and the other chiefs were in a small
room, preparing manifestoes and signing decrees.
They were curiously unaware of the movements of

the Convention. An aggressive attack by the party
of authority upon the party of insurrection was unknown in the tradition of revolt. They had an easy
assurance that at daybreak their forces would be
prepared once more to tramp along the familiar road
westwards. It was now half-past two. Robespierre
had just signed the first two letters of his name to a
document before him, when he was startled by cries
and uproar in the Place below. In a few instants he
lay stretched on the ground, his jaw shattered by a
pistol-shot. His brother had either fallen or had
leaped out of the window. Couthon was hurled over
a staircase, and lay for dead. Saint-Just was a
prisoner.

Whether Robespierre was shot by an officer of the
Conventional force, or attempted to blow out his own
brains, we shall never know, any more than we shall
ever be quite assured how Rousseau, his spiritual
master, came to an end. The wounded man was
carried, a ghastly sight, first to the Committee of
Public Safety, and then to the Conciergerie, where
he lay in silent stupefaction through the heat of the
summer day. As he was an outlaw, the only legal
preliminary before execution was to identify him.
At five in the afternoon, he was raised into the cart.
Couthon and the younger Robespierre lay, confused
wrecks of men, at the bottom of it. Hanriot and
Saint-Just, bruised and begrimed, completed the
band. One who walks from the Palace of Justice,
over the bridge, along the rue Saint Honoré, into the

rue Royale, and so to the Luxor column, retraces the *via dolorosa* of the Revolution on the afternoon of the Tenth of Thermidor.

The end of the intricate manœuvres known as the Revolution of Thermidor was the recovery of authority by the Convention. The insurrections, known as the days of the Twelfth Germinal, First Prairial, and Thirteenth Vendémiaire, all ended in the victory of the Convention over the revolutionary forces of Paris. The Committees, on the other hand, had beaten Robespierre, but they had ruined themselves. Very gradually the movement towards order, which had begun in the mind of Danton, and had gone on in the cloudy purposes of Robespierre, became definite. But it was in the interest of very different ideas from those of either Danton or of Robespierre. A White Terror slowly succeeded the Red Terror. Nine months after the death of Robespierre the reaction was strong enough to smite his colleagues of the two Committees. The surviving Girondins had come back to their seats in the Convention : the Dantonians had not forgiven the execution of their chief. These two parties were bent on vengeance. In April 1795, a decree was passed banishing Billaud-Varennes, Collot d'Herbois, and Barère. In the following month the leaders of the Committee of General Security were thrown into prison. The Revolution had passed into new currents. We cannot see any reasons for thinking that those currents would have led to any happier results if Robespierre had won the battle. Tallien, Fouché, Barras, and the rest may have been thoroughly bad men. But then what qualities had Robespierre for building up a state ? He had neither strength of practical character, nor firm breadth of political judgment. When we compare him,—I do not say with Frederick of Prussia, with Jefferson, with Washington,—but with the group of able men who made the closing year of the Convention honourable and of good service to France, we have a measure of Robespierre's incompetence.

VICTOR HUGO'S *NINETY-THREE.*

' HISTORY has its truth, Legend has its truth.
Legendary truth is of a different nature from historic
truth. Legendary truth is invention with reality for
result. For the rest, history and legend have the
same aim—to paint under the man of a day eternal
humanity.' These words from his new and latest
work (ii. 4) [1] are a repetition of what Victor Hugo had
already said in the introduction to his memorable
Legend of the Ages. But the occasion of their application is far more delicate. Poetry lends itself naturally
to the spacious, distant, vague, highly generalised
way of presenting real events. A prose romance, on
the other hand, is of necessity abundant in details,
in special circumstances, in particularities of time
and place. This leaves all the more room for historic
error, and historic error in a work of imagination
dealing with actual and known occurrences is
obviously fatal, not only to legendary truth, but to
legendary beauty and poetic impressiveness. And
then the pitfalls which lie about the feet of the

[1] The references are to the *Édition Définitive* in two
volumes.

Frenchman who has to speak of 1793,—the terrible year of the modern epoch! The delirium of the Terror haunts most of the revolutionary historians, and the choicest examples in all literature of bombast, folly, emptiness, political immorality, inhumanity, formal repudiation of common sense and judgment, are to be found in the rhapsodies which men of letters, some of them men of eminence, call histories of the Revolution, or lives of this or that actor in it.

It was hardly a breach, therefore, of one's allegiance to Hugo's imaginative genius, if one had misgivings as to the result of an attempt, even in his strong hands, to combine legend with truth on a disastrous field, in which grave writers with academic solemnity had confounded truth with the falsest kind of legend. The theme was so likely to emphasise the defects incident to his mighty qualities; so likely to provoke an exaggeration of those mannerisms of thought no less than of phrase, which, though never ignoble nor paltry, yet now and then take something from the loftiness and sincerity of the writer's work. Wisdom, however, is justified of her children, and Hugo's genius has justified his choice of a difficult and perilous subject. *Quatrevingt-treize* is a monument of its author's finest gifts; and while those who are happily endowed with the capacity of taking delight in nobility and beauty of imaginative work will find themselves in possession of a new treasure, the lover of historic truth who hates to see abstrac-

tions passed off for actualities and legend erected in
the place of fact, escapes with his sensibilities almost
unwounded.

The historic interlude at the beginning of the
second volume is undoubtedly open to criticism from
the political student's point of view. As a sketch
of the Convention, the scene of its sittings, the
stormful dramas that were enacted there one after
another for month after month, the singular men
who, one after another, rode triumphant upon the
whirlwind for a space, and were then mercilessly
swept in an instant into outer darkness; the com-
moner men who cowered before the fury of the storm,
and were like ' smoke driven hither and thither by
the wind,' and laboured hard upon a thousand schemes
for human improvement, some admirable, others
mere frenzy, while mobs filed in and danced mad
carmagnoles before them—all this is a magnificent
masterpiece of accurate, full, and vivid description.
To the philosophy of it we venture to demur. The
mystic, supernatural view of the French Revolution,
that is so popular among French writers who object
to the supernatural and the mystical everywhere
else, is to us a thing incredible, most mischievous.
People talk of '93, as a Greek tragedian treats the
Tale of Troy divine, or the terrible fortunes of the
house of Atreus, as the result of dark invincible fate,
the unalterable decree of the immortal gods. Even
Victor Hugo's strong spirit does not quite overcome
the demoralising doctrine of a certain revolutionary

school, though he has the poet's excuse. Thus, of the Convention:

Minds all a prey to the wind. But this wind was a wind of miracle and portent. To be a member of the Convention was to be a wave of the ocean. And this was true of its greatest. The force of impulsion came from on high. There was in the Convention a will, which was the will of all, and yet was the will of no one. It was an idea, an idea resistless and without measure, which breathed in the shadow from the high heavens. We call that the Revolution. As this idea passed, it threw down one and raised up another; it bore away this man in the foam, and broke that man to pieces upon the rocks. The idea knew whither it went, and drove the gulf of waters before it. To impute the Revolution to men is as one who should impute the tide to the waves. The Revolution is an action of the Unknown. . . . It is a form of the abiding phenomenon that shuts us in on every side and that we call Necessity. . . . In presence of these climacteric catastrophes which waste and vivify civilisation, one is slow to judge detail. To blame or praise men on account of the result, is as if one should blame or praise the figures on account of the total. That which must pass passes, the storm that must rage rages. The eternal serenity does not suffer from these boisterous winds. Above revolutions truth and justice abide, as the starry heaven abides above the tempests (i. 188-189).

As a lyric passage, full of the breath of inspiration; as history, superficial and untrue; as morality, enervating and antinomian. The author is assuredly far nearer the mark in another place when he speaks of '*that immense improvisation* which is the French

Revolution' (ii. 35)—an improvisation of which every step can be rationally explained.

After all, this is no more than an interlude. Victor Hugo only surveys the events of '93 as a field for the growth of types of character. His instinct as artist takes him away from the Paris of '93, where the confusion, uproar, human frenzy, leave him no background of nature, with nature's fixity, sternness, indifference, sublimity. This background he found in La Vendée, whose vast forests grow under the pencil of the master of all the more terrible and majestic effects, into a picture hardly less sombre and mighty in its impressiveness than the memorable ocean pieces of his *Toilers of the Sea*. If the waves are appalling in their agitation, their thunders, their sterility, the forest is appalling in its silence, its dimness, its rest, and in the invisibleness of the thousand kinds of life to which it gives a shelter. If the violence and calm and mercilessness of the sea penetrated the earlier romance with transcendent fury, so does the stranger, more mysterious, and in a sense even more inhuman life of the forest penetrate its successor. From the opening chapter down to the very close, even while the interlude takes us for a little while to the Paris café where Danton, Robespierre, and Marat sit in angry counsel, even while we are on the sea with the royalist Marquis and Halmalo, the reader is subtly haunted by the great Vendean woods, their profundity, their mystery, their tragic and sinister beauties.

2 B

The forest is barbarous.

The configuration of the land counsels man in many an act. More than we suppose, it is his accomplice. In the presence of certain savage landscapes, you are tempted to exonerate man and blame creation : you feel a silent challenge and incitement from nature ; the desert is constantly unwholesome for conscience, especially for a conscience without light. Conscience may be a giant ; that makes a Socrates or a Jesus : it may be a dwarf ; that makes an Atreus or a Judas. The puny conscience soon turns reptile ; the twilight thickets, the brambles, the thorns, the marsh waters under branches, make for it a fatal haunting place ; amid all this it undergoes the mysterious infiltration of ill suggestions. The optical illusions, the unexplained images, the scaring hour, the scaring spot, all throw man into that kind of affright, half-religious, half-brutal, which in ordinary times engenders superstition, and in epochs of violence, savagery. Hallucinations hold the torch that lights the path to murder. There is something like vertigo in the brigand. Nature with her prodigies has a double effect ; she dazzles great minds, and blinds the duller soul. When man is ignorant, when the desert offers visions, the obscurity of the solitude is added to the obscurity of the intelligence ; thence in man comes the opening of abysses. Certain rocks, certain ravines, certain thickets, certain wild openings of the evening sky through the trees, drive man towards mad or monstrous exploits. We might almost call some places criminal (ii. 21).

With La Vendée for background, and some savage incidents of the bloody Vendean war for external machinery, Victor Hugo has realised his conception of '93 in three types of character : Lantenac, the royalist marquis ; Cimourdain, the puritan turned Jacobin ; and Gauvain, for whom one can as yet

find no short name, he belonging to the millenarian
times. Lantenac, though naturally a less original
creation than the other two, is still a bold and
striking figure, drawn with marked firmness of
hand, and presenting a distinct and coherent conception. It is a triumph of the poetic or artistic part
of the author's nature over the merely political part,
that he should have made even his type of the old
feudal order which he execrates so bitterly, a heroic,
if ever so little also a diabolic, personage. There is
everything that is cruel, merciless, unflinching, in
Lantenac; there is nothing mean or insignificant.
A gunner at sea, by inattention to the lashing of
his gun, causes an accident that breaks the ship
to pieces, and then he saves the lives of the crew
by hazarding his own life to secure the wandering
monster. Lantenac decorates him with the cross
of Saint Louis for his gallantry, and instantly afterwards has him shot for his carelessness. He burns
homesteads and villages, fusillades men and women,
and makes the war a war without quarter or grace.
Yet he is no swashbuckler of the melodramatic stage.
There is a fine reserve, a brief gravity, in the delineation of him, his clear will, his quickness, his intrepidity,
his relentlessness, that make of him the incarnation
of aristocratic coldness, hatred, and pride. You
might guillotine Lantenac with satisfaction, and
yet he does not make us ashamed of mankind.
Into his mouth, as he walks about his dungeon,
impatiently waiting to be led out to execution, Victor

Hugo has put the aristocrat's view of the Revolution. Some portions of it (ii. 224-226) would fit amazingly well into Renan's notions about the moral and intellectual reform of France.

If the Breton aristocrat of '93 was fearless, intrepid, and without mercy in defence of God and the king— and his qualities were all shared, the democrat may love to remember, by the Breton peasant, whether peasant follower or peasant leader—the Jacobin was just as vigorous, as intrepid, as merciless in defence of his Republic. ' Pays, Patrie,' says Victor Hugo, in words that perhaps will serve to describe many a future passage in French history, ' ces deux mots résument toute la guerre de Vendée ; querelle de l'idée locale contre l'idée universelle ; paysans contre patriotes ' (ii. 22).[1] Certainly the Jacobins were the patriots of that era, the deliverers of France from something like the process of partition that further east was consummated in this very '93. We do not mean the handful of odious miscreants who played fool and demon in turns in the insurrectionary Commune and elsewhere : such men as Collot d'Herbois, or Carrier, or Panis. The normal Jacobin was a remarkable type. He has been described by Louis Blanc as something powerful, original, sombre ; half agitator, half statesman ; half puritan, half monk ; half inquisitor, half tribune. These words of the

---

[1] In corroboration of this view of the Vendean rising as democratic, see Mortimer-Ternaux, *Hist. de la Terreur*, vol. vi. bk. 30.

historian are the exact prose version of the figure
of Cimourdain, the typical Jacobin of the poet.
'Cimourdain was a pure conscience, but sombre.
He had in him the absolute. He had been a priest,
and that is a serious thing. Man, like the sky, may
have a dark serenity; it is enough that something
should have brought night into his soul. Priesthood
had brought night into Cimourdain. He who has
been a priest is one still. What brings night upon
us may leave the stars with us. Cimourdain was full
of virtues, full of truths, but they shone in the midst
of darkness ' (i. 123). If the aristocrat had rigidity,
so had the Jacobin. 'Cimourdain had the blind
certitude of the arrow, that only sees the mark and
makes for it. In revolution, nothing so formidable
as the straight line. Cimourdain strode forward
with fatality in his step. He believed that in social
genesis the very extreme point must always be solid
ground, an error peculiar to minds that for reason
substitute logic ' (i. 127). And so forth, until the
character of the Jacobin lives for us with a precision,
a fullness, a naturalness, such as neither Carlyle nor
Michelet nor Quinet has been able to clothe it with,
though these too have the sacred illumination of
genius. Victor Hugo's Jacobin is a poetic creation,
yet the creation only lies in the vivid completeness
with which the imagination of a great master has
realised to itself the traits and life of an actual
personality. It is not that he has any special love
for his Jacobin, but that he has the poet's eye for

types, politics apart. He sees how much the aristocrat, slaying hip and thigh for the king, and the
Jacobin, slaying hip and thigh for the Republic,
resembled one another. 'Let us confess,' he says,
' these two men, the Marquis and the priest [Lantenac
and Cimourdain], were up to a certain point the self-
same man. The bronze mask of civil war has two
profiles, one turned towards the past, the other
towards the future, but as tragic the one as the other.
Lantenac was the first of these profiles, Cimourdain
was the second; only the bitter rictus of Lantenac
was covered with shadow and night, and on the
fatal brow of Cimourdain was a gleam of the dawn '
(ii. 91).

And let us mark Victor Hugo's signal distinction
in his analysis of character. It is not mere vigour
of drawing, nor acuteness of perception, nor fire of
imagination, though he has all these gifts, and truest
of their kind. But then Scott had them too, and yet
we feel in Victor Hugo's work a seriousness, a significance, a depth of tone that never touches us in the
work of his famous predecessor in romance, delightful
as the best of that work is. Balfour of Burley is one
of Scott's most commanding figures, and the stern
Covenanter is nearly in the same plane of character
as the stern Jacobin. Yet Cimourdain impresses
us more profoundly. He is as natural, as human,
as readily conceivable, and yet he produces something of the subtle depth of effect that belongs to
the actor in a play of Æschylus. Why is this?

Because Hugo makes us conscious of the tragedy of temperament, the sterner Necessity of character, the resistless compulsion of circumstance, that is the modern and positive expression for the old Destiny of the Greeks, and in some expression or other is now an essential element in the highest presentation of human life. Here is not the Unknown. On the contrary, we are in the very heart of science ; tragedy to the modern is not τύχη, but a thing of cause and effect, invariable antecedent and invariable consequent. It is the presence of this tragic force underlying action that gives to all Hugo's work its lofty quality, its breadth, and generality, and fills both it and us who read, with pity and gravity and an understanding awe.

The action is this. Cimourdain had the young Gauvain to train from its earliest childhood, and the pupil grew up with the same rigid sense of duty as the master, though temperament modified its form. When the Revolution came, Gauvain, though a noble, took sides with the people, but he was not of the same spirit as his teacher. ' The Revolution,' says Hugo, ' by the side of youthful figures of giants, Danton, Saint-Just, and Robespierre, has young ideal figures, like Hoche and Marceau. Gauvain was one of these figures ' (ii. 34). Cimourdain has himself named delegate from the Committee of Public Safety to the expeditionary column of which Gauvain is in command. The warmth of affection between them was undiminished, but difference in

temperament bred difference in their principles.
They represented, as the author says, the two poles
of the truth; the two sides of the inarticulate,
subterranean, fatal contention of the year of the
Terror. Their arguments with one another make
the situation more intelligible to the historic student,
as they make the characters of the speakers more
transparent for the romance.

This is Cimourdain:

.Beware, there are terrible duties in life. Do not
accuse what is not responsible. Since when has the
disorder been the fault of the physician? Yes, what
marks this tremendous year is being without pity.
Why? Because it is the great revolutionary year.
This year incarnates the Revolution. The Revolution
has an enemy, the old world, and to that it is pitiless,
just as the surgeon has an enemy, gangrene, and is
pitiless to that. The Revolution extirpates kingship in
the king, aristocracy in the noble, despotism in the
soldier, superstition in the priest, barbarity in the judge,
in a word whatever is tyranny in whatever is tyrant.
The operation is frightful, the Revolution performs it
with a sure hand. As to the quantity of sound flesh that
it requires, ask Boerhave what he thinks of it. What
tumour that has to be cut out does not involve loss of
blood? . . . The Revolution devotes itself to its fated
task. It mutilates but it saves. . . . It has the past in
its grasp, it will not spare. It makes in civilisation a
deep incision whence shall come the safety of the human
race. You suffer? No doubt. How long will it last?
The time needed for the operation. Then you will live,
etc. (ii. 65-66).

'One day,' he adds, 'the Revolution will justify
the Terror.' To which Gauvain retorts thus:

Fear lest the Terror be the calumny of the Revolution. Liberty, Equality, Fraternity, are dogmas of peace and harmony. Why give them an aspect of alarm? What do we seek? To win nations to the universal public. Then why inspire fright? Of what avail is intimidation? It is wrong to do ill in order to do good. You do not pull down the throne to leave the scaffold standing. Let us hurl away crowns, let us spare heads. The Revolution is concord, not affright. Mild ideas are ill served by men who do not know pity. Amnesty is for me the noblest word in human speech. I will shed no blood save at hazard of my own. . . . In the fight let us be the enemies of our foes, and after the victory their brothers (ii. 67).

These two together, Cimourdain and Gauvain, make an ideal pair of the revolutionists of '93. Strip each of them of the beauty of character with which the poet's imagination has endowed them, add instead passion, violence, envy, egoism, malice; then you understand how in the very face of the foreign enemy Girondins sharpened the knife for the men of the Mountain, Hébertists screamed for the lives of Robespierrists, Robespierre struck off the head of Danton, Thermidorians crushed Robespierre.

Victor Hugo has given to this typic historical struggle of '93 the qualities of nobleness and beauty which art requires in dealing with real themes. Lantenac falls into the hands of the Blues, headed by Cimourdain and Gauvain, but he does so in consequence of yielding to a heroic and self-devoting impulse of humanity. Cimourdain, true to his temperament, insists on his instant execution.

Gauvain, true also to his temperament, is seized with a thousand misgivings, and there is no more ample, original, and masterly presentation of a case of conscience, that in civil war always must be common enough, than the struggle through which Gauvain passes before he can resolve to deliver Lantenac. This pathetic debate—'the stone of Sisyphus, which is only the quarrel of man with himself'—turns on the loftiest, broadest, most generous motives, touching the very bases of character, and reaching far beyond the issue of '93. The political question is seen to be no more than a superficial aspect of a deeper moral question. Lantenac, the representative of the old order, had performed an exploit of signal devotion. Was it not well that one who had faith in the new order should show himself equally willing to cast away his life to save one whom self-sacrifice had transformed from the infernal Satan into the heavenly Lucifer?

Gauvain saw in the shade the sinister smile of the sphinx. The situation was a sort of dread crossway where the conflicting truths issued and confronted one another, and where the three supreme ideas of man stood face to face—humanity, the family, the fatherland. Each of the voices spoke in turn, and each in turn declared the truth. How choose? Each in turn seemed to hit the mark of reason and justice, and said, Do that. Was that the thing to be done? Yes. No. Reasoning counselled one thing; sentiment another; the two counsels were contradictory. Reasoning is only reason; sentiment is often conscience; the one comes from man, the other from a loftier source. That is why sentiment has less

distinctness, and more might.   Yet what strength in the
severity of reason !   Gauvain hesitated.   His perplexity
was so fierce.   Two abysses opened before him : to
destroy the marquis, or to save him ?   Which of these
two gulfs was duty ?

The whole scene (ii. 206-219) is a masterpiece of
dramatic strength, sustention, and flexibility—only
equalled by the dramatic vivacity of the scene in
which Cimourdain, sitting as judge, orders the
prisoner to be brought forward, to his horror sees
Gauvain instead of Lantenac, and then condemns
the man whom he loves best on earth to be taken
to the guillotine.

The tragedy of the story, its sombre tone, the
overhanging presence of death, are prevented from
being oppressive by the variety of minor situation
and subordinate character with which the central
figures are surrounded.   No writer living was so
consummate a master of landscape, and besides the
forest we here have an elaborate sea-piece, full of
the weird, ineffable, menacing suggestion of the sea
in some of her unnumbered moods ; and there is a
scene of late twilight on a high solitary down over
the bay of Mont Saint Michel, to which a reader
blessed with sensibility to the subtler impressions
of landscape will turn again and again, as he visits
some actual prospect where the eye procures for the
inner sense a dream of beauty and the incommensur-
able.   Perhaps the palm for exquisite workmanship

will be popularly given, and justly, to the episode
humorously headed *The Massacre of Saint Bartholomew*, at the opening of the third volume. It is the
story of three little children, barely out of infancy,
awaking, playing, eating, wondering, slumbering, in
solitude through a summer day in an old tower. As
a rule the attempt to make infancy interesting in
literature ends in failure. But at length the painters
have found an equal, or more than an equal, in an
artist whose medium lends itself less easily than
colour and form to the reproduction of the beauty
and life of childhood. In his poetry Victor Hugo
had already shown his rare sensibility to the
pathos of the beginnings of our life ; witness *Chose
vue un jour de printemps, Les Pauvres Gens*, the
well - known pieces in *L'Année terrible*, and a
hundred other lively touches and fragments of
finished loveliness and penetrating sympathy. In
prose it is a more difficult feat to collect the trivial
details that make up the life of the tiny human animal
into a whole that shall be impressive, finished, and
beautiful. And prose can only describe by details
enumerated one by one. This most arduous feat is
accomplished in the children's summer day in the
tower, and with enchanting success. Intensely real-
istic, yet the picture overflows with emotion—not
the emotion of the mother, but of the poet. There
is infinite tenderness, pathos, love, but all heightened
at once and strengthened by the self-control of
masculine force. A man writing about infants

seems able to place himself outside, and thus to gain more calm and freedom of vision than the yearning of women permits to them in this field of art. Not a detail is spared, yet the whole is full of delight, pity, humour. Only one lyric passage is allowed to poetise and accentuate the realism of the description. Georgette, some twenty months old, scrambles from her cradle and prattles to the sunbeam.

What a bird says in its song, a child says in its prattle. 'Tis the same hymn; a hymn indistinct, lisping, profound. The child has what the bird has not, the sombre human destiny in front of it. Hence the sadness of men as they listen, mingling with the joy of the little one as it sings. The sublimest canticle to be heard on earth is the stammering of the human soul on the lips of infancy. The confused chirruping of a thought, that is as yet no more than an instinct, has in it one knows not what sort of artless appeal to eternal justice ; or is it a protest uttered on the threshold before entering, a protest meek and poignant? This ignorance, smiling at the Infinite, compromises all creation in the lot that shall fall to the weak defenceless being. Ill, if it shall come, will be an abuse of confidence.

The child's murmur is more and is less than words ; there are no notes, and yet it is a song ; there are no syllables, and yet it is language. . . . This poor stammering is a compound of what the child said when it was an angel, and of what it will say when it becomes a man. The cradle has a Yesterday as the grave has a Morrow ; in that strange cooing the Morrow and the Yesterday mingle their twofold mystery. . . .

Her lips smiled, her eyes smiled, the dimples in her cheeks smiled. There came forth in this smile a mysterious welcome of the morning. The soul has faith

in the ray. The heavens were blue, warm was the air.
The fragile creature, without knowing or recognising, or
understanding anything, softly afloat in musings that
are not thought, felt itself safe in the midst of nature,
among those friendly trees and that guileless greenery,
in the pure and peaceful landscape, amid the rustle of
nests, of flowing springs, of insects, of leaves, while over
all there glowed the great innocency of the sun (ii. 104).

As an eminent man has written about Words-
worth's most famous Ode, there may be some bad
philosophy here, but there is assuredly noble and
touching poetry.

If the carelessness of infancy is caught with this
perfection of finish, there is a tragic companion piece
in the horror and gnawing anguish of the wretched
woman from whom her young have been taken—her
rescue from death, her fierce yearnings for them like
the yearnings of a beast, her brute-like heedlessness
of her life and her body in the cruel search.

So the poet conducts us along the strange excur-
sive windings of the life and passion of humanity.
The same hand that draws such noble figures as
Gauvain—and the real Lanjuinais of history was
fully as heroic and noble as the imaginary Gauvain
of fiction—is equally skilful in drawing the wild
Breton beggar who dwells underground among the
branching tree-roots; the monstrous Imânus, the
barbarous retainer of the Lord of the Seven Forests;
Radoub, the sergeant from Paris, a man of hearty
oaths, hideous, heroic, humoursome, of a bloody
ingenuity in combat. And the same hand that

described the silent sundown on the sandy shore of the bay, and the mysterious darkness of the forests, and the blameless play of the little ones, gives us the prodigious animation of the night surprise at Dôl, the furious conflict at La Tourgue, and, perhaps most powerful of all, the breaking loose of the gun on the deck of the *Claymore*. You may say that this is only melodrama ; but if we turn to the actual events of '93, the melodrama of the romancer will seem but tame compared with the melodrama of the faithful chronicler. And so long as the narrative of melo-dramatic action is filled with poetry and beauty, there is no reproach in uncommon situation, in intense passion, in magnanimous or subtle motives that are not of every day. Of Hugo's art we may say what Newman has said of something else : *Such work is always open to criticism and it is always above it.*

There is poetry and beauty, sure enough, in the common lives about us, if we look at them with imaginative and sympathetic eye, and we owe much to the art that reveals to us the tragedy of the parlour and the frock-coat, and analyses the bitterness and sorrow and high passion that may underlie a life of outer smoothness and decorum. Still, no criticism will accept this as the final and exclusive limitation of imaginative work. Art is nothing if not catholic and many-sided, and it is certainly not exhausted by mere domestic possibilities. Goethe's fine, lumin-ous feeling for practical life, that has given such depth of richness and wisdom to his best prose writing, fills us with a delightful sense of satisfaction and of what is adequate ; and yet why should it not leave us with a mind eagerly open for the larger and more inventive romance, in which nature is clothed with some of the awe and might and silent contemplation of the puny destinies of man, that used to surround the conception of the supernatural ? Hugo seeks strong and extraordinary effects ; he is a master of terrible image, profound emotion, audacious fancy; but then these are as real, as natural, as true to fact, as the fairest reproduction of the moral poverties of the world. Let it be added that while he is without a rival in the dark mysterious heights of imaginative effect, he is equally a master in strokes of tenderness and all that is most delicate in human sympathy. *Ninety-three* seems to contain pieces that surpass every other book of Hugo's in the latter range of qualities, and not to fall at all short in the former. And so, in the words of the man of genius recently writing on Victor Hugo,[1] ' As we pity ourselves for the loss of poems and pictures which have perished, and left of Sappho but a fragment and of Zeuxis but a name, so are we inclined to pity the dead who died too soon to enjoy the great works we have enjoyed. At each new glory that " swims into our ken," we surely feel that it is something to have lived to see that too rise.'

[1] Swinburne.

FRANCE IN THE EIGHTEENTH CENTURY.

THE announcement that one of the most ingenious and accomplished men of letters in Europe was engaged upon a history of the French Revolution, raised some doubts among those who have thought most about the qualifications proper to the historian. M. Taine has the quality of the best type of a man of letters; he has the fine critical aptitude for seizing the secret of an author's or an artist's manner, for penetrating to dominant and central ideas, for marking the abstract and general under accidental forms in which they are concealed, for connecting the achievements of literature and art with facts of society and impulses of human character and life. He is the master of a style which, if it seems to lack the breadth, the firmness, the sustained and level strength of great writing, is yet always energetic, and fresh, and alive with that spontaneous reality and independence of interest which distinguishes the genuine writer from the mere weaver of sentences and the servile mechanic of the

---

[1] *Les Origines de la France contemporaine.* Tom. i. *L'Ancien Régime.* Par H. Taine. Paris: Hachette. 1876.

2 C

pen. The matter and form alike of M. Taine's best
work—and we say best, for his work is not without
degrees and inequalities of worth—prove that he has
not shrunk from the toil and austerity of the student,
from that scorn of delight and living of laborious
days, by which only can men either get command
of the art of just and finished expression, or gather
to themselves much knowledge.

But with all its attractiveness and high uses of its
own, the genius for literature in its proper sense is
distinct from the genius for political history.   The
discipline is different, because the matter is different.
To criticise Rousseau's *Social Contract* requires one
set of attainments, and to judge the proceedings of
the Constituent Assembly or the Convention requires
a set of quite different attainments.   A man may
have the keenest sense of the filiation of ideas, of
their scope and purport, and yet have a very dull or
uninterested eye for the play of material forces, the
wayward tides of great gatherings of men, the rude
and awkward methods that sometimes go to the
attainment of wise political ends.

It would perhaps not be too bold to lay down this
proposition ; that no good social history has ever been
written by a man who has not either himself taken a
more or less active part in public affairs, or else been
an habitual intimate of persons who were taking such
a part on a considerable scale.   Everybody knows
what Gibbon said about the advantage to the historian
of the Roman Empire of having been a member of the

English parliament and a captain in the Hampshire grenadiers. Thucydides commanded an Athenian squadron, and Tacitus filled the offices of prætor and consul. Xenophon, Polybius, and Sallust, were all men of affairs and public adventure. Guicciardini was an ambassador, a ruler, and the counsellor of rulers ; and Machiavel was all these things and more. Voltaire was the keen-eyed friend of the greatest princes and statesmen of his time, and was more than once engaged in diplomatic transactions. Robertson was a powerful party chief in the Assembly of the Scotch Church. Grote and Macaulay were active members of parliament, and Hallam and Milman were confidential members of circles where affairs of State were the staple of daily discussion among the men who were responsible for conducting them to successful issues. Guizot was a prime minister, Finlay was a farmer of the Greek revenue. The most learned of contemporary English historians a few years ago was twice pressed to contest a county, and was habitually inspired in his researches into the past by his interest in the politics of the present. The German historians, whose gifts in reconstructing the past are so valuable and so singular, have for the most part been as actively interested in the public movements of to-day, as in those of any century before or since the Christian era. Niebuhr held more than one political post of dignity and importance ; and of historical writers in our time, one has sat in several Prussian parliaments ; another, once the tutor of a Prussian prince, has lived in the atmosphere of high politics; while all the best of them have taken their share in the preparation of the political spirit and ideas that have restored Germany to all the fullness and exaltation of national life.

It is hardly necessary to extend the list. It is indeed plain on the least reflection that close contact with political business, however modest in its pretensions, is the best possible element in the training of any one who aspires to understand and reproduce political history. Political preparation is as necessary as literary preparation. There is no necessity that the business should be on any majestic and imperial scale. To be a guardian of the poor in an East-End parish, to be behind the scenes of some great strike of labour, to be an active member of the parliamentary committee of a Trades Council or of the executive committee of a Union or a League, may be quite as instructive discipline as participation in mightier scenes. Those who write concrete history, without ever having taken part in practical politics, are, one might say, in the position of those ancients who wrote about the human body without ever having effectively explored it by dissection. Carlyle, it is true, by force of penetrating imaginative genius, has reproduced in stirring and resplendent dithyrambs the fire and passion, the rage and tears, the many-tinted dawn and the blood-red sunset of the French Revolution; and the more a man learns about the details of the Revolution, the greater is his admiration for Carlyle's magnificent performance. But it is dramatic presentation, not social analysis; a masterpiece of literature, not a scientific investigation; a prodigy of poetic insight, not a sane and quantitative exploration of the complex processes, the deep-lying economical, fiscal, and political conditions, that prepared so immense an explosion.

We have to remember, it is true, that M. Taine is not professing to write a history in the ordinary sense. His book lies, if we may use two very pompous but indispensable words, partly in the region of historiography, but much more in the region of sociology. The study of the French Revolution cannot yet be a history of the past, for the French still walk *per ignes suppositos,* and the Revolution is still some way from being fully accomplished. It was the disputes between the Roman and the Reformed churches which inspired historical research in the sixteenth and seventeenth centuries; it is the disputes among French parties that now inspire what professes to be historiography, but what is really a sort of experimental investigation in the science of society. They little know how long and weary a journey lies before them, said Burke, who undertake to bring great masses of men into the political unity of a nation. The process is still going on, and a man of M. Taine's lively intellectual sensibility can no more escape its influences than he can escape the ingredients of the air he breathes. We may add that if his work had been really historic, he must inevitably have gone further back than the eighteenth century for the 'Origins' of contemporary

France.   The very slight, vague, and unsubstantial
chapter with which he opens his work cannot be
accepted as a substitute for what the subject really
demanded — a serious summary, however condensed
and rapid, of the various forces, accidents, deliberate
lines of policy, which, from the breaking up of the
great fiefs down to the death of Louis the Fourteenth,
had prepared the distractions of the monarchy under
Louis's descendants.

Full of interest as it is, M. Taine's book can hardly
be described as containing much that is new or
strikingly significant.   He develops one idea, indeed,
which we have never before seen stated in its present
form, but which, if it implies more than has been often
advanced by previous writers in other forms, cannot
be accepted as true.   This is perhaps a point better
worth discussing than any other which his book raises.
The rest is a very elaborate and thorough description
of the structure of society, of its physiognomy in
manners and characteristics, the privileges, the burdens,
the daily walk and conversation of the various classes
which made up the French people between the
Regency and the Revolution.   M. Taine's method of
description does not strike one as altogether happy.
It is a common complaint against French historians
that they are too lax about their authorities, and too
heedless about giving us chapter and verse for their
assertions.   M. Taine goes to the contrary extreme,
and pours his note-books into his text with a steady-
handed profusion that is excessively fatiguing, and

makes the result far less effective than it would have been if all this industrious reading had been thoroughly fused and recast into a homogeneous whole. It is an ungenerous trick of criticism to disparage good work by comparing it with better; but the reader can scarcely help contrasting M. Taine's overcrowded pages with the perfect assimilation, the pithy fullness, the pregnant meditation, of De Tocqueville's book on the same subject. When we attempt to reduce M. Taine's chapters to a body of propositions standing out in definite relief from one another, yet conveying a certain unity of interpretation, we soon feel how possible it is for an author to have literary clearness along with historic obscurity.

In another respect we are inclined to question the felicity of M. Taine's method. It does not convey the impression of movement. The steps and changes in the conflict among the organs of the old society are not marked in their order and succession. The reader is not kept alive to the gradual progress of the break-up of old institutions and ideas. The sense of an active and ceaseless struggle, extending in various stages across the century, is effaced by an exclusive attention to the social details of a given phase. We need the story. You cannot effectively reproduce the true sense and significance of such an epoch as the eighteenth century in France, without telling us, however barely, the tale, for example, of the long battle of the ecclesiastical factions, and the yet more important series of battles between the judiciary and the crown. If M

Taine's book were a piece of abstract social analysis, the above remark would not be true. But it is a study of the concrete facts of French life and society, and to make such a study effective, the element of the chronicle, as in Lacretelle or Jobez, cannot rightly be dispensed with.

Let us proceed to the chief thesis of the book. The new formula in which M. Taine describes the source of all the mischiefs of the revolutionary doctrine is this. 'When we see a man,' he says, 'who is rather weak in constitution, but apparently sound and of peaceful habits, drink eagerly of a new liquor, then suddenly fall to the ground, foaming at the mouth, delirious and convulsed, we have no hesitation in supposing that in the pleasant draught there was some dangerous ingredient; but we need a delicate analysis in order to decompose and isolate the poison. There is one in the philosophy of the eighteenth century, as curious as it was potent: for not only is it the product of a long historic elaboration, the final and condensed extract in which the whole thought of the century ends; but more than that, its two principal elements are peculiar in this, that when separated they are each of them salutary, yet in combination they produce a poisonous compound.' These two ingredients are, first, the great and important acquisitions of the eighteenth century in the domain of physical science; second, the fixed classic form of the French intelligence. 'It is the classic spirit which, being applied to the scientific acquisitions of the time, produced the philosophy of the century and the doctrines of the Revolution.' This classic spirit has in its literary form one or two well-known marks. It leads, for instance, to the fastidious exclusion of particulars, whether in phrases, objects, or traits of character, and substitutes for them the general, the vague, the typic. Systematic arrangement orders the whole structure and composition from the period to the paragraph, from the paragraph to the structural series of paragraphs ; it dictates the style as it has fixed the syntax. Its great note is the absolute. Again, 'two principal operations make up the work of the human intelligence: placed in face of things, it receives the impression of them more or less exactly, completely, and profoundly ; next, leaving the things, it decomposes its impression, and classifies, distributes, and expresses more or less skilfully the ideas that it draws from that impression. In the second of these processes the classic is superior.' Classicism is only the organ of a certain reason, the *raison raisonnante ;* that which insists upon thinking with as little preparation and as much ease as possible ; which is contented with what it has acquired, and takes no thought about augmenting or renewing it ; which either cannot or will not embrace the plenitude and the complexity of things as they are.

As an analysis of the classic spirit in French literature, nothing can be more ingenious and happy than these pages (p. 241, etc.) But, after all, classic is only the literary form preferred by a certain turn of intelligence; and we shall do well to call that turn of intelligence by a general name, that shall compre-hend not only its literary form but its operations in every other field. And accordingly at the end of this very chapter we find M. Taine driven straightway to change classic for mathematic in describing the method of the new learning. And the latter description is much better, for it goes beneath the surface of literary expression, important as that is, down to the methods of reasoning. It leads us to the root of the matter, to the deductive habits of the French thinkers. The mischief of the later speculation of the eighteenth century in France was that men argued about the complex, conditional, and relative propositions of society, as if they had been theorems and problems of Euclid. And M. Taine himself is, as we say, com-pelled to change his term when he comes to the actual facts and personages of the revolutionary epoch. It was the geometric, rather than the classic, quality of political reasoning, which introduced so much that we now know to have been untrue and mischievous.

Even in literary history it is surely nearer the truth to say of the latter half of the century that the revolutionary movement began with the break-up of classic form and the gradual dissolution of the classic spirit. Indeed this is such a commonplace of criti-cism, that we can only treat M. Taine's inversion of it as a not very happy paradox. It was in literature that this genius of innovation, which afterwards ex-tended over the whole social structure, showed itself

first of all. Rousseau, not merely in the judgment
of a foreigner like myself, but in that of the very
highest of all native authorities, Sainte-Beuve, effected
the greatest revolution that the French tongue had
undergone since Pascal. And this revolution was
more remarkable for nothing than for its repudiation
of nearly all the notes of classicism that are enumerated
by M. Taine. Diderot, again, in every page of his
work, whether he is discussing painting, manners,
science, the drama, poetry, or philosophy, abounds
and overabounds in those details, particularities, and
special marks of the individual, which are, as M.
Taine rightly says, alien to the classic genius. Both
Rousseau and Diderot, considered as men of letters,
were conscious literary revolutionists, before they were
used as half-conscious social revolutionists. They
deliberately put away from them the entire classic
tradition as to the dignity of personage proper to art,
and the symmetry and fixed method proper to artistic
style. This was why Voltaire, who was a son of the
seventeenth century before he was the patriarchal sire
of the eighteenth, could never thoroughly understand
the author of the *New Heloïsa*, or the author of the
Père de famille and *Jacques le fataliste*. Such work
was to him for the most part a detestable compound
of vulgarity and rodomontade. 'There is nothing
living in the eighteenth century,' M. Taine says, 'but
the little sketches that are stitched in by the way and
as if they were contraband, by Voltaire, and five or
six portraits like Turcaret, Gil Blas, Marianne, Manon

Lescaut, Rameau's Nephew, Figaro, two or three hasty sketches of Crebillon the younger and Collé ' (p. 258). Nothing living but this ! But this is much and very much. We do not pretend to compare the authors of these admirable delineations with Molière and La Bruyère in profundity of insight or in grasp and ethical mastery, but they are certainly altogether in a new vein even from those two great writers, when we speak of the familiar, the real, and the particular, as distinguished from old classic generality. And, we may add in passing, that the social life of France from the death of Louis XIV. downwards was emancipated all round from the formality and precision of the classic time. As M. Taine himself shows in many amusing pages, life was singularly gay, free, sociable, and varied. The literature of the time was sure to reflect, and does reflect, this universal rejection of the restraints of the past age when the classic spirit had been supreme.

Apart from this kind of objection to its exact expression, let us look at the substance of M. Taine's dictum. 'It was the classic spirit, which, when applied to the scientific acquisitions of the time, produced the philosophy of the century and the doctrines of the Revolution.' Even if we substitute geometric or deductive spirit for classic spirit, the proposition remains nearly as unsatisfactory. What were the doctrines of the Revolution ? The sovereignty of the people, rights of man, liberty, equality, fraternity, progress and perfectibility of the species—these were the main articles of the new creed. M. Taine, like too many French writers, writes as if these ideas had never been heard of before 1789. Yet the most important and decisive of them were at least as old as the Reformation, were not peculiarly French in any sense, and were no more the special products of the classic spirit mixing with scientific acquisitions than they were the products of Manicheanism. It is extraordinary that a writer who attributes so much importance to Rousseau, and who gives us so ample an account of his political ideas, should not have traced these ideas to their source, nor even told us that they had a source wholly outside of France. Rousseau was a Protestant; he was a native of the very capital and mother city of Protestantism, militant. and democratic; and he was penetrated to his heart's core by the political ideas which had arisen in Europe at the Reformation. There is not a single principle in the Social Contract which may not be found either in Hobbes, or in Locke, or in Althusen, any more than there is a single proposition of his deism which was not in the air of Geneva when he wrote his Savoyard Vicar. If this be the case, what becomes of the position that the revolutionary philosophy was worked out by the *raison raisonnante*, which is the special faculty of a country saturated with the classic spirit? If we must have a formula, it would be nearer the truth to say that the doctrines of the Revolution were the product, not of the classic spirit applied to scientific acquisitions, but, first, of

the democratic ideas of the Protestant Reformation, and then of the fictions of the lawyers, both
of them allied with certain urgent social and political
necessities.

So much, then, for the political side of the 'philosophy of the century,' if we are to use this too
comprehensive expression for all the products of a
very complex and many-sided outburst of speculative
energy. Apart from its political side, we find M.
Taine's formula no less unsatisfactory for its other
phases. He seems to us not to go back nearly far
enough in his search for the intellectual origins, any
more than for the political origins, of his contemporary
France. He has taken no account of the progress of
the spirit of Scepticism from Montaigne's time, nor of
the decisive influence of Montaigne on the revolutionary thinkers. Yet the extraordinary excitement
aroused in France by Bayle's *Dictionary* was a proof
of the extent to which the sceptical spirit had spread
before the Encyclopædists were born. The great
influence of Fontenelle was wholly in the same sceptical direction. There was a strong sceptical element
in French Materialism, even when materialism was
fully developed and seemed most dogmatic.[1] Indeed,
it may sometimes occur to the student of such a man
as Diderot to wonder how far materialism in France
was only seized upon as a means of making scepticism
both serious and philosophic. For its turn for scepticism is at least as much a distinction of the French

---

[1] See Lange's *Geschichte des Materialismus*, i. 298.

intelligence as its turn for classicism. And, once more, if we must have a formula, it would be best to say that the philosophy of the century was the product, first of scepticism applied to old beliefs which were no longer easily tenable, and then of scepticism extended to old institutions that were no longer practically habitable.

And this brings us to the cardinal reason for demurring to M. Taine's neatly rounded proposition. His appreciation of the speculative precursors of the Revolution seems to us to miss the decisive truth about them. He falls precisely into those errors of the *raison raisonnante*, about which, in his description of the intellectual preparation of the great overthrow, he has said so many just and acute things. Nothing can be more really admirable than M. Taine's criticism upon Montesquieu, Voltaire, Rousseau, Diderot, as great masters of language (pp. 339-361). All this is marked by an amplitude of handling, a variety of approach, a subtlety of perception, a fullness of comprehension, which give a very different notion of M. Taine's critical soundness and power from any that one could have got from his account elsewhere of our English writers. Some of the remarks are open to criticism, as might be expected. It is hard to accept the saying (p. 278) that Montesquieu's 'celebrity was not an influence.' It was Montesquieu, after all, who first introduced among the encyclopædic band a rationalistic and experiential conception of the various legal and other conditions of the social

union, as distinguished from the old theological explanation of them. The correspondence of Voltaire,
Rousseau, Diderot, D'Alembert, is sufficient to show
how immediately, as well as how powerfully, they
were influenced by Montesquieu's memorable book.
Again, it is surely going too far to say that Montesquieu's *Persian Letters* contained every important
idea of the century. Does it, for instance, contain
that thrice fruitful idea which Turgot developed in
1750, of all the ages being linked together by an
ordered succession of causes and effects?   These and
other objections, however, hardly affect the brilliance
and substantial excellence of all this part of the book.
It is when he proceeds to estimate these great men,
not as writers but as social forces, not as stylists but
as apostles, that M. Taine discloses the characteristic
weaknesses of the bookman in dealing with the facts
of concrete sociology.   He shows none of this weakness in what he says of the remote past. On the
contrary, he blames, as we have all blamed, Voltaire,
Rousseau, and the rest of the group, for their failure
to recognise that the founders of religions satisfied a
profound need in those who accepted them, and that
this acceptance was the spontaneous admission of their
relative fitness.   It would be impossible to state this
important truth better than M. Taine has done in
the following passage :—

'At certain critical moments in history,' he says,
'men have come out from the narrow and confined
track of their daily life and seized in one wide vision

the infinite universe; the august face of eternal nature is suddenly unveiled before them; in the sublimity of their emotion they seem to perceive the very principle of its being; and at least they did discern some of its features. By an admirable stroke of circumstance, these features were precisely the only ones that their age, their race, a group of races, a fraction of humanity, happened to be in a condition to understand. Their point of view was the only one under which the multitudes beneath could place themselves. For millions of men, for hundreds of generations, the one access to divine things was along their path. They pronounced the unique word, heroic or tender, enthusiastic or tranquillising; the only word that, around them and after them, the heart and the intelligence would consent to hearken to ; the only one adapted to the deep-growing wants, the long-gathered aspirations, the hereditary faculties, a whole moral and mental structure,—here to that of the Hindu or the Mongol, there to that of the Semite or the European, in our Europe to that of the German, the Latin, or the Slav; in such a way that its very contradictions, instead of condemning it, were exactly what justified it, since its diversity produced its adaptation, and its adaptation produced its benefits ' (p. 272).

It is extraordinary that a thinker who could so clearly discern the secret of the great spiritual movements of human history, should fail to perceive that the same law governs and explains all the minor

2 D

movements in which wide communities have been suddenly agitated by the word of a teacher. It is well—as no one would be more likely to contend than myself, who have attempted the task—to demonstrate the contradictions, the superficiality, the inadequateness, of the teaching of Rousseau, Voltaire, or Diderot. But it is well also, and in a historical student it is not only well, but the very pith and marrow of criticism, to search for that 'adaptation,' to use M. Taine's very proper expression, which gave to the word of these teachers its mighty power and far-spreading acceptance. Is it not as true of Rousseau and Voltaire, acting in a small society, as it is of Buddha or Mahomet acting on vast groups of races, that 'leur point de vue était le seul auquel les multitudes échelonnées au - dessous d'eux pouvaient se mettre'? Did not they too seize, 'by a happy stroke of circumstance,' exactly those traits in the social union, in the resources of human nature, in its deep-seated aspirations, which their generation was in a condition to comprehend,—liberty, equality, fraternity, progress, justice, tolerance?

M. Taine shows, as so many others have shown before him, that the *Social Contract*, when held up in the light of true political science, is very poor stuff. Undoubtedly it is so. And Quintilian—an accomplished and ingenious Taine of the first century —would have thought the Gospels and Epistles, and Augustine and Jerome and Chrysostom, very poor stuff, compared with the—

> Mellifluous streams that watered all the schools
> Of Academics old and new, with those
> Surnamed Peripatetics, and the Sect
> Epicurean, and the Stoic severe.

And in some ways, from a literary or logical point of view, the early Christian writers could ill bear this comparison. But great bodies of men, in ages of trouble and confusion, have an instinctive feeling for the fragment of truth which they happen to need at the hour. They have a spontaneous apprehension of the formula which is at once the expression of their miseries and the mirror of their hope. The guiding force in the great changes of the world has not been the formal logic of the schools or of literature, but the practical logic of social convenience. Men take as much of a teacher's doctrine as meets their real wants : the rest they leave. The Jacobins accepted Rousseau's ideas about the sovereignty of the people, but they seasonably forgot his glorification of the state of nature and his denunciations of civilisation and progress. The American revolutionists cheerfully borrowed the doctrine that all men are born free and equal, but they kept their slaves.

It was for no lack of competition that the ideas of the *Social Contract*, of Raynal's *History of the two Indies*, of the *System of Nature*, of the *Philosophical Dictionary*, made such astounding and triumphant way in men's minds. There was Montesquieu with a sort of historic method. There was Turgot, and the school of the economists. There were seventy thousand of the secular clergy, and sixty thousand of the regular clergy, ever proclaiming by life or exhortation ideas of peace, submission, and a kingdom not of this world. Why did men turn their backs on these and all else, and betake themselves to revolutionary ideas? How came those ideas to rise up and fill the whole air? The answer is that, with all their contradiction, shallowness, and danger, such ideas fitted the crisis. They were seized by virtue of an instinct of national self-preservation. The evil elements in them worked themselves out in infinite mischief. The true elements in them saved France, by firing men with social hope and patriotic faith.

How was it, M. Taine rightly asks, that the philosophy of the eighteenth century, which was born in England and thence sent its shoots to France, dried up in the one country, and grew to overshadow the earth in the other? Because, he answers, the new seed fell upon ground that was suited to it, the home of the classic spirit, the country of *raison raisonnante*. Compare with this merely literary solution the answer given to the same question by De Tocqueville :—' It was no accident that the philosophers of the eighteenth century generally conceived notions so opposed to those which still served as the base of the society of their time ; *these ideas had actually been suggested to them by the very sight of that society, which they had ever before their eyes*' (*Ancien Régime*, 206). This is the exact truth and the whole truth. The greatest enterprise achieved by the men of letters in the period of intellectual preparation was the Encyclopædia ; and I have elsewhere tried to present what seemed to be ample evidence that the spirit and aim of that great undertaking were social, and that its conductors, while delivering their testimony in favour of the experiential conception of life in all its aspects, and while reproducing triumphantly the most recent acquisitions of science, had still the keenest and most direct eye for the abuses and injustice, the waste and disorder, of the social institutions around them. The answer, then, which we should venture to give to M. Taine's question would be much simpler than his. The philosophy of the eighteenth century fared differently in England and in France, because its ideas did not fit in with the economic and political conditions of the one, while, on the contrary, they were actively warmed and fostered by those of the other. It was not a literary aptitude in the nation for *raison raisonnante,* which developed the political theories of Rousseau, the moral and psychological theories of Diderot, the anti-ecclesiastical theories of Voltaire and Holbach. It was the profound disorganisation of institutions that suggested and stimulated the speculative agitation. 'The nation,' wrote the wise and far-seeing Turgot, 'has no constitution ; it is a society composed of different orders ill assorted, and of a people whose members have few social bonds with one another ; where consequently scarcely any one is occupied with anything beyond his private interest exclusively,' and so forth. [1] Any student, uncom-

[1] *Œuvres,* ii. 504.

mitted to a theory, who examines in close detail the wise aims and just and conservative methods of Turgot, and the circumstances of his utter rout after a short experiment of twenty months of power, will rise from that deplorable episode with the conviction that a pacific renovation of France, an orderly readjustment of her institutions, was hopelessly impossible. '*Si l'on avait été sage!*' those cry who consider the Revolution as a futile mutiny. If people had only been prudent, all would have been accomplished that has been accomplished since, and without the sanguinary memories, the constant interpolations of despotism, the waste of generous lives and noble purpose. And this is true. But then prudence itself was impossible. The court and the courtiers were smitten through the working of long tradition by judicial blindness. If Louis XVI. had been a Frederick, or Marie Antoinette had been a Catherine of Russia, or the nobles had even been stout-hearted gentlemen like our Cavaliers, the great transformation might then have been gradually effected without disorder. But they were none of these, and it was their characters that made the fate and doom of the situation. As for the court, Vergennes used an expression which suggests the very keyword of the situation. He had been ambassador in Turkey, and was fond of declaring that he had learnt in the seraglio how to brave the storms of Versailles. Versailles was like Stamboul or Teheran, oriental in etiquette, oriental in destruction of wealth and capital, oriental in anti-

pathy to a reforming grand vizier. It was the queen,
as we now know by incontestable evidence, who persuaded the king to dismiss Turgot, merely to satisfy
some contemptible personal resentments of herself
and her creatures.[1] And it was not in Turgot's case
only that this ineptitude wrought mischief. In June
1789 Necker was overruled in the wisest elements of
his policy and sent into exile by the violent intervention of the same court faction, headed by the same
queen, who had procured the dismissal of Turgot
thirteen years earlier. And it was one long tale
throughout, from the first hour of the reign down to
those last hours at the Tuileries in August 1792;
one long tale of intrigue, perversity, and wilful incorrigible infatuation.

Nor was the queen only to blame. Turgot, says
an impartial eye-witness—Creutz, the Swedish ambassador—is a mark for the most formidable league
possible, composed of all the great people in the
kingdom, all the parliaments, all the finance, all the
women of the court, and all the bigots. It was
morally impossible that the reforms of any Turgot
could have been acquiesced in by that emasculated
caste, who showed their quality a few years after his
dismissal by flying across the frontier at the first
breath of personal danger. 'When the gentlemen
rejoiced so boisterously over the fall of Turgot, their
applause was blind; on that day they threw away,

---

[1] *Cor. entre Marie Thérèse et le Comte Mercy-Argenteau.* vol
iii.

and in a manner that was irreparable, the opportunity
that was offered them of being born again to political
life, and changing the state-candlestick of the royal
household for the influence of a preponderant class.
The nobility, defeated on the field of feudal privilege,
would have risen again by the influence of an assembly
where they would have taken the foremost place; by
defending the interests of all, by becoming in their
turn the ally of the third estate, which had hitherto
fought on the side of the kings, they would have
repaired the unbroken succession of defeats that had
been inflicted on them since Louis the Fat.'[1]   It
would be easy to name half a dozen patricians like
the Duke d'Ayen, of exceptional public spirit and
capacity, but a proud order cannot at the first exi-
gency of a crisis change its traditional front, and
abandon the maxims of centuries in a day.   As has
been said more than once, the oriental policy of
the crown towards the nobles had the inevitable effect
of cutting them off from all opportunity of acquiring
in experience those habits of political wisdom which
have saved the territorial aristocracy of our own
country.   The English nobles in the eighteenth century had become, what they mostly are now, men of
business; agriculturists at least as much as politicians; land agents of a very dignified kind, with very
large incomes.   Sully designed to raise a working
agricultural aristocracy, and Colbert to raise a working commercial aristocracy.   But the statesman cannot

---

[1] *Turgot, philosophe et économiste.* Par A. Batbie, p. 380.

create or mould a social order at will. Perhaps one reason why the English aristocracy became a truly agricultural body in the eighteenth century was the circumstance that many of the great landowning magnates were Tories, and remained sulking on their estates rather than go to the court of the first two kings of the Hanoverian line ; just as the dependence of these two sovereigns of revolutionary title upon the revolution families is one reason why English liberties had time to root themselves thoroughly before the monarchical reaction under George III. In France, for reasons which we have no room to expatiate upon, the experiments both of Sully and of Colbert failed. The result may be read with graphic effect in the pages of Arthur Young, both before the Revolution broke out and again after Burke's superb rhetoric had biassed English opinion against it.

M. Léonce de Lavergne, it is true, in his most interesting book upon the Provincial Assemblies under Louis XVI., has endeavoured to show that in the great work of administrative reform all classes between 1778 and 1787 had shown themselves full of a liberal and practical spirit. But even in his pages we see enough of apprehensions and dissensions to perceive how deep was the intestine disorganisation ; and the attitude of the nobles in 1789 demonstrated how incurable it was by any merely constitutional modifications. Sir Philip Francis, to whom Burke submitted the proof-sheets of the *Reflections*, at once

with his usual rapid penetration discerned the weak
ness of the anti-revolutionary position. 'The French
of this day,' he told Burke, 'could not act as we did
in 1688. They had no constitution as we had to
recur to. They had no foundation to build upon.
They had no walls to repair. Much less had they
*the elements of a constitution very nearly as good as
could be wished.* A proposition so extraordinary as
this last ought to have been made out *in limine*, since
the most important deductions are drawn from it.'[1]
But, though Burke insisted on drawing his deductions
from it with sweeping impetuosity, neither he nor
any one else has yet succeeded in establishing that
all-important proposition.

What we desire to say, then, comes, in short, to
this, that M. Taine has given an exaggerated importance to the literary and speculative activity of the
last half-century of the old monarchy. In measuring
the force of the various antecedents of the Revolution,
he has assigned to books and philosophical ideas a
place in the scale of dissolvent conditions that belongs
more rightly to decayed institutions, to incompetent
and incorrigible castes, to economic incongruities that
could only be dealt with trenchantly. Books and
ideas acquired a certain importance after other things
had finally broken up the crumbling system. They
supplied a formula for the accomplished fact. 'It
was after the Revolution had fairly begun,' as a contemporary says, 'that they sought in Mably and

---

[1] Burke's *Correspondence*, iii. 157.

Rousseau for arms to sustain the system towards which the effervescence of some hardy spirits was dragging affairs. It was not the above-named authors who set people's heads aflame. M. Necker alone produced this effect, and determined the explosion.'[1]

The predominance of a historic, instead of an abstract, school of political thought could have saved nothing. It could have saved nothing, because the historic or conservative organs and elements of society were incompetent to realise those progressive ideas which were quite as essential to social continuity as the historic ideas. The historic method in political action is only practicable on condition that some, at any rate, of the great established bodies have the sap of life in their members. In France not even the judiciary, usually the last to part from its ancient roots, was sound and quick. 'The administration of justice,' says Arthur Young, 'was partial, venal, infamous. The conduct of the parliament was profligate and atrocious. The bigotry, ignorance, false principles, and tyranny of these bodies were generally conspicuous.'[2] We know what the court was, we know what the noblesse was, and this is what the third great leading order in the realm was. We repeat, then, that the historic doctrine could get no fulcrum or leverage, and that only the revolutionary doctrine, which the eighteenth century had got ready

[1] Sénac de Meilhan, *Du gouvernement en France*, 129, etc. (1795).　　[2] *Travels in France*, i. 603.

for the crisis, was adequate to the task of social renovation.

Again, we venture to put to M. Taine the following question. If the convulsions of 1789-94 were due to the revolutionary doctrine, if that doctrine was the poison of the movement, how would he explain the firm, manly, steadfast, unhysterical quality of the American Revolution thirteen years before? It was theoretically based on exactly the same doctrine. Jefferson and Franklin were as well disciplined in the French philosophy of the eighteenth century as Mirabeau or Robespierre. The Declaration of Independence recites the same abstract and unhistoric propositions as the Declaration of the Rights of Man. Why are we to describe the draught which Rousseau and the others had brewed, as a harmless or wholesome prescription for the Americans, and as maddening poison to the French? The answer must be that the quality of the drug is relative to the condition of the patient, and that the vital question for the student of the old *régime* and the circumstances of its fall is what other drug, what better process, could have extricated France on more tranquil terms from her desperate case? The American colonists, in spite of the over-wide formulæ of their Declaration, really never broke with their past in any of its fundamental elements. They had a historic basis of laws and institutions which was still sound and whole, and the political severance from England made no breach in social continuity. If a different result followed in

France, it was not because France was the land of the
classic spirit, but because her institutions were inadequate, and her ruling classes incompetent to transform
them.

M. Taine's figure of the man who drains the
poisonous draught, as having been previously ' a little
weak in constitution, but still sound and of peaceful
habits,' is entirely delusive.   The whole evidence
shows that France was not sound, but the very reverse of sound, and no inconsiderable portion of that
evidence is to be found in the facts which M. Taine
has so industriously collected in his own book.   The
description of France as a little weak in constitution,
but still sound and of peaceful habits, is the more
surprising to us because M. Taine himself had in
an earlier page (p. 109), when summing up the results
of Privilege, ended with these emphatic words : 'Déjà
avant l'écroulement final, la France est dissoute, et
elle est dissoute parce que les privilégiés ont oublié
leur caractère d'hommes publics.'   But then is not
this rather more than being only a little weak in constitution, and still sound ?

AN EASTER DIGRESSION.

Of all the views of the world possible to a poetical mind in the Cæsarean age this was the noblest and most ennobling, that it is a benefit for men to be released from a belief in the immortality of the soul, and thereby from the evil dread of death which steals over men like terror creeping over children in a dark room.—MOMMSEN.

I.

THE approach of Easter had tempted us towards the scene of a poet's musings on the same day years before—'the great sinful streets of Naples.' But time was too short, hygienic memories of a last visit were not seductive, and weather seemed more propitious to such changes of mind as a library might promise. So, with Hobbes's warning at heart, that we should either work or play, but never loiter, I stayed in my library, my Penseroso from beneath his helm-like bonnet watching me with what Ruskin calls that ghostly vitality of his.

I began a holiday by turning over a little sheaf of desultory collectanea, including a slender volume of *Les grands hommes qui sont morts en plaisantant,* and another on students killed in climbing from their ladders to high bookshelves. I took out some of them that had a sort of connection with one another, bound by the mortal link that must concern us always, holidays and workdays alike. Here are one or two of my scattered specimens; they will at least do no harm.

QUEEN ELIZABETH. (*Philosophy of the man of action.*) —As for me, I see no such great reason why I should either be proud to live, or fear to die. I have had good experience of this world. I have known what it is to be a subject, and I now know what it is to be a sovereign. Good neighbours I have had, and I have met with bad; and in trust, I have found treason. I have bestowed benefits on ill deservers; and where I have done well, I have been ill reputed and spoken of. When I call to mind things past, behold things present, and look forward to things to come, I *count them happiest that go hence soonest.* Nevertheless . . . I am armed with better courage than is common in my sex, so that whatsoever befalls me, death shall never find me unprepared.

LEIGHTON. (*The Scotch divine of the time of the Restoration, indifferently episcopal and presbyterian, the friend of Bishop Burnet who reports this of him.*)— There were two remarkable circumstances in his death. He used often to say that if he were to choose a place to die in, it should be an inn, it looking like a pilgrim's going home, to whom this world was all an inn, and who was weary of the noise and confusion of it. He added that the officious tenderness of his friends was an entanglement to a dying man, and that the unconcerned attendance of those that could be procured in such a place would give less disturbance. He had his wish.

SWIFT. (*His tragic letter when he heard in London that Stella was dead or dying.*)—'If you believe,' he writes, 'she cannot hold out till my return, I would not think of coming to Ireland. . . . I would not for the universe be present at such a trial of seeing her depart. She will be among friends that upon her own account and great worth will tend her with all possible care, where I should be a trouble to her, and the greatest torment to myself. . . . I am of opinion that there is not a greater folly than to contract too great and intimate a friendship, which must always leave the survivor miserable.'

SIR WILLIAM TEMPLE. (*To the Countess of Essex, 1674, on her grief at the death of her only daughter. A long eloquent letter, of which this is the wholesome kernel.*)—Your complaints ought to be turned into acknowledgments, for the goods or blessings of life are usually esteemed to be birth, health, beauty, friends, children, honour, riches. Now when your ladyship has fairly considered how God Almighty has dealt with you in what He has given you of all these, you may be left to judge yourself how you have dealt with Him in your complaints for what He has taken away. But if you look about you and consider other lives as well as your own, and what your lot is in comparison with those that have been drawn within the circle of your knowledge ; if you think how few are born with honour, how many die without name or children, how little beauty we see, how few friends we hear of, how many diseases and how much poverty there is in the world, you will fall down upon your knees, and instead of repining at one affliction, will admire so many blessings as you have received at the hand of God.

GLADSTONE. (*Cranmer at the stake.*)—Do you remember Jeremy Collier's sentence on his bravery at the

2 E

stake, which I count one of the grandest in English prose ? ' He seemed to repel the force of the fire, and to overlook the torture by strength of thought.' Thucydides could not beat that.

SIR HENRY VANE.—'Death holds a high place in the policy and great communities of the world. . . . It is the part of a valiant and generous mind to prefer some things before life, as things for which a man should not doubt nor fear to die. . . . True natural wisdom pursueth the learning and practice of dying well, as the very end of life, and indeed he hath not spent his life ill that hath learned to die well. It is the chiefest thing and duty of life. The knowledge of dying is the knowledge of liberty, the state of true freedom, the way to fear nothing, to live well, contentedly, and peaceable. . . . It is a good time to die, when to live is rather a burden than a blessing, and there is more ill in life than good.' When his hour came, Vane's actual carriage on Tower Hill was as noble and resolute as his words.

PLUTARCH. (*Death of Pericles.*)—When he was near his end, the best of the citizens and those of his friends who were left alive, sitting about him, were talking of the greatness of his merits, and his powers, and reckoning up his famous actions, and the number of his victories. They talked thus together among themselves, as though he were unable to mind what they said, and that his senses were gone ; he took notice of every word, and speaking out among them, said that he wondered they should commend and take notice of things which were as much owing to fortune as to anything else, and at the same time should not make mention of that which was the most excellent and greatest thing of all. 'For,' said he, 'no Athenian, through my means, ever wore mourning.'

LA FONTAINE. (*Death and the Woodcutter.*)—Bent

under the weight of his faggots and the long toil of
years, striving for his hovel of a home, at length he casts
down his logs, and thinks of his hard lot. What pleasure
has he ever had, often without bread, always without rest
—his wife, his children, soldiers, taxes, debts, forced
labour? He calls aloud for Death. Coming in an
instant Death bids him say what it is he wants. 'To
help me,' entreats the Woodcutter, 'to hoist the load up
on my back again ; it won't take you long.' Better to
go on suffering than to die. Such is ever the motto of
mankind.

MONTAIGNE.—Look on earth and at the poor people
scattered over it, bowed and bent, intent on their work,
knowing nothing of Aristotle or Cato, either of example
or precept ; from them day after day nature exacts
lessons of constancy and patience, purer and more unsophisticated than those we study with such care in the
school ; how many of them do I regularly see who make
little of poverty ; how many who would fain die, and
who pass death without fright or affliction. The man
there digging my garden has this morning buried his
father or his son. The names by which they call their
maladies take off their edge and soften them ; phthisis
is for them a cough, dysentery only a looseness, pleurisy
no more than a stitch ; and as they name them gently, so
they bear them ; they must be grievous indeed to stay
their everyday toil ; they never keep to their beds save
to die.

VICTOR HUGO. (*Death on the midnight field at
Waterloo.*)—Si quelque chose est effroyable, s'il existe une
réalité qui dépasse le rêve, c'est ceci : vivre, voir le soleil,
être en pleine possession de la force virile, avoir la santé
et la joie, rire vaillamment, courir vers une gloire qu'on
a devant soi éblouissante, se sentir dans la poitrine un
poumon qui respire, un cœur qui bat, une volonté qui
raisonne, parler, penser, espérer, aimer, avoir une mère,

avoir une femme, avoir des enfants, avoir la lumière,—
et tout à coup, le temps d'un cri, en moins d'une minute,
s'effondrer dans un abîme, tomber, rouler, écraser, être
écrasé, voir des épis de blé, des fleurs, des feuilles, des
branches, ne pouvoir se retenir à rien, sentir son sabre
inutile, des hommes sous soi, des chevaux sur soi, se
débattre en vain, les os brisés par quelques ruades dans
les ténèbres, sentir un talon qui vous fait jaillir les yeux,
mordre avec rage des fers de chevaux, étouffer, hurler, se
tordre, être là-dessous, et se dire : tout à l'heure j'étais un
vivant.[1]

SCOTT (*on a rule of nature*).—We speak freely of her
whom we have lost, and mix her name with our ordinary
conversation.   This is the rule of nature.   All primitive
people speak of their dead, and I think virtuously and
wisely.   The Highlanders speak of their dead children
as freely as of their living members, how poor Colin or
Robert would have acted in such or such a situation.   It is
a generous and a manly tone of feeling.

[1] 'If anything in the world is frightful, if there exists a
reality that exceeds dream, 'tis this : to be alive, to see the sun,
to be in full possession of a man's strength, to have health and
gladness, to laugh in brave spirits, to hasten towards a glory
in full front of you, dazzling; to feel in your breast a lung
that breathes, a heart that beats, a will with reason ; to speak,
to think, to hope, to love ; to have a mother, to have a wife, to
have children, to have light . . . then all at once, the time
for a cry, in less than a minute, to crash down into an abyss,
falling, crushing, crushed ; to see wheat-stalks, flowers, leaves,
branches ; to find nothing to cling to—to feel your sword no
use ; men beneath you, horses on top of you.   To struggle in
vain, bones all broken by rearings in the dark ; to feel a
horse-hoof that makes your eyes burst out, to bite the horse-
shoes in mad rage, to writhe, shriek, stifle ; to lie there and to
say : A moment ago and I was a live creature.'

II

I took it into my head that I might do worse than give a day or two to reviving memories of Lucretius, the ancient poet who fits in so closely with leading thoughts, and contests of thought, in our present day, to say nothing of Helvétius, d'Holbach, and others, on whom I had exercised mind and pen of old. It evidently matters much what book, prose or verse, lays hold of a man and of what book he happens by temperament, teaching, training, or accident to lay hold. *The Nature of Things* can hardly be called a book to live with, but it is full of grandeur, sympathetic feeling, sublime sonorous music, that a reader may be glad and all the better for having near him. Lucretius like Machiavelli is one of the great figures in literature who have gone through long spells of what is called immortality, bearing all the time a bad name. Singular is his story. His life was ' invisible and dim.' His one poem was never completed. Its duration hung upon a single manuscript. The manuscript appeared and disappeared for successive centuries. Whether his influence persisted in traces obscure and rare through the theologies and philosophies of the Middle Ages, scholars earnestly dispute. Some contend that in influence he was only second to Aristotle, and in continuous popularity only second to Virgil. Poet, savant, philosopher, he claims a place in three spheres. Nobody, I should think, reads his unique poem literally through. Mommsen finds Lucretius as savant absolutely unreadable. Others measure the poet, and insist that if you take a round figure for what you have a right to call poetry, you come to no more than 1800 lines out of 7400. More fastidious persons will have it there are only 700 really fine or memorable lines in the whole six books. About numbers this quarrel, like so many if not most quarrels of taste, is trivial. Even those who firmly choose to skip three-quarters still are conscious of the sound of a voice that is sublime, and the might of an imagination that soars on triumphant pinions beyond the flaming ramparts of the world. Whatever definition of poetry we may borrow from the poets themselves — whether 'a speaking picture' or 'invention' (Johnson) or 'articulate music' (Dryden)—the tense, defiant, concentrated, scornful, fervid, daring, and majestic verse of Lucretius is unique and his own.

It is not hard to see why he should have had this bad name. He was vehemently unorthodox on sacred fundamentals—a pagan, without religion, or the feeling for it. This last is what mankind are slowest to forgive. It is curious that, as I think, Dante finds no place for Lucretius in any of his three spheres of the other world, Inferno, Purgatory, or Paradise. Again, to readers who did not go much below the surface, he was what in our days is loosely, and somewhat promiscuously, labelled Pessimist. Pessimism—which, let us recollect, is a very different thing from misanthropy—has many a shape, and voices beyond counting. A learned Grecian of our time has assured us that Æschylus, though a strictly religious pagan, like Pindar, may well be called a pessimist, nay, ' the very patriarch and first preacher of pessimism,' and of this the Grecian finds his illustration in Prometheus, who redeems men from the low estate in which they were born, instructs them in all art and knowledge to lift them up from their sorry plight, discovers without disparagement or blame that they listen without hearing, and in the end is repaid by cruel exile in iron chains upon the frosty Caucasus.   However this may be, pessimism ranges from the passionate laments of Israel; the clear-eyed melancholy of the Greek; the savage and unholy imaginations of the man like Swift, who on his birthday ever read Job's third chapter; the crystal lustre of Leopardi's unchangeable despair and lacerating irony; the transitory effusions of German *Weltschmerz*, or the effronteries of Zara-thustra.   Lucretius stands alone in the controversial force and energy with which the genius of negation inspires him, and transforms into sublime reasons for firm act, so long as living breath is ours, the thought that the life of a man is no more than a dream of a shadow, the generation of men no more than the generation of leaves, putting forth to air and sky, then scattered by autumn winds to earth.

His philosophy was borrowed from a Greek, but Lucretius was Roman, and the furious havoc of

Rome in his day may well have awakened in him energetic thought on the problems of the world, such as may happen even to men with none of his commanding genius in any age, ancient or our own, who have the misfortune to be brought into sight of the like ruin of distracted States and insensate men.

Among the most singular of those who have tried their hands at turning Lucretius into English must be counted the wife of the famous puritan, Colonel Hutchinson. She turned him into verse, as she says, out of youthful curiosity to understand things she heard so much discourse of at second hand. In time the admirable woman grew to be as angry with Lucretius as if he had been an episcopalian royalist, with his ' foppish casual dance of atoms,' and the other senseless superstitions.

Later than Jeremy Taylor a verse translation by a writer, now unknown for other things, was printed by Creech in 1682, and went through many editions. Then the task fell by way of experiment into mightier hands. Having, with much ado, got clear of Virgil, Dryden undertook some pieces of Lucretius, in whom he found as his distinguishing character a certain kind of noble pride. Our untold debt to Dryden as the most splendid master of English prose, can by no means content us with the verse into which he Englished some of the finest lines in poetry :

'Tis pleasant safely to behold from shore
The rolling ship and hear the tempest roar. . .

And so forth, in a style that has no note of either the vigour or the music of its original.[1]

Crossing a long tract of time, from the seventeenth century to the end of the nineteenth, we still find English and French poets coming on to Lucretian ground. The most popular English poet of our Gladstonian era perhaps did not make the worthiest

[1] The French ecclesiastic, famous in his day for erudition, polite and skilful diplomacy, and for a collection of Roman antiques, which Frederick the Great bought for Berlin, came across Bayle, who was the purest sceptic of his own, or perhaps of any age. 'I am a protestant,' said Bayle to Polignac, 'for in my soul I protest against all that I hear said, and all that I see done.' Among other things he much impressed the cardinal by his references to Lucretius. Polignac, a sincere and honest man, set to work on a Latin poem, *Anti-Lucrèce* (1747), which made a great stir in the literary world all over Europe. Voltaire in a thoughtless moment too handsomely complimented its author as a mixture of Virgil and Plato, the avenger of heaven and the conqueror of Lucretius. By and by Voltaire changed his mind, and the work speedily became a poem without poetry and philosophy, without reason, a thing of dry bones which everybody praised and nobody could read. Some said that the simplest anti-Lucretius was to be found in his own poem and its pretty palpable incoherences, and perhaps the same point might have spared us many elaborate volumes of animadversion on many other books besides *The Nature of Things*. Even of great Aristotle one of his translators has said that no progress can be made in the study of him by an art of interpretation which aims only at reconciling an author with himself. At any rate *Anti-Lucrèce* no more extinguished *The Nature of Things* than Frederick's *Anti-Machiavel* extinguished *The Prince*. The world had come upon a time when the *memento mori* of the Middle Ages was losing its iron command, and this mood Lucretius suited.

choice when he tacked his lofty, solemn, powerful verses called *Lucretius* on to a repellent, and not well-supported, myth about an amatory potion.

Sully-Prudhomme was a zealous Lucretian, in the respectable conviction that

> Pour dissiper l'horreur de notre nuit profonde,
> Le soleil ne peut rien, ni le jour éclatant,
> Mais la Nature parle et la Raison l'entend !

He even began a translation, but was not sorry to find himself anticipated by what he felt bound to regard as the definitive version of Lefèvre (1876). Nor can an English ear be sorry either, for somehow the great open diapason of the Lucretian hexameter is grievously missing in this effort of a poet of proved grace and modern elegance.

Still stranger is it to find Lucretius invoked as his partner in devotion to the philosophic muse by Lamartine—that singular and winning genius, who was not only a poet, but, as competent French critics say, the very spirit of poetry itself; and who besides his poetry, by way of passing episode, over-turned a throne by a book—a book of which the most potent contemporary novelist wittily said that it raised history to the level of fiction. Lamartine courageously risked his life in victorious encounters with the Paris mob of 1848; he fascinated, persuaded, overwhelmed, ruled them in some of their stormiest hours. 'Physical nature,' he said, 'was the theme of Lucretius; moral nature is mine.' Far indeed is the journey from Lamartine's delicate faculty in gifts of poetic beauty to the Roman poet's unsparing wrestle with false divinities, misjudged destinies, a universe of desolating law. Yet in both of them glowed the like vivid sympathies of soul.

Macaulay does justice to Lucretius's general poetic strength and elevation, even placing him before Virgil among the wearers of poetic crowns, but he despatches the philosophy as, for the most part, utterly worthless. This comes to much the same as Mommsen's verdict that Lucretius, dealing with atoms and void and the rest of his science, is unreadable. Most such verdicts rather miss the mark of history. The scientific theories were unverified, as they were bound to be, and so the philosophy associated with them was but the shadow of a system with no clear root in sound method. Yet the aerial labour of his imagination brought him marvellously far on the path towards the mountain heights of modern speculation. The world in which we live, and all the business of the elements, has become a sounding house of vast general laws. Of these laws it is the nature of things to be their subject. They are no sport of arbitrary, changeful, and capricious deities. Far distant, aloof, remote, dwell those divine beings. The doctrines of the Atom, again, the doctrines of special affinities, leave their traces after many centuries in the prevailing guesses of our present time upon the constitution of matter. Then in fine comes the great key-note from which we started. The relations of body and soul, the poet argues, well considered in all their analogies and phenomena in the universe of sentient being, bid us shake ourselves free from that terror of death, and the mysterious dread of the continuity of conscious individual life in an unknown hereafter, which so darkly overshadows, distracts, and paralyses the life of 'momentary man.' Of all the countless hosts of poets, preachers, philosophers, and theologians who, with every variety of aspect and approach, have held, by way either of promise to the good or menace to the bad, that all philosophy of life is in essence *commentatio mortis*, Lucretius is most strenuous, lofty, and insistent on enforcing the sombre lesson taught by the ancient Hebrew long ages before him : ' Whatsoever thy hand findeth to do, do it with thy might ; for there is no work, nor knowledge, nor wisdom in the grave, whither thou goest.'

It was impossible that our own glorious literature should not contain, in prose and verse alike, a thousand things of superlative beauty about this universal theme, from Raleigh's ' *O eloquent, just and mighty death*,' or the thrilling dialogues in Claudio's prison, down to the most melting and melodious single verse in all the exercises of our English tongue, ' *After life's fitful fever he sleeps well*,' the tender summary of it all. Still, the famous passage of Lucretius at the close of his third book is of such quality that I hardly find in my heart to quarrel with the accomplished critic of to-day who suggests that ' its lofty passion, its piercing tenderness, the stately roll of its cadences, is perhaps unmatched in human speech.'

> 'Iam iam non domus accipiet te læta, neque uxor
> Optima, nec dulces occurrent oscula nati
> Præripere et tacita pectus dulcedine tangent :
> Non poteris factis florentibus esse, tuisque
> Præsidium : misero misere,' aiunt, 'omnia ademit
> Una dies infesta tibi tot præmia vitæ. . . .

Now no more shall a glad home and a true wife welcome thee, nor darling children race to snatch thy first kisses and touch thy heart with a sweet and silent content ; no more mayest thou be prosperous in thy doings and a defence to thine own ; 'alas and woe !' say they, 'one disastrous day has taken all these prizes of thy life away from thee'—but thereat they do not add this, 'and now no more does any longing for these things beset thee.' This did their thought but clearly see and their speech follow, they would release themselves from great heartache and fear. 'Thou, indeed, as thou art sunk in the sleep of death, wilt so be for the rest of the ages, severed from all weary pains ; but we, while close by us thou didst turn ashen on the awful pyre, made unappeasable lamentation, and everlastingly shall time never rid our heart of anguish.' Ask we then this of him, what there is that is so very bitter, if sleep and peace be the conclusion of the matter, to make one fade away in never-ending grief ?—MACKAIL.

Then there is the half of the fifth book which Munro pronounces unsurpassed, if not unequalled, in all Latin poetry for varied beauty, earnest satire, and sublimity.

Critics have complained of *Paradise Lost* that Milton has taken a scheme of life for life itself. Of

Lucretius at least this is not true. Though his own days are 'invisible and dim,' his poem is rich and glowing in the essence and spirit of the life of the world in itself. His gospel is a gospel of active energy and of sympathy all through the world of sentient being. I have already copied a short piece of Montaigne's, and there is a touch of the same feeling in Lucretius's thought of the aged ploughman after the ease and fruitfulness of earth's golden days have passed away—how the husbandman shakes his head and with deep sigh upon sigh thinks that the labour of his hands comes to so little ; how we wear out the strength of labouring men and their oxen. We do not know what Lucretius would have made of Liberty, Equality, and Fraternity, but Freedom, Justice, Pity is no bad battle-cry, and it is Lucretian. We may well be as indifferent as we like about atom and void, but it is pleasant to read of ' light-sleeping dogs with faithful hearts in their breasts, and woolly flocks, and beasts of burden whom we protect and feed in requital of their useful services.' Or the picture of the Molossian hounds, ' when they essay fondly to lick their whelps with their tongue, or toss them with their feet, and snapping at them make a feint with lightly closing teeth of swallowing, though with gentle forbearance they caress them with a yelping sound greatly different from that which they utter when left alone in a house they bay, or when they shrink away with a crouching body howling from blows.'

III.

The place of death in Lucretius naturally brings a reader, with good authors at his elbow, to Lessing's *Laocoön*—' dear Lessing,' as George Eliot called him —one of the rare books that, like Grotius or Adam Smith, startled the world by a sudden shaft of new light diffusing itself over changed tracts of thought for all time to come. Though first suggested to him by Burke's *Sublime and Beautiful*, of which Lessing made himself translator, it was a fruitful surprise in the originality of its contribution to the philosophy of art, and the conditions of poetry and painting. Not any less remarkable, and it brings him involuntarily into line with Lucretius, is the little tract with which he shortly followed *Laocoön*, on the images of death in ancient art—a plea against the notion that to the classic world the symbol of death took the repulsive shape of the skeleton, the Arch Fear in a visible form. Goethe records how, in his youth, they were all enchanted with the beauty of the thought that the ancients represented Death as the brother of Sleep, each in form the semblance of the other, twin brothers in the arms of Night. The enchantment was not universal, for in common faith death is the penalty of Sin; hence it was natural to symbolise it by a terrifying image. Lessing's reply was that the Christian faith has not revealed this dreadful truth in order to make us despair, but promises a blessed end to devout resignation and contrition of heart. The Scripture itself, moreover, he goes on, speaks of the Angel of Death : why should not the artist give up the hateful skeleton, and put us in possession of the better image of an angel ? ' Only religion misconceived can draw us away from the beautiful, and it is an evidence for the true religion properly understood, the more it everywhere restores us to beauty.' Whether or not he accurately divined all the transformations and conclusions by which the skeleton came to be taken for the image of death, Lessing was felt to have carried his law of beauty into supreme heights of art and life. In those days, sang Schiller in *Die Götter Griechenlands*, ' no grisly skeleton entered the chamber, and stood before the deathbed.' So, in short, the skeleton was displaced on the funereal monument by a gracious genie bearing in all simplicity a reversed torch or some symbol of the resurrection.

To nobody, we might well have supposed, was the spirit of Lucretius so little congenial as it was to Goethe, the stormiest of poets to the most composed. Yet, as it appeared, when Goethe came back from his travels in Italy, he was full-blown pagan, and was not slow to express high thoughts of *The Nature of Things*. For some twenty years he encouraged its first translation into German (1820), and even took an active share in the task. Vitally different as the vast march of time had made them, the two stand out, each of them a grand compound of poetry, scientific aim, and practical philosophy. Goethe applauds Lucretius as a diligent observer and explorer of nature, as master of strange powers of living delineation of nature's phenomena. All these, joined to an amazing elevation of mind and speech, assured his immortality as man, Roman, philosopher, and poet all in one. His book, says Goethe, who does not often show much care for historic values, is one of the most remarkable documents in the world, because it shows how men thought and felt on the secrets of the universe between the sixth and eighth decades before the Christian era.

It is interesting to note how in the latest hours at which the Christian era has yet arrived, Lucretius is still a living combatant as he was in the pagan era. The most brilliant English apologist of our day, I should think, has been Martineau, and when the apologist comes to deal with the ' great mountain-chain of death,' and life to come, it is to the rolling hexameters from Lucretius he goes for adverse texts that he made it his business to overthrow. Goethe himself, so widely counted ' Europe's sagest head,' may well be said to be the founder, guide, and oracle of an informal, nameless, and unorganised communion of his own—men and women content to live their lives independently of two articles of such profound and saturating belief as those against which Lucretius waged his impassioned war. Some would say the Greeks found it all out long before either Roman or German, and end the matter in some plangent lines in a fragment of Euripides :

Γαῖα μεγίστη καὶ Διὸς αἰθήρ,
ὁ μὲν ἀνθρώπων καὶ θεῶν γενέτωρ,
ἡ δ' ὑγροβόλους σταγόνας νοτίας
παραδεξαμένη τίκτει θνατούς,
τίκτει δὲ βορὰν φῦλά τε θηρῶν·
ἔθεν οὐκ ἀδίκως
μήτηρ πάντων νενόμισται.

χωρεῖ δ' ὀπίσω
τὰ μὲν ἐκ γαίας φύντ' εἰς γαῖαν,
τὰ δ' ἀπ' αἰθερίου βλαστόντα γονῆς
εἰς οὐράνιον πάλιν ἦλθε πόλον·
θνήσκει δ' οὐδὲν τῶν γιγνομένων,
διακρινόμενον δ' ἄλλο πρὸς ἄλλον
μορφὴν ἑτέραν ἐπέδειξεν.

Earth the most great, and Heaven on high :
    Father is He to man and god ;
    And She, who taketh to her sod
The cloud-flung rivers of the Sky

And beareth offspring, men and grass
    And beasts in all their kinds, indeed
    Mother of All.   And every seed
Earth-gendered back to Earth shall pass,

And back to Heaven the seeds of Sky ;
    Seeing all things into all may range
    And, sundering, show new shapes of change,
But never that which is shall die.
                              GILBERT MURRAY.

Or the better-known lines :

    τοῦτον εὐτυχέστατον λέγω
ὅστις θεωρήσας ἀλύπως, Παρμένων,
τὰ σευνὰ ταῦτ', ἀπῆλθεν ὅθεν ἦλθεν ταχά,
τὸν ἥλιον τὸν κοινόν, ἄστρ' ὕδωρ νέφη
πῦρ· ταῦτα κἂν ἑκατὸν ἔτη βιῷς, ἀεὶ
ὄψει παρόντα, κἂν ἐνιαυτοὺς σφόδρ' ὀλίγους
σεμνότερα τούτων ἕτερα δ' οὐκ ὄψει ποτέ.

I hold him happiest
Who, before going quickly whence he came,
Hath looked ungrieving on these majesties,
The world-wide Sun, the stars, water and clouds
And fire. Live, Parmeno, a hundred years,
Or a few weeks, these thou wilt always see,
And never, never, any greater things.

Ibid.

This is Menander. For him Goethe had the liveliest admiration. He calls him pure, noble, cheerful, altogether invaluable, even though unhappily but a fragment. Yet if one demands an antistrophe to this strophe of Menander, I can think of none more apt than Goethe's own famous and beautiful psalm of life, known as *Das Göttliche.* From a very different point of view Browning's readers will not forget his sombre lines under the title *Prospice.*